Praise for A.A. Gill is Further Away

'Gill applies his acerbity on Sudan, India, Cuba, Germany and California, uncovering the personality of each place much as he does with his celebrity interviewees'
National Geographic Traveller

'Describing each location with equal wonder, he makes Morris dancers sound as exotic as Madagascan tribes' *Shortlist*

'Whatever his methods, not many writers can so succinctly drill down into a destination ... punctuated with thoughts and ideas pulsating with wisdom' *Business Traveller Reuters*

'If you like travel, brilliant writing and truly original thinking, then join the queue' *Vanity Fair*

'As this collection of stories shows, few writers can get under the skin of a place as evocatively or effectively' *Wanderlust*

'[Gill] never fails to write with power and wit'
Lonely Planet Magazine

'A highly diverting collection' *Good Book Guide*

A.A. Gill was born in Edinburgh. He is the author of two novels, *Sap Rising* (1997) and *Starcrossed* (1999), books on two of London's most famous restaurants, The Ivy and Le Caprice. He is also the author of several non-fiction books, and is the TV and restaurant critic for the *Sunday Times*. He lives in London and spends much of his year travelling.

By A.A. Gill

A.A. Gill is Away
The Angry Island
Previous Convictions
Table Talk
Paper View
A.A. Gill is Further Away

A.A. GILL
IS FURTHER AWAY
helping with enquiries

A.A. Gill

photographs by Tom Craig

PHOENIX

A PHOENIX PAPERBACK

First published in Great Britain in 2011
by Weidenfeld & Nicolson
This paperback edition published in 2012
by Phoenix,
an imprint of Orion Books Ltd,
Orion House, 5 Upper St Martin's Lane,
London WC2H 9EA

An Hachette UK company

1 3 5 7 9 10 8 6 4 2

A CIP catalogue record for this book
is available from the British Library.

ISBN 978-0-7538-2929-5

Typeset by Input Data Services Ltd,
Bridgwater, Somerset

Printed and bound by CPI Group (UK) Ltd,
Croydon, CR0 4YY

www.orionbooks.co.uk

To Edith and Isaac

Contents

Acknowledgements

Thanks to all the editors, sub-editors and libel lawyers on the various publications in which these pieces first appeared – the *Sunday Times*, *Vanity Fair*, *GQ* and *National Geographic*. Thanks also to Alan Samson, Celia Hayley, Lucinda McNeile and Carole Green, to Ed Victor and Charlie Campbell, and to Amy Turner. And, as ever, to Nicola.

Foreword

A weather-beaten man with a pale eye, a halting hip and the bony grip of a chap who has been holding on to the frayed tether end of dear life in boys' own circumstances, shook my soft hand at the Royal Geographical Society in Kensington Gore, and said, 'It's the young ones I feel sorry for, the ones just setting off. It's all over. There's nowhere left to discover. Nothing worth exploring. The globe has been wrested from the hands of adventurers and explorers and passed to geographers and stocktakers. It's all computer models and statistics, squalor and rainfall, plastic bags and refugees. The world has passed its found-by date.' I smiled enigmatically, sphinx-like I hoped. I couldn't have disagreed more. But this has become an arguable truism, the most profoundly depressing orthodoxy of our age: our world is only fit for salvage, and travelling in it is a selfish indulgence. And the only stories worth telling, or that should be told, are those that conform to the essential grim truth: that we are curators of a midden.

Like so much familiar wisdom, so many pikestaff-plain plausible certainties, it's not just untrue, it's the about-face opposite of the confronted truth. The moment I step out of the familiar and the unconsidered, I'm overwhelmed by excitement, beauty and the astonishing variety of it all, and the near-universal bright optimism of the world. It is a more wonderful and gratifying place than it has ever been. Not least because for the first time we can get to all of it. I've just turned down a trip to the Antarctic. In my grandfather's day only a handful of people had ever set foot in the Antarctic. In his father's day, no one ever had. Now, you can book passage on a cruise ship for a tour. And that's supposed to be a disastrous thing? As are journeys to the Kalahari, up the Orinoco, weekend breaks to Florence and Reykjavik, even walking on the downs. This practised pessimism, this green, whole-earth snobbery that arrives as 'I am a traveller, you are a tourist, they are trippers', implies that the world is traversed by the wrong sort of people having the wrong sort of good time. But my experience, everything I've learnt being a journalistic tripper tells me that travel is a good thing. A brilliant, inspiring, heart-filling, head-expanding, great thing. That almost everyone is better off for it, both the visitor and the visited. More of the fear and unhappiness in the world is caused by insularity and closed doors than by openness and crowds. The greatest inventions of the age are the jet engine and the airport, those magical portals of escape and romance. Tourism is a greater force for peace, harmony, economies, education and stability than the United Nations, all its agencies and every NGO bundled together in Bermuda shorts. As for the age of discovery and exploration being over, doesn't that really depend on where you start and who's being discovered?

There is a perverse snobbery about first-person travel writing: 'I'm here, and you, well, you're not here.' The implication is that *here* is particularly marvellous because you're *there*, and we'd be awfully pleased if the rest of you would keep it that way. That sort of journalism excludes, leaves you feeling mildly envious and annoyed, and aware that in reading it you're paying for someone else to trip barefoot along the shore at sunset. I'm always conscious that the first thing I have to do is to bring whoever picks up this page with me.

This collection is not all far and wide. Half of it is prosaically close, and bits of it, like Old Age and The Guinea Pig Club, are journeys and destinations of a more profound and metaphorical kind. No two people's worlds look the same. Many hate travelling, dread 'abroad', only want a hotel and a pool or some snow and a mountain, the smell of lavender, a hammock, cheap wine and hot nipples. But ever since I started peripatetic writing two decades ago, I've had this insatiable craving, this ravenous curiosity for 'out there', for it all. Hot, cold, sodden, arid, luxurious or stony, I'm constantly aware that the sand is running through the glass and the road still stretches ahead. So many places, so many people, the pages are falling off the calendar like late autumn leaves. And somewhere, just over the horizon, my days will stop and my final regret, with shrunken shank, sans teeth, sans eyes, sans taste, sans everything, won't be not enough sex or caviar, it won't be not enough cashmere or laughter – it will be that I didn't get to see the Northern Lights or Timbuktu, that I haven't been to the Atacama Desert or met the Nagas of Nagaland, I never saw the monkey puzzle forests of Chile. It will be places that I regret, and it will be places that I remember. We pass this way but once. As I get older and the horizon draws in, the list of what is possible or likely grows shorter and closer. Realistically, I'm not going to climb the Matterhorn or run a desert marathon. The vastness of the deep will be forever second-hand. But I'm growing more inquisitive about things closer to home. Travel is never about distance. Over the road from the Royal Geographic Society is Hyde Park and Kensington Gardens, the destination for one of my favourite stories from this collection.

On most of my trips, I work with a photographer. The photographer I work with most is Tom Craig. I don't know how many stories we've done together, but they stretch from Spitsbergen to Tasmania, from Chad to Haiti. These days it's rare for a journalist and a photographer to have such a close and continuous jobbing relationship, but to find that words and pictures are working to complement each other, not as illustrations or captions, but in tandem, synchronised but separate, is the abiding, quiet joy and pride of my job. I call it hacking; he calls it painting with light. But working with Tom is, and I hope continues to be, a particularly satisfying dovetailing of crafts.

As I write this, the journey that has moved and preoccupied me most over the last year is one I didn't take. I wasn't there. I was the passive reader. My daughter Flora was on her gap year. She asked my advice about where she should go with her three friends. I told her about the monkey puzzle forests and the Northern Lights, I suggested the footsteps of Herodotus and Stanley. I produced books and maps. She ignored it all, and like every other released-into-the-public public school child, took a trip to Thailand and Laos and Cambodia, Vietnam, Malaysia and Singapore, to get drunk on a thousand steamy beaches, float in sullen seas, eat burgers in palm-roofed bars. I sighed and gave her the benefit of my disappointed, selective travel snobbery. And five months later she returned. I met a child who had been indelibly changed by a new-minted globe; by a journey that for her was all bright discovery, all exploration. She had swum in incandescent seas under tropical moons, seen temples and ruins, trekked through rough jungles, slept with bedbugs and cockroaches, and in bus stations, travelled in tuk-tuks and flip-flops. She was filled with it. Travel may broaden your mind, but you really want it to widen your soul and infect you with the longing. Sometimes, she says, she lies awake and knows that it's all still out there, all the places she went to, and beyond them, all the other places she has yet to see, that they're all going on just over the horizon, a few hours away. And she said: 'I want to go back, I really want to go back, and then go on and on and on.'

NEAR

Morris Dancing

You think you know all about Essex: pram-gobby, ponytail face-lifts, Juicy Couture buttcrack, Friday night alco-doner vomit, wheelie-bin doggy shags, Burberry and Chardonnay, effing and bling. We all know about Essex, but that's only the half of it. There's the fat-thighed slags' bottom halves, the metro overspill, the East End outreach. And then, in the north, just past Stansted, yards from the slip roads and interlocking roundabouts, there is another country.

The transformation is as sudden as it is beautiful. The utilitarian Esperanto landscape becomes the soft lilt of ancient fields, thickly edged with poppies and elderflower. The roads bend and drop, following an older topography, the memory of more circuitous journeys.

Twenty minutes from the airport is Thaxted. It crawls up a hill. Georgian and Victorian rural cottages and shops lean on each other for support. The streets are free of the cloned monopolies of building societies and mini-supermarkets. There is an over-indulgence of pubs, and a church that is too grand for this market town, and beside it a windmill. It was paid for by the great post-feudal wool boom.

This neat and congenial town, with its greens, a clock mender and merchants' houses, is surrounded by a vale of gently decrepit farmland. It is everything the vile Cotswolds aspire to plagiarise. But it's a little more than it seems. This big church is a cradle of unconventional radicalism. It had a famous vicar, Conrad Noel, who preached Christian socialism, and another, Peter Elers, one of the first openly gay vicars in the Church of England, who blessed a lesbian 'marriage' in 1976 on the understanding that, if the Church blessed battleships and budgerigars, it ought to find it in its heart to bless men and women in love. Gustav Holst lived here, and, a couple of doors away, so did Dick Turpin.

Early on a blissful blue and bright morning, Thaxted is quiet and elegantly somnambulant. Stepping out of the long shadows, I catch sight of two men in white – unusually early cricketers perhaps – and then another man, in a coat of rags, talking to a pantomime dragon. In the distance I can hear the rhythmic timpani of sleigh bells. There are more men lifting their beer-blown faces to the sun. Men in straw hats with ribbons, men with bright waistcoats.

Thaxted's insurgent heretical secret isn't canonical bolshevism or buggery, it's folklore. The glorious weekend is the annual coming together of Britain's morris men. Not just a run-of-the-mill summer ritual line-up of hanky wavers and broomstick bashers, but the seventy-fifth anniversary of the Thaxted Morris Ring – the quango of morris dancing and mumming. This little market town is the heart of the mysterious cult of the morris. This will be the largest get-together of morris men in living memory.

The day starts with various teams going out to Essex villages and doing their jiggy business as a pub crawl before converging on Thaxted high street. We start off in Finchingfield, a village of idiotic prettiness. There's a green, a pond with ducks, a church, cottages, burgeoning flowers, simple yokels leaning on sticks, tow-haired children in smocks delivering wholemeal bread, and an antiques shop with a prominent welcoming message pointing out that this isn't a museum, everything is for sale and if you don't want to buy stuff then sod off. And there's a pub, a real pub-on-the-green called the Fox.

Inside, the moment it opens, there is a gimpy collection of morris men in stripy waistcoats and straw hats with plastic flowers, sinking the first pint like fire engines taking on supplies. They tip out on to the lawn and, after a lot of toing and froing and bad-breath backchat, a team of blokes arrange themselves in a ragged line with a fiddle, an accordion and a penny whistle, and strike up the familiar sound of summer weekends in rural Middle England. Their bright and gaudy costumes make the picture complete as they go after each other like fat, rheumatic game hens, chaffing and puffing and heavily skipping through routines that would bore an infant school. Morris dancers are one of the most riotously risible and despised groups in Britain. Yet they caper on regardless. To be a morris man is to live a regardless life. These are men apart, oblivious of or immune to the mockery and the curled lips. They keep alive an uncared for and unwanted tradition – simply for the pleasure of a thing itself, and their own company, and bladder-deforming quantities of beer. Sir Thomas Beecham's advice to try anything once except incest and folk dancing has wrapped the morris in a received wisdom of disdain. For most people it is bizarre and tasteless Terpsichorean graffiti, like animated garden gnomes.

A pair get up and do a jig with each other. Nobody watches. I notice that one of them is wearing Velcro comfy-fit shoes of the sort advertised in the back of the *Sunday Telegraph*. Behind the dancers there is that eternal punctuation mark of English villages, the comforting war memorial that chimes the knell of passing days, the names resonant of another England; Ernest and Tom Purkiss, Portor Choat, Tom Juniper, Percy Wiffen, T. O. Ruggles-Brice. They seem to belong to the accordion and the tinny round-elay, the clack of wands and the beery 'ya' of bucolic voices. The pub is advertising a Neil Diamond tribute evening.

In the nearby village of Cornish Hall End, the morris men mill about, unclipping their personal tankards from their elasticated belts to sink pints through Lovelace-gaping gullets before forming up in a ragged square and skipping their simple circular pattern. In the beer garden, families lounge, children run in mobs, nobody takes much notice. The Horse and Groom is having a Blues Brothers tribute evening.

The Morris Ring rules the dance. It has been based in Thaxted for all its seventy-five years. This year is its three-quarter century, and promises particularly splendid meetings of the nation's dance troupes. They are all based in villages, and vary in their particulars, but, like football teams, they obey the niceties. Each has a leader, a treasurer and a coach. They dance traditional dances identified by their places of origin. They also have fools who caper with bladders – theirs and pigs'. There are men on hobbyhorses, men who dress up as women, often representing Maid Marian or Queen Victoria, and sometimes they 'go molly' – that is, in blackface.

There are also men who are animals – deer, dragons and horses – and it's always men. There are no women in the Ring. Nobody knows the origins of morris dancing – the name probably comes from 'Moorish'. It may have been born in North Africa or Spain; it may have come back with the crusades. There was certainly Elizabethan morris dancing. Shakespeare's comic actor Will Kempe famously took nine days to dance from London to Norwich.

Seventy-five years is really not that old for a governing association for an ancient rural folk art. Ping-pong is half a century older, and the rugby football association is nearly twice as old as the Morris Ring. What we see is a recreation – or, perhaps better, a resurrection. The great fire and brimstone, steam and grind of the industrial upheaval of the nineteenth century dislocated, and in many places extinguished, a whole canon of frail, delicate, English rural culture.

Factories and mines broke the legs of the Celtic and Saxon patchwork of time and magic. The mass march of the working classes from hoes to picks, moved from village greens to the satanic mills and smog of back-to-backs. But just as the morris faded to white, so a few urban middle-class musicologists and folklorists stepped out back down the rutted lanes to the extremities of green England and began to piece together the vanished life. Cecil Sharp collected thousands and thousands of folk tunes. They were used by composers such as Elgar, Vaughan Williams, Holst and Britten. The Arts and Crafts movement enthused hundreds of Hampstead socialists to get in touch with their pointy toed roots and to look to a new medievalism of weaving and pottery, husbandry, cottage gardens and vegetarianism. They grew unironic beards and dressed their children in homespun smocks, and occasionally, like Eric Gill (no relation), they lived entirely recreated medieval lives and slept with their children. The folklore of the morris got a worthy and self-conscious kiss of life. It got polite, and a hierarchy, and snobbery, and rules. Like the druid and bardic movements in Wales, a few proselytising enthusiasts became the bottomless butt of jokes for the metropolitan masses.

Writers such as Orwell, Waugh and Betjeman mocked the beer and beards, the lentils and earnestness of the morris. The dance became emblematic of a certain sort of Fabian – humourless and sexless, worthy socialism. But nobody really knew what the original meanings or intentions of the dance had been, and they didn't seem to care much. It was enough that they could make it fit this Hardyesque and patronising vision of a peasant, elfin England.

Anthropologists tend to explain all rural ritual, craft and culture as 'fertility', or harvest thanksgiving. They're the catch-all explanations for rude behaviour that doesn't come with a manual. It seems that there may well be connections with ancient mystical characters and pre-Christian beliefs – the Green Man appears and Herne the Hunter, lord of the forest. There are animistic spirits of flowers and green things, but it never really gets let out from under the tasteful and picturesque hey nonny nonny of pub bores and country tourist posters.

At the next village pub, something quite different happens. They release the beast. In the car park by the wheelie bin, the Saddleworth Morris Men from Yorkshire arrive, trotting like pit ponies, bells on their black clogs, wearing hanging baskets of flowers and feathers on their heads, led by a meaty man with a whip. There is none of the hop, skip and whack about this troupe. They have a muscular, purposeful swagger. Their dance is physical and masculine, and beautifully aggressive under their great flowered hats. They have the gimlet-eyed, tuber-featured faces of the north, and suddenly the morris is captivating. The rhythm stamps out darker motifs and bellicose camaraderie. The patterns they make stay in the mind's eye. You can see them weave spells.

My small boy offers a swan's feather he found to one of the dancers, who takes off his hat to put it in. The boy's mother asks if she can see the hat. 'You mustn't put it on,' the dancer warns like a woodland troll in a fairy story. 'I don't like to say in front of your man, but if a lass wears the hat she has to have . . . you know . . . go to bed with the morris man. That's the rule.' Nicola thinks about it for a moment, and hands back the hat with an apologetic, maybe-next-time smile.

For all its fecund heritage and its promise of seed time and harvest, morris dancing is incontrovertibly the least sexy jigging in the world. Unlike the folk dances of the rest of Europe, with their silly dressing up and geometric patterns, or the leaping reelers of the Celtic edges of the British Isles, the morris is perversely and defiantly not the vertical expression of a horizontal desire. They not only do not dance with women, but they don't dance for or at women. Indeed, you get the feeling they don't really dance for anyone but themselves.

There is something admirable about this – the absence of showmanship. Nobody could accuse these men of overt displays of vanity. Their vast stomachs held in by sweaty nylon shirts like warm mozzarellas, their blotched faces, the pallor of lives lived on a slow bar stool. They exhibit the stamina and grace of shopping trolleys, with beards that loom like badly eaten Weetabix and hair that has given up under the torture of middle-aged ponytails. Morris dancing never had a golden age. It never grasped the zeitgeist. There was no morris Woodstock or summer of love. It was reborn beyond the aesthetic pale and, contrarily, there is something wonderful about that, something brave and properly, collectively eccentric.

While the bien pensants snigger and change their beliefs and preferences with the season, the morris dancers skip on, knowing that every year will be like the year before, knowing they will always be the back marker of the least 'now' occupations on earth, just ahead of incest, yet continuing, convinced of their own inverted rightness, free of whim or caprice, excused riches, vanity, ambition, celebrity or cachet. And then, as if to prove the utter imperviousness to aesthetics, along come the Britannia Coco-nut Dancers of Bacup.

You've never heard of them, or seen them, unless you're from north Lancashire, and even then you might have given them a wide berth. They rarely travel from their home village – this is the first time they've been to Thaxted, and they only came because the Saddleworth team was here to look after them. They are small, nervous men. And so they might be, for they are wearing white cotton night bonnets of the sort sported by Victorian maids, decorated with sparse ribbons. Then black polo-neck sweaters, like the Milk Tray man, with a white sash, black knee breeches, white stockings and black clogs. As if this weren't enough, someone at some point has said: 'What this outfit really needs is a red and white hooped miniskirt.' 'Are you sure?' the dancers must have replied. And he was. But it doesn't finish there. They have black faces, out of which their little bright eyes shine anxiously. On their hands are strapped single castanets. A single castanet is the definition of uselessness. The corresponding castanet is worn on the knee. To say you couldn't make up the Coconutters would be to deny the evidence of your astonished eyes.

The dance begins with each Nutter cocking a hand to his ear to listen to something we human folk can't catch. They then wag a finger at each other, and they're off, stamping and circling, occasionally holding bent wands covered with red, white and blue rosettes that they weave into simple patterns. It's not pretty and it's not clever. It is simply, awe-inspiringly, astonishingly other. Morris men from southern troupes come and watch in slack-jawed silence. Nothing in the civilised world is quite as elementally bizarre and awkwardly compelling as the Coco-nutters of Bacup. What are they for? What were they thinking of? Why do they do these strange, misbegotten, dark little incantations? It's said that they might have originally been Barbary corsairs who worked in Cornish tin mines and travelled to Lancashire, and that the dance is about listening underground, a sign language of miners. And then there's all the usual guff about harvest and spring and fecundity, but that doesn't begin to describe the strangeness of this troupe from the nether folk world.

At teatime in Thaxted, the crowds stumble out of the pubs and line the main street that dips down the steep hill and escapes out into the countryside, which glints with the shimmering gilt of nostalgia, waiting for the return of haystacks and corn dollies and scarecrows. This is distant Albion in the afternoon. From the top of the hill, the morris men parade en masse with their attendant fiddlers and accordionists, drummers and whistlers, hobbyhorses, mystical animals, female impersonators and capering fools. From the bottom of the hill a corresponding group starts up. It's like the final illustration from a compendium of nursery rhymes and cautionary tales. A scene of the Day of Judgement from a half-forgotten, half-recreated lexicon of English folklore and fairy stories. The vivid swag of all the bright pomp and rhythm drags you along, exorcises the ridicule and the patronage, the lifelong received metropolitan wisdom of disdain. This is a lost part of what we once were, and who we still are. The two groups meet and dance their dances, turn swords into pentangles, sticks into eaves and hankies into hankies. They prance and skip and jig, the bells jingle, they shout and clack and cheer and canter, calling up the great lost way of being. The morris twitches like an amputated limb from a body that has been long since buried. It is the last rite of a belief that nobody can recall. The movements and the tune and nonsense, an ancient language that's bereft of the life that formed it.

But as you watch, there is a tingle, a spasm of recognition, a lightness in the stomach, a tightness in the throat, and the faint spark of connection. A distant echo, a folk memory, of what all this once was, what we once were. In the great, Gadarene dash for progress and industry, for the brick and stone and concrete, for the iron and smoke, we broke something vital, severed a link in the chain of ourselves, and there was no going back. There is a realisation that the dislike and the mockery of the morris is not wholly rational or deserved – that if this was some other nation's rural culture we'd watch with polite interest and inquisitive enjoyment. But because it's so close, it comes with the buttock clench of embarrassment, the guilt and the squirm. Like seeing photographs of ourselves in foolish fancy dress at drunken student parties, this is not who we grew up to be.

But the morris men dance on anyway, propitiating they know not what, an awkward family heirloom that doesn't go with anything else and is all we have left of our pre-industrial heritage. The dance is a kiss on the forehead of a skull that has sunk back into the earth and the dappled fields that in turn have become the ring roads, roundabouts, runways, shopping centres and starter-home cul-de-sacs of the postmodern age. They dance anyway. No longer for us, but despite us.

The sun goes down, the accordions play on, the pewter tankards slop, and, at eleven, the clamour and the shouting and the clapping and singing fade away, as if someone has pulled a plug, letting out all the noise. The lights of the town go out, and under the heavy, early summer moon there is a faint sound of a distant violin.

Down a winding cobbled street from the church trips the Abbots Bromley Horn Dance, the most evocative and strangely dramatic of all morris dances, performed for perhaps hundreds of years, conceivably for thousands. They are led by a single fiddler, dressed in a rag coat, playing a tune that is childlike and simple, but also full of sadness and an ethereal, mordant power, like the soundtrack of a dream. Behind him come men carrying antlered fallow deer heads in front of their faces. Behind them, a man-woman, a hunter and a hobbyhorse. They dance in silence, slowly. The hunt turns and turns, casting patterns in the moonlight. You feel its mossy, shadowed meaning beyond understanding. A ghost dance, a silently keening sadness. The things we misplace always bear a heavier loss than the things we choose to grasp with white knuckles. And in the darkness, quite unexpectedly, I feel tears of mourning on my cheek.

Hyde Park

Like all great journeys, trysts, campaigns and fresh starts, Hyde Park begins at dawn. It's the longest weekend of the year, and the grand and imperious gates are open to let in the sullen grey morning. Hyde is the most famous park in the world. Gethsemane may be older, the Bois de Boulogne bigger, but Hyde is the great green daddy; the space that fathered an international patchwork of geomorphic spaces. Wherever men design new cities for free and happy citizens with a sense of aspiration, leisure and culture, they plant the seed of Hyde Park. It is more than just an area without buildings, more than a bit of random green belt caught inside the intestines of concrete like trapped wind. Parks are a counterpoint to tarmac and brick, the obverse of the one-way, mind-your-step, roaring angular, analytically civic. They are places that remind the city of what it really is, and what it actually isn't, what it grew out of, and what it aspires to be.

Hyde Park has grown to look like an imaginary land from a children's book: it has open plains and secret dells, wild places, ruins and follies, fountains and palaces. It is Britain's biggest tourist attraction – it has five million visitors a year. There are six hundred organised events here, from political rallies and the Proms to the Tour de France and Sunday brass bands. And there are thousands and thousands of disorganised events: games of football and rounders, office parties, lonely hearts get-togethers and keep-fit runs.

I've been coming to the park since I was a child. I've lost boats, failed to fly kites, played cricket, lain in the long grass with girlfriends, walked dogs, pushed prams, taught my children to ride bikes here. If I claim to belong to any piece of country, if

I feel a bond with any place, then it's with this park. This is its story for a day.

At 6.15 a.m., the Household Cavalry are up and at 'em, ready to take the horses for the watering parade. There used to be a Georgian barracks here; its classical pediments are still stuck like a bandage above the ceremonial goods entrance. Knightsbridge Barracks is probably the ugliest building in London, with the most beautiful view. It was designed by Sir Basil Spence, who managed to construct vertical bomb damage out of horizontal bomb damage. The barracks, with its timid brutalism, is the one building visible from everywhere in the park.

The troopers stamp around with that winningly martial mixture of arresting, boyish teasing and determined, robotic purpose. There is an end-of-term, exhausted euphoria about them: they've just finished their ceremonial year. The horses are being sent to Norfolk and Windsor for holidays; the relentless clip-clop, polishing and waddling is slowing down. Cavalry walk with extreme and hilarious difficulty in their great delta-winged boots, into which giggling foreign girls occasionally slip their phone numbers. If you've ever wondered what happens to the tons of horse shit produced daily by the Queen's mounted guard, it's shovelled into a clever dumb-waiter chute affair and taken away by lorry. Where to, I ask the captain in charge. He looks challenged. 'Just away.'

The guard at the goods entrance steps into the carriageway, his assault rifle at the high port: it's the best way to stop traffic. And the troop walk out, their hooves sounding brittle and beautiful in the damp early morning. We step lightly up the eastern march of the park. The great avenue of London planes flutter and syncopate, camouflaging the misty green where early morning t'ai chi and pilates exercises make strange hieroglyphs of bodies in the middle distance, looking like figures lost from medieval frescoes of purgatory.

If you look carefully from Park Lane, you can see the remains of the earthworks that were the Parliamentary defence of London from Royalist attack in the civil war. This was the very edge of the city in the seventeenth century.

A hundred yards out from the barracks, the officer bellows like a man coming round from anaesthetic, and the troop smartly turn eyes left. They're passing the small box-hedged memorial to men killed by an Irish republican car bomb. They do this every time. It seems to commemorate not just the dead, but a time of quainter, home-made terrorism. Ceremony and hindsight can make anything heritage.

West Londoners occasionally wake in the early hours imagining they can hear horses' hooves, like an echo of Kipling in the dawn. Mostly they turn over and go back to sleep to dream of centaurs. Where the cavalry go is up to the officer in charge. Today's it's Notting Hill Gate. Through the northern boundary of the park they trot into a little side street, and there, in a cul-de-sac, the men dismount. The officer borrows a tenner from his sergeant and takes orders. Five coffees, three teas. He marches to a workmen's café, where the Middle Eastern owners give him a discount and beam at his boots and buttons. The troop stand around holding the horses, sucking back-handed cigarettes, and get on with the unending rounds of military teasing. The officer serves them coffee. It's just like being behind the bike sheds at school with the cool gang. Above us, a man opens his curtains and rubs his eyes and closes them again. 'Once, we were parked up,' the captain says, 'Robert De Niro came past. Didn't bat an eye. He was in London, so of course the Household Cavalry were taking tea in a mews in South Kensington at 6.30 in the morning.'

At 7.30 a.m. the Serpentine Swimming Club meets. It's not a nice morning for a dip. Even the geese have all been blown into a dirty corner by the squally weather. The Serpentine swimmers are one of those peculiar English associations that are invariably prefaced with 'intrepid' and 'eccentric'. They've been meeting here since 1864. They're a good-natured bunch who tip up in clothes bought for frugality and longevity rather than style. They clutch towels that are as thin and balding as are a good many of them.

Standing on the edge of the lake in distressingly skimpy

Speedos and rubber caps, they look like shelled turtles. I can't help casting their biopic as an Ealing Comedy. They range from MPs and retired architects to hotel doormen and taxi drivers. Many of them have swum the Channel. They swim here every week, including Christmas Day. There's no mucking about, no splashing or dive bombs or lilos: today they're racing. A chap with a barrel chest, a clipboard and a stopwatch starts them in a relaxed, staggered handicap. 'Dave, where are you? Dave, get in.' They dive into the turgid, scummy water and flap their arms with a wiry purpose. After a few minutes the water looks like a war film after the torpedo. The swimming club has a small unisex changing room full of old kit and grinning photographs. It's crowded with the raucous and morbidly pale, knobbly bodies, sawing at themselves with gritty towels.

Outside, there's a little ceremony. The winner is a man called Squirrel. There's a good-natured cheer; he gets a little silver cup. A lady, presumably Mrs Squirrel, mocks him fondly. 'Happy Birthday!' someone shouts. Squirrel is eighty-four today. Swimmers depart to breakfast radiating mad, rude immortality.

The Serpentine was made by damming the Westbourne, one of the lost rivers of London. It was built by Queen Caroline. They say that, but I doubt if she lifted a finger. It is an ornamental water feature that needed an Act of Parliament and a titanic amount of money, but it set off a trend for grand, natural looking lakes in grand, natural looking landscapes all over the parks of England. The other stretch of water here is the Round Pond, where model-yacht clubs sail their grounds for divorce. The geese that have always been here have recently been joined by puffy, hissy flotillas of swans. There used to be only one swan, a psychotic old male who kept the others away. Now he's gone, all the riffraff have moved in.

For most Londoners, Hyde Park and Kensington Gardens are synonymous. They flow one into the other, connected by the Serpentine. Kensington Gardens was the private backyard of Kensington Palace, and slowly grew into public use. George II was once mugged here. He asked the robber to let him keep the seal from his fob watch. The man agreed on the condition that the King promised not to tell anyone. He promised, and he never did. Rotten Row, the sandy bridle path along the south of the park, is a mispronunciation of Route du Roi. It was the other King's Road from the Palace of Kensington to the Palace of Westminster. It was the first London street to get lighting, to make sure the monarch didn't get robbed again.

Hyde Park was taken by Henry VIII from Westminster Abbey; he used it as a hunting ground. It became common ground on the edge of London, a meeting place for mobs, the illicit and the sexually commercial. The two parks have quite different atmospheres. Kensington Gardens is a polite and parochial, a dog-walking, pram-pushing park. Hyde Park is more public and political; it hosted the great reforming marches, student rallies and save-the-world pop concerts. Here was the reformers' tree, a post office for political reform and Tyburn. The licence given to the hanged to shout a final plea, prayer or curse to the public became Speakers' Corner. Every Sunday, comfortingly like every other Sunday, the diktat of stern religion, extreme unelectable politics and bizarre dietary advice is shouted out in single-issues raps. The Pre-Berlin Wall communists and pre-Darwin Christians offer a sort of puppet show of free speech – a mime with volume. The audience is mostly amused tourists. For all the blood and broken necks that bought it, you sense that this freedom of speech is not the cornerstone of a democracy. The foundation, the load-bearing beam of a free society, is not shouting: it's being able to make people listen.

In the centre of the park is a police station with an old-fashioned blue light and a red pillar box. The royal parks stand apart from the boroughs and districts that they float in: they have their own laws and customs, and the man in charge of policing them is Superintendent Simon Ovens, whose office is papered with positively enforcing aphorisms. His favourite is 'The main thing is to make the main thing the main thing'. 'I must say that a dozen times a day,' he tells me. He's very proud of the park and the policing of it. There's always a response car circling; they can be at any point within three or four minutes. There are officers on foot, on bikes and on horses. There are, on average, two reported incidents a day; there is also an astonishing 44 per cent clear-up rate, which makes the park not just the safest area of comparable size in the city but, by miles, the most efficiently and effectively policed.

What I'm surprised by is that this isn't done with zero-tolerance, obsessive zealotry. 'Look,' says the superintendent, 'with all the bylaws, it's probably technically illegal to do everything in the park, but our job is to see that the people who use it get to do what they want without interfering with the rights of others to do what they want. We have a lot of conflicting interests here, lots of different cultures. Middle Eastern families bring picnics; they don't necessarily get on with the dog-walkers [there are a million visits by accompanied dogs a year], and the most complaints are about cyclists.' Football games have to go on beside hen parties and capoeira classes; women in burkas have to put up with girls lying in their bras and pants. But there is something about the park that seems to make people decent citizens. 'I have events with sixty thousand people here. We have to get them in and out safely with a handful of officers. If that was a football crowd, I'd need at least two thousand policemen.'

The park is innately a well-mannered, liberal, live and let live place. What about sex? He leans back in his chair. 'Well, there's a lot of it. That's traditionally what a lot of people come to parks for. You've been down to the Rose Garden? It's a gay meeting place and has been for years, it's near the barracks. It's not my officers' job to go and poke around bushes to catch people doing what they're doing. We've all moved on from that. If they want to discreetly go behind an arbour, no one's going to come looking for them. If, on the other hand, you're going to have sex on a bench in front of passers-by, then you'll get nicked. But gay men are a vulnerable group – robbery, homophobic violence and blackmail. A lot of them are married, so this is clandestine and they have a right to protection. So we have a presence in the garden. Officers in high-vis jackets with torches patrol the central walk. We're there to protect gay men. They have a right to the park like everyone else.'

There is a lot of sex in the park. It is in the nature of nature to flirt and ogle and for kids to practise with their new hormones. You notice that the couples are either very young or surprisingly middle-aged. There are also a lot of mixed-race couples and a lot of discreet Asians holding hands. All the people who would get a room if they could but can't. The park exists as a great, damp, free bedsit for those who need a place to get squirmy and intense. Couples look like mating frogs washed up on river banks, clothes hoicked and snagged on cruxes, fingers inching the attrition of ardour across buckles and buttons and bra clasps, suckered in interminable thoughtless lockjawed snogs. And on benches, the office romances and infidelities, the coy shared sandwiches, fumbled intense kisses, the stroking and clasping and the gazing.

On any summer Friday, the park pullulates with couples dry-humping before going back on commuter trains to their rightful owners in the suburbs. The Rose Garden, which at night slips into the gay rut, is by day at its most beautiful, a frothing flower garden. Tourists sit on the benches, tramps compete with the scent; families stand in front of the perilous piles of petals and grin to have their pictures taken, to be stuck in albums around the globe.

All the formal gardening in Hyde Park is meticulous, endlessly captivating. Hidden in the middle of the park is a compost heap the size of the Dome. Along with the army of gardeners, there are arboriculturists and wildlife wardens looking after 62 genera of trees, 130 species and 120 subspecies. On the Hyde Park side, the prominent species is the London plane. They don't just give off oxygen; their flaky bark absorbs pollution. Generations of children have known that their round seeds are fairy eggs. In Kensington Gardens, the dominant species are the chestnuts. There are walks of mulberries; a family of Cypriot women collect unripe almonds on Lovers' Walk in Hyde Park. Through the high summer, there is a fugitive, sweet smell that's like moving through the rooms of an invisible bordello – it's the flowering limes. The park has large areas of set-aside heather, wild barley and meadow grass. One woman regularly leaves death threats for the park manager on his answering machine because the seeds get caught in her dog's paws.

Over the years, Hyde Park has accumulated knick-knacks, memorials, statues, ornaments, like granny furniture. They grow to be abided and occasionally loved. There's a Wellington memorial on the south-eastern corner made out of boiled cannons, paid for by the women of Britain. It is a colossal rendering of Achilles in his rage; he's classically naked. He was the first naked man to stand in London. The mothers and the nannies of Kensington were outraged, so a fig leaf was slapped on him like a prurient parking ticket. They might have been more outraged if they had realised his fury was due to the death of his boyfriend. Now he glares in his leafy thong at Byron over Park Lane.

There is a stone monolith to the Holocaust in Hyde Park, and a lump of granite given by the grateful people of Norway. There is the original statue that inspired part of the Rhodes Memorial in Cape Town, and the sad obelisk to Speke, who killed himself after discovering the source of the Nile. And there's Albert in his derided Gothic-revival space rocket, now gleaming gold, surrounded by more pulchritudinous allegory than even a serious German could bear. The corner groups represent the four continents; the houri from Asia on the elephant has the best pair of stone tits in London. Outside Kensington Palace, there's William of Orange – a gift from the Kaiser, and a statue of Queen Victoria, who was born and lived here in relative regal poverty. It's sculpted by her daughter. And there's a little terrier with his bottom in the air standing in a drinking fountain, in memory of Esmé Percy, an actor who died in 1957 and instantly became so utterly forgotten he might never have existed. As far as I can discover, he specialised in walk-on aristocrats and once played Ali, the grand eunuch, in the 1935 film *Abdul the Damned*.

Most magically and memorably, there is Peter Pan, the Frampton statue that is one of the most famous monuments in the world. It is certainly the most poignantly beloved and beautiful in London. It appeared overnight and was commissioned and paid for by Barrie, the author who invented him. He met the Llewelyn Davies children and their mother and their dog in the gardens and they were the inspiration for the greatest fairy story ever written. But Kensington Gardens isn't just the place where infants lost by forgetful nannies get taken to Neverland: it *is* Neverland. Every scene in the book belongs here. The weeping beech that Peter sleeps in is still living in the flower walk. The statue is on the shore of the Long Water, where he lands after his voyage in the birds' nest. Peter stands on a pixelated plinth of fairies and animals. He's hidden in an alcove of foliage, so you come upon him all of a sudden.

I sat for an hour and watched the parents bring their children, and the odd thing is that although the kids find the little mice and the rabbits in the sculpture with delight, it is the grown-ups who really get knocked back by Peter. Some to tears. This man-child playing his pipes, blowing a tune whose pitch is too high and fragile for us to hear any more, forcefully reminds them that Barrie's story is not about children but grown-ups. At the heart of the adventure, the romance and the swashbuckling is the saddest truth ever told, that we all grow up and that what we leave behind is more precious than what we gain.

And then there's Princess Diana. How naturally one follows the other. The votive cult of the dead Diana has added a million visitors to Kensington Gardens. Her pilgrimage path is marked out by the ugly goitres in the road like maudlin speed bumps. I've wandered the park for years and I still have no idea where they lead. There is the memorial children's playground with its pirate ship, a ghostly ironic nod to Pan, and there is the great, grudging, temper-filled fountain that was the lavatorial focus for so much regurgitated bile and sour resentment when it opened. Actually now, when nobody's watching, it looks rather chic and elegantly pale. The water rolls and tumbles in a pleasing way and lots of people come to dabble and just stare into the distance in a bashful, shy, enigmatic way.

I stood on the bank and the chap in a bit of a uniform came up and said: 'You can't stand on the memorial. You can sit on it, lie on it or wade in it, but you can't stand on it.' How do I get to sit on it without standing on it first? 'I don't know,' he said, and shook his head. This was the great central mystery of his calling which wasn't primarily as a vestal guard but as a contract cleaner. He works for the private company that maintains the princess's water-work. What's it like? 'Hard work, man. She needs scrubbing out every day. She grows mould and slippery.' You can see her being cleaned in the early morning as the guards go for their coffee trot.

The fountain has its own deep aquifer and uses hundreds of gallons of water that are then pumped into the Serpentine. At its conception and construction, the horizontal Diana fountain seemed like a particularly vacuous committee choice. But now, ten years later, it looks slyly appropriate, elegant, shallow and exceedingly high maintenance, with a deep colonic most mornings, but despite everything rather winning.

Hyde Park is a polyglot pan-national place. All the tongues and customs of the world come here. A park is an internationally understandable place – streets, shops and coffee bars may seem intimidating to foreigners, but everyone speaks park. In the lunch hour, men unroll their mats and make their prayers facing Whiteleys, next to couples sharing bacon sandwiches. Filipino maids lift their faces to the sun and little gangs of Polish lads go about their laddie business. A big Ghanaian skates backwards, legs crossing and uncrossing down the boulevard, arms flailing like a man falling from a high window.

There is always a sadness to the park, an elusive atmosphere of melancholy punctuated by the squeals of pre-school games lessons and toddlers in hard hats slumped on fat, slow ponies, the parties of butt-cheeky girls with bottles of Pinot Grigio. The park is where people come to bring their sadness and loneliness. For every pair of young lovers, there is a broken heart on a solitary bench; hunched men with furrowed brows take clouds of depression to walk the aimless paths as medication. The mad and maddened come to mutter and shout at the wood nymphs and zephyrs. In the wild grass in the north of the park, a lost vicar with a suitcase and a spaniel stops and asks if we can remind him of the redeeming truth of existence. He's quietly desperate, politely overwhelmed by unhappiness.

Hyde Park, without instruction, direction, government or judiciary, has grown to be a model of a just and benign society, where people behave well not because they're made to, but because they can. Where crowds come and depart freely and in good temper. On a summer Saturday there may be 20,000 people here who will let each other be with grace and politeness. Every race, religion, age and class can play or read or eat in an egalitarian beauty and safety. You can do things here that you would never dare do anywhere else; it relieves you of embarrassment or shame; it is a small liberal proof that if you trust people, they behave with manners and care. The park is the vindication of a quiet, levelling English anarchy. The streams of rush-hour cyclists race each other westwards like flocks of Day-Glo geese; the park grows quiet; the sun balances on top of St Mary Abbot's steeple on the southern carriageway; seven herons and a fox wait in a flowerbed to be fed by a deranged lady with an unspeakable sack.

Kensington Gardens closes at dusk. Hyde Park stays open till midnight. The darkness creeps through the trees, which become home to foxes, moths and pipistrelle bats and Central European builders looking for a place to sleep. The park is lit by Victorian gaslights; they cast an ethereal pale glow, and through the avenues of planes the harsh neons of the red and white city streets glint and hiss, but here in the pearly blue quietness the park grows bewitchingly enchanted, a hint of a parallel utopia, that other Eden.

Fatherhood

I

There are any number of design glitches in the human frame: the precipitous decision to stand upright instead of trundling on all fours, which embarrassingly rearranged the visibility of our gonads thereby demanding the manufacture of the Y-front; a columnar spine instantly invented the chiropractor. But as consolation we got oversized female breasts as a secondary compensation for having made their lady bits downward facing instead of backward facing at nose level.

But perhaps the worst of all ergonomic glitches was that we were born not knowing how to blow our noses. I don't expect this worries you much because you've probably got nose-blowing covered and most of the people you want to kiss are pretty tidy in the nose department. But you weren't born like that. There was a time in your life when the contents of your nose ran free.

I'd forgotten about the magic of nasal flubber until my new two both got colds on Christmas Day and one grew a geological outcrop that resembled an inverted Old Man of Hoy and the other had two spigots of effluvia that trickled on to her extended tongue. Neither had any idea of the concept of blowing but they did instantly glean that bogies were edible, which is an interesting Darwinian footnote. We are obviously born with the pick and chew gene.

The sight of them, blocked and soggy, reminded me of something I saw in Africa. I was covering the war in Darfur from a refugee camp on the border with Chad in an old tent that passed a Médecins Sans Frontières (MSF) waiting room packed with women and their desperately dying children. There was one mother who stood out as strikingly beautiful. I mean, really memorable looking. A face that was strong and implacable – huge eyes and cheekbones cast in toffee-coloured bronze, framed in a single bright shawl. I signalled to Tom the photographer to take her picture. It was an easy opening spread. She regarded him and his camera with her obsidian eyes devoid of emotion; she was as beautifully inscrutable as a sphinx.

As he kept snapping, the child was wrapped in the folds of her shawl, making that soft mewing that is the exhausted way of children who are losing the light. Shrivelled with dehydration and malnutrition, her nose was clotted with a huge soggy goitre of snot. The mother never took her eyes from Tom's lens, and slowly and deliberately lent down and gently put her mouth over her child's little nose and sucked, then swallowed. It was properly shocking on so many levels.

First, of course, it was disgusting, an act passively aimed at the gaze of strange men from a woman who had probably lost her husband, her family, who had nothing but this little scrap of life in a shawl. Many of the women in this room had been raped. Her face was a terrible liability. The act was overtly sexual but repellent, but that's not the overriding image or the memory that I carry. It was a profound act of love.

At the edge of coping, there was very little this woman could do for her child; she had nothing left to give. No more milk, no more protection, no more security or hope. But she could clean it. And at the margin of life, when all the options are spent, what's important is the simple and practical. And love is like that. Messy and basic and animal. It isn't romantic or subtle when it's all we have left.

The first lesson of being a parent, of being a man, is that you have no idea of what love is, or like, or for. That urgent, delicious groin-magnet feeling that you understand as being love is the tease, the taster, the glimpse – it is a warm bath compared to the riptide of the real thing. And that arrives with fatherhood. Up until then you've just been paddling in love. Nobody ever tells you this, nobody ever explains that you can't feel the bottom, that you drown in the stuff. Other men never mention that love, which is remiss of us, and our dads never tell us, never really tell us. You can write 'love you' on a birthday card, whisper love to a sleeping tousled head, but to explain to an adolescent, a teenager, that terrifyingly transcendent fundamental act of nature that is loving your children, is too difficult and choking. But you should know, you should be aware, that you can't be prepared for it, nothing prepares you. But you shouldn't be surprised. The funny and sad thing is, that the time when it's easiest to say it, when there is the greatest paternal emotion, when it's most obvious and strong, you never remember. Those first years when you can't blow your own nose, when your father picked you up and rocked you and watched you speechlessly as you slept, are blank. Later, as you grow up, the relationship is muddled with practicality, with the resentment and the accidents, with the dull rigmarole of discipline and bedtimes and homework, inappropriate behaviour, tantrums and tiredness. And that's what you know of your childhood. You remember dodging through it. But there were four scant years when you slept in an ocean of love and your father never forgets and it never goes away and it will come to you.

And you realise the greatest design fault of human beings is that they don't remember their childhood and you can't recall their first words or first steps – the first time they tasted chocolate or falling asleep on their father's shoulders in dark kitchens. You need to know it's coming and you need to know it's already there.

II

A wise man once said – actually, it was Billy Crystal, in *When Harry Met Barry* – 'All the philosophy a man needs for a full life is contained in *The Godfather*'. It has a parable for all occasions.

I'm writing this in the very early morning in New York. It's so early the night doesn't even know it's died yet. I can't sleep. You fly across the Atlantic and think, 'At least I won't be woken up by teething wet babies at an ungodly hour', and then you lie awake because your body thinks you're still at home waiting for a baby to cry.

The Godfather: I watched *Part III* on the plane. That's how bad the movies were.

It starts with a monologue. Old Michael says, 'The only wealth in this world is children.' Not family, but children. Every other possession is dust and ashes. No amount of cousins, nieces and nephews or godchildren or dachshunds compare. And *The Godfather* is the story of how not to have kids. But every father has a Corleone inside him. Until you do it, you've no idea how much of parenting is based on fear and vengeance. All the pastel PR, the cards and the wrapping paper say it's ducklings and bunnies. It's not: it's fear and fury.

The papers are full of stories about children not being allowed to play, never going outside, their lives organised into supervised prison visits to other house-arrest toddlers. No one kicks a ball in the street, complains the *Daily Mail*, or sits in the dust with a stick. The media wisdom is that we're terrified for our kids. But that's only part of it. What parents are really frightened of is what would happen to them if their kid got hurt or died. What unspeakable cocktail of caustic emotion would we be dipped in every day for the rest of our lives? The inner Godfather comes with the stork. We all get our inner *capo di tutti capi*. You never know he's lurking until you see your child bullied.

I have an HD memory of the day my elder daughter came home from nursery school and sat silently on the edge of her bed, chin on chest, fingers pulling at her mittens. Something was the matter. Getting information out of a four-year-old is like unpicking wet wool. Finally, the lip quivered, she dissolved and sobbed that she'd been picked on. Her coloured tissue-paper picture of fish had been scribbled on and the two girls who were her friends had giggled and whispered.

I felt myself go cold and light-headed. I've never believed it when defendants say a red mist descended and they didn't know what they were doing until they came round in a spatter of gore and meaty chunks. For me it's really clear and cold like Novocain. I got a rush of concentrated rage that was biblical. I've been angry, peeved, miffed, pissed off, irritated. I spend most of my waking life dabbing in the pink to puce colour swatch of hacked-off. But this feeling was off the register. I would have killed those girls. Without a second thought, without remorse, sod the consequences. But first I'd have garrotted and flayed their pets. Then impaled their grandparents on sharpened stakes. Rubbed out their favourite cartoon characters. And if that sounds such a schlock overreaction that it's funny, let me underline: I really meant it.

It wasn't so much the desire to wreak vengeance on infants that was shocking, it was that it came out of nowhere. It belonged to my inner Godfather. The need to protect your kids is so ancient it's pre-bipedal. Pre-anger management. Pre-arbitration. My hunter-gatherer instinct to prevent my DNA becoming a sabre-toothed snack has remained unreformed and can be accessed by a four-year-old girl's bad afternoon.

I lay awake that night palpitating with the aftershock, astonished at how instant and overpowering the feeling was, how instantly 10,000 years of reason, culture and civilisation can be swept off the table. And then I thought, how am I going to get through the next thirty years? How's it going to feel when this gets serious, if they're really bullied? What do I do when the first bastard breaks her heart?

The point of all this is that psychotic terror stalks parents. There is no bottom line, no court of appeal, no point where you cut your losses and walk away. If it gets hideous you will go nuclear. You would watch the world burn for a child. Which is extreme and weird. The next thing that happens, of course, is that the phone goes and a man you've never met with a catch in his voice who's just holding it together tells you that his little girl had a fight with your daughter who wouldn't let her play in the Wendy house and called her ginger and now he's comforting a small, hopeless thing whose whole world has dissolved and what, he says half-pleading, half-threatening, are you gonna do about it?

And you think, 'Oh, honestly, get a grip. Get some perspective. Pull yourself together.' And you reply, breezily, 'Sorry, but they're just being kids. It'll be someone else tomorrow. I'll have a word.' And you put the phone down and snigger. There is no empathy, no fraternal sense of 'I know what you're going through, mate. I've lain in the dark my eyes full of tears, too.' You just think, 'Well, she's a ginger. What do they expect?' And that's shaming.

My daughter's now seventeen. When she goes out I give her cash. I tell her to keep her phone on. To be careful. I say it every time and she smiles that little grin that's flattened me ever since she discovered that's what that little grin would do. And really what I want to say is, be careful, because you are carrying around the most delicate and dangerous thing I have. Look both ways. Don't get into cars driven by boys. Don't get into cars driven by men. Don't drink in corners. Don't drink outside. Don't take things, trust strangers ... Because you don't understand the prehistoric grenade of fury you take from me. No one ever said that's what parents are: frightened, frightened and furious, haunted by the misery from which there is no return.

III

Gandhi had four sons. The oldest was Harilal. Harilal was a bit of a lad. A sulky, difficult disappointment. A problem. He drank too much. Fought with his dad. And in a major fit of the fuck-yous, converted to Islam. And then he missed his dad's funeral.

Gandhi was assassinated and, in the tradition of Hindus, was cremated on a pile of sandalwood, cedar and ghee in public. It's the eldest son's obligation to light the fire and scatter the ashes in the Ganges. Mahatma Gandhi's funeral: you can imagine. A billion people mourning and our boy Harilal doesn't turn up. He's too drunk.

Now, missing your dad's funeral is a big deal. There's no way you can shrug it off and say the alarm didn't work. Burying your father is a thing. A huge thing. One of the biggest lumps you've got to swallow as a man. That's the handover. That's where you pick up, do up your top button, get the key to the shed. That's when you're on your own. No one behind you to steady you when you wobble, no one to palm you a tenner. On the day of your dad's funeral you really haven't anything better to do. Now imagine your dad's the most famous, inspirational man in the world, father not just to you, not just to the nation, but the whole subcontinent. It doesn't bear thinking about. But Harilal had to think about it. He had to think about it for the rest of his life. And there was no old man there to tell him it was fine, they'd do it again in the summer holidays.

I got a couple of e-mails from readers after the first column. Most of them from sons talking about the difficulty of dealing with their dads. Fascist dads, controlling dads, feckless, forgetful, embarrassing dads, dads who never said well done and were never proud. But there were a couple who said how great their fathers were. One in particular sent a long letter, an articulate lad, said his dad was a brick. When he got expelled, his dad had been there for him. When he'd been nicked for dealing, his dad had stood by him. The business with the knife, and the drug addiction, the lying, the thieving and arguments, he'd always been there, and when the boy had done a stretch he'd looked after the illegitimate grandson. An old geezer who'd worked all his life for the gas board, never given up for a moment, never faltered with the quiet, strong love.

The son said he still had some problems, was cleanish and soberish, couldn't find a job, was living on his old man's sofa. He was his best friend and he couldn't thank him enough. Now, you can read that and you'll probably think, 'What a great bloke. What a good man. I hope my dad would do that for me. I hope I'd manage to do that for my son.' But then, if you read that story in every Wednesday column in every paper you'd get it the other way round. The nation's greatest problem: feckless, feral, violent, vicious, drunk, cowardly, gutless, entitled gobshite youth, all the fault of their parents. You'd read that and you'd say it's the fathers I blame. No discipline. No limits. No firm hand.

Do you think they said that to Gandhi? His Congress mates, while they were sitting in the hot dust, waiting to get their peaceful heads split by frightened fathers' sons from the Tyne? Did they say, 'So Mohandas, how's that boy of yours doing? Still drunk? Still cheeking his mum? Still think the world owes him a living?

What that boy needs is a clip around the ear. I know you don't agree with that sort of thing but, trust me, he'd learn some manners if you took a belt to him.'

The perfectly obvious point, of course, is that good parents and good children don't necessarily go together like happy families. We like to imagine that our family is the product of nature: stout genes and breeding. 'Ooh, he's got his grandpa's nose! And his auntie's smile! And a really stubborn streak. That'll be the Welsh side of the family.' And then we like to think that everyone else's family is solely the responsibility of nurture, learnt or more likely unlearnt behaviour. 'Look at them. What do you expect with parents like that?'

When my first child was born, I had a list of things I wanted to do with it as long as a footballer's fiancée's shopping list. Music it had to hear, things it'd read, places we'd go. Lots of fun, a bit of character building. Likes, politics, tastes, would all be carefully poured into the empty vessel. Hapless, dumb, naïve idiot that I was. I imagined that life was a set of binary decisions. Straight or gay. Labour or Tory. Rugby or football. Beatles or Stones.

For a start, 'it' turned out to be 'her'. And before she'd even said a word or stamped her foot, before she'd seen Robert De Niro or Jack Nicholson, *Godfather I* or *II*, she was already plainly, unarguably, unchangeably, a creature of her own imagining. She wasn't like her grandparents, she didn't have the mythical qualities of her nation, neither was she baked from my personal recipe. She was simply a self-conceived person. And so it continued with all my children. I offer them anchovies and oysters, Auden and Brookner, Molière and Peckinpah, and they hand me back Nutella and Sunny Delight, Dahl and the Flaming Lips, Jack Black and YouTube.

I'm pleased they have the courage of their culture but it's despite me, not because of me. I don't take responsibility for their shortcomings, or their appalling haircuts. But then neither do I take credit for their many shy attributes. We are each and all of us unanswerable, authors of our own triumph and disaster. But it's easier to deal with both those things if you're not alone. And it's not about good parent and bad parent. It's about being a constant parent. All the time, every day. Until one of them comes and puts a match to you.

Gandhi had a brother. You know what he was? A copper.

IV

We can measure the ages of man by the functions we have to go to wearing a tie. We start with the birthday parties: goodie bags, face-painting paedophiles and tears. The end-of-term exam parties: cider on wet grass, reciting poetry. Engagement parties, graduation dos and the long, tedious decades of stag nights and weddings where you eke out your holiday allowance sitting at Stansted waiting for Ryanair to take you to Helsinki wearing a T-shirt that boasts 'Shag Your Women Drink Your Beer: Gary's Last Weekend Of Freedom' and where every summer Saturday is a furious dash up the M4 for ivory silk, love divine and the joke about the MILF, the sunburn and the razor.

Then there are the years of christening and house-warming followed by the divorced dinner parties and the purgatory of charity events and auctions. Then, blessedly, there is a lull where the dinner jacket can entertain moths on your behalf and you can watch TV in the nude before the funerals start.

I am now in the foothills of elegy bye-byes and this, I expect, is as far as we go before the end of the party line until the great reunion in the sky. The first people to die on you are generally your grandparents. You get to practise mourning on a rabbit and a couple of goldfish and then there is the long period where death is a real shock, an unfair abomination, too fast, too young. Slowly it becomes commonplace and predictable. The cancers flourish like a cottage's herbaceous borders. The arteries mould. The malign and disgusting sickness of decrepitude creeps over your generation.

The age of funerals and memorials kicks off with your parents, and at the moment all my contemporaries seem to be burying their fathers. Let me warn you this is far sadder than you are prepared for. Someone said that no boy is truly a man till his father dies. And I was talking about this with a friend the other day who'd just come from distributing his incinerated dad over bluebells in Sussex. He was, he said, with a catch in his voice, 'not just my dad but my best friend'.

I found my solicitously concerned face of comfort had turned into a rictus of barely disguised disgust. If there is one new age, touchy-feely Dear Deirdre received truism that turns my heart to flint, withers sympathy on the tongue, it is the notion that our parents can also be our friends. That a relationship between father and son isn't quite special enough, it needs to be iced with mateyness.

The idea comes from both sides: boys want their dads to be mates because mates don't tell you off, make you feel guilty, ask what you're doing with your life and tell you to get an early night because you've got work in the morning. And more pathetically, fathers curry their kids' friendship because it seems to be a way of standing off old age. A short cut back to youth, permission to behave like a juvenile and again pick up the embarrassing bollocks of childhood. But the cost is that they lay down the responsibility of guardianship.

It's one thing to have a drink with your dad, play golf with him, but think it through. There's a whole list of matey stuff you don't want to do with him. You don't want to go on a lad's holiday to Corfu. You don't want to watch porn. You don't want to lie to his bird about where he was last night. You don't want to play-fight with towels in the changing room.

I once asked my dad to come to a party I was throwing. His face lit up. He was pleased to be asked and then added that he probably wouldn't. 'Why not?' I asked. 'It'll be fun.'

'Well, it's your friends.'

'What's wrong with my friends?'

'Nothing. They're a fine collection of young people. But they're your friends. They're not people I would choose as my friends. Because sweet, funny, charming and pretty as they may be, they're also rather boring. How could they not be? Their joy is all in their potential. The vitality is all promise.'

'But,' I asked, 'does that mean you think I'm boring?'

He thought for a moment. 'No, you're my son. Everything you ever said and did, everything you will ever say or do is of immense interest, concern and occasionally pride to me. But if you were someone else's son, I'd find you a glib, smug, shallow young man squandering his assets, who I wouldn't want anywhere near my daughter.' Fair point.

Think back over your life. Remember the stages you've already been through – all those parties. And now remember who your best friend was at each of them. Unless you're Rodney Bewes, there will have been at least half a dozen best friends in your life. And you grow up. You grow apart. Friends are the best thing in life. But they're replaceable. If not replaceable, then changeable. A party with your dad is a pair of deckchairs. To make your father your best friend is to swap something that is unique for something ubiquitous. To make your son your best friend is to quit on the most important job you ever had. We will all bury many friends, but only one father.

V

The nanny just came back with my children, my pink-eyed, damp and matted twins. Their mother is exultant. Edith was the best in swimming class by miles (perhaps that should be fathoms). She can do 'The Clam Song', sitting quietly, and was brilliant k-k-kicking and putting her head underwater. Much better, apparently, than the other little girl, who was four months older. 'What about my boy?' I asked. 'How did he do?' The voice drops an octave. 'He just drinks the water.' Oh. I felt a pang for the lad. I understand. He wasn't trying to drink the pool. He was trying to put off drowning by removing the water. I feel for him. I know swimming is a misnomer. It's just prolonged drowning. It is an empirical watery truth that in the end all swimmers sink.

But today the important thing in this house is that Edith is better at holding her breath underwater than some other little muppet. So that's it. It has started. And I never heard the gun. I've had them for barely a year. They don't walk or talk but already my twins have been entered in life's race, or the race of life. If any of you still harboured vague doubts about the utter murderous veracity of Darwin's *The Origin of Species*, go and spend two minutes on the touchline of a primary school football match. You will see the vicious genetic imperative, watch parents jerk to the triumphant tune of their DNA. The need to know that your kid is going to be heads up in a position to nick the sausages, soft furnishings and bitch of an infant next door when the time comes is not rational. It's not nice. But the ancient lizard bit of our brains says it's inevitable. Like children in high chairs, falling jammy side down, we're programmed to march to the Nazi-like triumph of our genes.

The Football Association has just banned league tables and the publishing of results for primary school football leagues. They say the competition is too much for kids who just want to kick a ball about. But the parents are beside themselves with fury, incandescent that they have been cheated of their pint-sized victory. All this is perhaps the toughest and most humiliating part of parenthood. This unseemly desire to see your kid defeat every other kid, along with all the other things nobody ever tells you. Nobody ever tells you that when you become a father you also become a fan. You get a lifetime membership. What you see there lying in the pram in a warm *crème brûlée* of its own curdled shit is your team. You will support that with every atom of your being, with every octave in your throat for the rest of your life. There will never be a transfer. The thing is, you'll feel it but you'll also know it's wrong.

As a parent you spend a lot of time having fights on your internal terrace with your inner fan. My big boy, Ali, played rugby for a season. I never played rugby. I have no idea how rugby works. Nobody with a straight nose knows how rugby works. But I was proud. My inner fan suddenly got a Welsh accent. 'How's the rugby going?' I asked. 'I'm not doing that this year, Dad. I'm doing farm work instead.' My inner Taffy fan gasped in pain and anguish. But the me that's writing this said, 'Good, good lad. That's nice. Mucking out sheep. Great. Bet you can do it faster than the other kids.'

Personal failure has a lot to do with the commitment of your inner fan. We have to be honest. This is all about getting a second shot. Build it and they'll come. I built the kid. Now bring on the glory. The failure and losses of our own past are the driving force. The fat fathers with nicotine fingers wheezing up and down the touchline are bellowing cathartic analysis, regretting with neonatal screams, releasing all that pent-up anger at the sad stored failures of childhood.

I went to the big kids' infant school once, and went to the loo, which was built to accommodate chimpanzees. I found a grown man sobbing over the Wendy sink. His son, his only son, had been winning the egg and spoon race. It had been there. He could taste the egg. Feel the spoon. And then the kid dropped it. And instead of picking it up and putting it back on the spoon and toddling over the line, he'd lobbed the cutlery into the crowd and lain face down on the grass having a tantie. It had dredged up feelings in his father that were so deep and bitter he'd had to retire to the bogs for a weep. 'Sorry,' he said, wiping his snot on his sleeve. 'I never do this. I haven't cried since ... I don't know ...' Since you lost the egg and spoon race, perhaps?

With me it's the opposite. It's the spark of success that terrifies. I never did sport. I did cynicism instead. My father had spent his childhood in a bath chair and had passed on a deep despise for the muddied oafs and flannelled fools. But at my very last sports day I nicked a younger boy's running spikes and got myself entered in the 100 metres. I won and set a new school record, to the consternation of everyone, not least me, and the fury of the games teacher. There was in that moment a bright, white-hot brand of glory that I have never completely lost. Like a scar. I can sense it. I can still feel the tape on my chest. It's poison. It's evil. It's that feeling I don't want to pass on to my children. Prowess, winning, may be a Darwinian imperative if you have to grow your own clothes and eat with your fingers but they're civilised and cultural dead ends.

The world we have created is not inherited by the fleet and strong, the bold or brave. It is invented and maintained by the collegiate, the cooperative, the committee people, the team players, the democrats, the humanists. The truth is that the first are rarely the best, they're just the first. The morals go to the smart, not the strong. The people you want to spend your life with are the pretty, witty ones, not the ones who can hold their breath longest underwater. And being a good grown up human being is realising that you only win when the last person has finished. We only turn out the light when everyone is in bed. And you don't want to be part of a world that leaves your kids behind.

Dyslexia

I didn't write this, I'm not writing this. Amy is writing this. Say: 'Hello, Amy.' I speak into Amy's crooked ear, and she types on my behalf. Amy can tell the difference between a lower case 'b' and a 'd' with one eye closed, after three gins. She minds her ps and qs, and she'll mind mine if I ask her. Amy is comfortable with all the many and subtle ways of 'ough'. Words are her open book, as simple as ACB. So she writes with an assured dexterity, without even looking down. But what you hear, the timbre, the cadence of the clusters and chicanes, those are mine. The voice that is whispering into your shell-like is mine. And that is a great and subtle alchemy. These squiggles, these secretive, revealing spoors are only desiccated sounds – the dried minestrone of speech. It's the voice that matters, warm from the mouth. Not these cold, black letters.

The first alphabet with vowels is Greek, eight hundred years before Christ. The word comes from alpha and beta, plagiarised from the Phoenicians: the pictograms for 'ox' and 'house'. A stable. The alphabet is a stable for words, for ideas, declarations, statements, jokes, orders, denials, rhymes, reasons, lies and last testaments. And you know what else stables are full of.

It was suggested that we should print this the way I write it, just so you could see, get some idea of the mess, the infantilely random alphabetti muesli of my fifty-five-year-old writing. You'd get a kick out of it. No, it would really amuse you. People still laugh at me on paper: 'Oh my God, is that real? Is that how you write? You've got to be joking.' I'm not immune, but I've grown thick-skinned, if a little defensive. After all the awards, the pats on the back, the gimpy words that put the kids through school and put a chicken in the pot, you can scoff all you like. You can scoff for free. I get paid for these words, and I gave up caring when I discovered the rest of you spell phonetic with a 'ph'.

There are better things to do on a miserably wet night than to come to a charmless church hall. Inside is the familiar setup of self-help: the table with pamphlets and privately published books of obsession, the industrial teapot, the semicircle of plastic chairs, the posters of concern and encouragement. There are perhaps twenty people here, talking in little groups, with the familiarity of a cause that is also a social life. A pair of women see me and beam. They are the vestal stewards of church halls everywhere: solid, energetic, intimidating. 'Ah, there you are!' says one. 'We're so pleased you could come. Have you got a cup of tea?' 'Have a biscuit,' says the other, producing a tin of chocolate ones. There's a plate of plain digestives. 'These are the VIP biscuits,' she whispers. This is probably the only hall where I'm a VIP: the monthly get-together of the Bexley, Bromley, Greenwich and Lewisham Dyslexia Association (founded 1974). And I am a dyslexic. A dyslexic who writes a lot – 1,500 words, give or take, a day. And if I let the spellchecker get its bureaucratic little pince-nez within squinting distance of any of them, it would say 1,000 are spelt wrongly. I am a grammar cripple, a functioning illiterate. Literally, I write for a living, and, like blind mountaineers and limbless golfers, I am a straw to be clutched at by these quietly desperate and bravely determined people whose lives and dreams for their children have been overwhelmed by twenty-six characters in search of orthodoxy.

The meeting gets under way. Four experts – an expert being someone who knows more than you do – sit in front of us: a teacher, a helper, a student and a learning-difficulties coach. The parents, mostly mothers, their faces taut with worry and incomprehension, listen intently. One or two have brought their children, who sit with their heads down, drawing, trying to be invisible. I'm with them. The questions swiftly become long, anguished stories of uncaring schools, intransigent authorities, lax teachers, jobsworth governors and thwarted children. At every hardship and symptom, the experts and regulars exchange knowing, conspiratorial grins and raised eyebrows. A desperate mother, twisting her fingers into knots, says the social services are trying to have her committed as an overanxious parent. There's a chance they'll take her child into care. The room shakes its head and tuts with the commiseration of the vindicated paranoid.

After too long, the meeting closes. It has answered all the questions with more questions. Doors have opened to reveal corridors filled with more doors. It has helped only to concern the concerned, whose anxieties mostly revolve around statements. Children with learning difficulties need to be statemented – that is, given a series of tests by a professional that take a long time and are, if not arbitrary, then not altogether precise, a bit like a *Cosmo* quiz for the semiliterate. They are useful, and they are craved by the parents of children who are failing.

A statement imposes a statutory obligation to give the child special attention. Education authorities and school boards don't want to do this because they don't have any money. They do have time. Time is everything. Children grow older, grow out of their shoes and, with luck, out of their schools. Everyone agrees that the sooner you treat dyslexia the better – so they connive to put off statementing. They don't return phone calls, they cancel appointments, lose forms and files, hoping the problem will go to another catchment area, another school, and probably the private sector. They're not uncaring or cruel. They know that the help they can give a dyslexic child will probably amount to no more than an unpaid, untrained teaching assistant doing a bit of nursery rhyme reading a couple of afternoons a week. Everybody understands that the urban comprehensive system isn't going to step up to the needs of a dyslexic child. Still, most parents have no choice but to make bigger and bigger nuisances of themselves. The children find they do have a choice: they can check out. They can turn up, but they can turn off. They can be in the room but not present. They can get their self-worth by being disruptive and too clever by half. They stop offering up their self-confidence to the blackboard to be squashed and mocked.

I hover by the book stand. There's a list of famous dyslexics –

Lee Ryan, Tommy Hilfiger, Benjamin Zephaniah, Steve Redgrave, Richard Branson, Zoë Wanamaker, Eddie Izzard, Toyah Willcox, Albert Einstein, Jackie Stewart. It sounds like a really horrible reality TV show. I could make a starrier list to advertise consumption or syphilis. 'We're a bit in two minds about Einstein,' says the book monitor. 'He was probably autistic.'

I buy a pamphlet called *The Perplexed Parent's Guide to Special Needs*. It is £8. It contains a glossary, four pages of jargon, eighty-seven learning abbreviations. So much easier to tell a parent their child has PMLD than 'profound and multiple learning difficulties'. The well-meaning ladies ask if I'll write for the dyslexic newsletter. I make my excuses. On the way out I am approached by a mother with her daughter, who's had her head bent over a notebook. She must be seven or eight. Her drawings are clever and accomplished, fluent doodles of fantasy things, things that aren't in this room. We smile at each other. 'So good at art,' says one of the vestal ladies. 'Typical dyslexic – so much creativity.'

Maybe I'm too hard on these people, but I've been avoiding meetings like this all my life. I've been avoiding writing this article for as long as I've been writing. I was diagnosed dyslexic when I was at a state junior school in north London, bottom of the class at pretty much everything except the nature table. We were given IQ tests, and apparently mine was disproportionately higher than my academic achievement. This was the way dyslexia was diagnosed in the 1960s. Although not a new disease – it was originally noted in the nineteenth century – it was new to the newly comprehensive school system, and a solid majority of teachers imagined it was either a dubious American import or a euphemism made up by middle-class parents for their dim sprogs. There was certainly no provision for it other than extra homework, which I got and resented, then lost and forgot, dropped in puddles, used as goalposts, fed to the neighbours' dog. So I was sent to a boarding school, St Christopher's, in Letchworth. They said they not only understood dyslexia, but could sensitively help.

At my interview the headmaster asked me to read from the

paper – the *Guardian*, naturally. The Commonwealth Conference was on in London. The first paragraph was an exotic list of African and Asian names. I fell at every one. He beamed. Seven years later, as he shook my hand and I left without a meaningful or useful qualification, he wished me good luck without conviction. The careers adviser had suggested a career in hairdressing. 'I'm sure you'll talk your way into something,' said the headmaster. 'I don't think we've ever had a pupil who's spent as much time doing special extra study on Saturdays.' And he laughed, and so did I. Neither of us meant it. It was only afterwards that I wondered if perhaps, after so many years of punishing my inability to under-stand, they might have thought of some alternative to taking away the only morning I had to myself.

In retrospect there was a prophetic encounter. I loved history. It was taught by a malevolent and bitter man who always gave me low marks for the work I struggled over at the expense of every other subject. One day I went to him in tears and said I thought my history was better than he gave me credit for. He said he thought my history was very good, but my writing was appalling, and he marked me as an examiner would: 'You have a problem with your writing, Gill.' And I thought, actually, no I don't. You have the problem with my writing. To me it makes perfect sense. And I pretty much decided then and there always to make my dyslexia someone else's problem.

There was, though, the 'one' teacher. The one that, if we're lucky, we all manage to find. He taught English. Peter Scupham. He didn't teach me how to write, he didn't do phonics or useful tricks to distinguish endings; he taught me how to read. He didn't even do that, really. He just showed me how to read. He read all the time – often out loud. He would come to our dormitory late at night and read M. R. James's ghost stories by the light of the full moon. He deconstructed Blake. 'The Sick Rose' was the first poem I ever learnt by heart. I read very slowly, but I forget very little. And it doesn't matter – books aren't a race. A book doesn't melt or go off. The author's still dead, the words still live. Peter Scupham showed me the breadth of what was possible. It wasn't

Dead Poets Society or Helen Keller, it was just going to the shelf. I found him very early one morning sitting on the floor of the English department, ripping up dozens of copies of Shakespeare. He looked up without surprise and said: 'You've got to show them who's boss.'

I was never going to make university or poly. I stumbled into art school via the labour exchange, manual and menial work: shops, warehouses, building sites, gardens, kitchens, waiting, nannying, modelling. And I did five years at Saint Martin's, then the Slade, where I took my art history exams with a dip pen. I cut my own quills and wrote with an elegantly illiterate, romantic scrawl. A lot of dyslexics end up in the art room or the drama department. Along with the worry of perceived dimness, there is a parallel and concomitant assumption among mothers that dyslexics are artistic. As amputees grow stronger in their remaining limbs, so children with deficient spelling will develop a heightened aesthetic, have natural affinity to line and colour, bias-cutting and spinning clay. In the church hall there'd been a lot of knowing smiles when I said I'd been at art school. 'Of course, we're all artistic, aren't we?' said the woman who claimed she hadn't discovered her inner dyslexia until after she'd completed her doctorate, and was wistfully still trying to uncover her innate creativity. I stayed with art until I was nearly forty. I got quite good at drawing. But I'd done it for twenty-five years, so I should have been competent. There is no proof that dyslexia makes you any more culturally sensitive or artistically dexterous than people who can spell. We end up holding brushes instead of pens because it's where we find some self-confidence. I don't regret the art, but when I finally did sit down to write, oh my God, it was like coming home. This is what I'd been trying to say with chiaroscuro and perspective. Why didn't I ever think of words? I was amazed at how easy writing is if you take away spelling and grammar. If you just say it.

Julian Elliott is a researcher into special needs, a teacher and an expert on dyslexia. Or, rather, he would be if he thought it existed. But last year he caused a lot of asterisks to be inserted into exclamations by questioning the very existence of dyslexia. I called him: I was rather looking forward to a fight. After all these years to discover that I'd been suffering from some imaginary disease, that I was just dim and backward all along. Happily, Professor Elliott's own written style is as wooden as Pinocchio's best-man speech. It is what's technically known as 'academic remedial'. Less fortunately, within three minutes I agreed with almost everything he said. Far from being a chalk dust and elbow patches grammarian, he's a liberal, sensitive soul.

His point is that dyslexia the label has become a meaningless catch-all. So many symptoms and conditions are attributed to it: word blindness, innumeracy, short-term memory loss, low self-confidence, truncated attention and untidiness, sensitivity to light, poor hand–eye coordination, inability to tell left from right, and various choice incapacities from the lighter end of the autistic spectrum. This is no longer a medical condition, it's a social one. He emphasises again that there is no link between IQ and dyslexia. We are not innately smarter, nor is there any provable link with artistic talent, theatricality or interior design. On the other hand, being a brilliant speller isn't an indicator of high IQ either, nor is reading a lot. But still, there is a huge weight of parental pressure behind the acceptance of dyslexia as a cause for special treatment and an indicator of aesthetic sensitivity.

Elliott does not deny that some children have difficulty reading and writing, but he says that the difficulty simply falls into the general bucket of special needs. The treatments for dyslexia and for other learning difficulties are identical, and if the cure is the same, so, possibly, is the condition. But there is consternation at the thought of disbanding the dyslexics' club, not only from parents but from a host of commercially interested schools and experts. There is a lucrative dyslexia industry. Where the state system has been unable and unwilling to offer help, it has colluded with the private sector, all too happy to offer a service and to exploit the worries and fears of parents. So now there are legions of specialists and gurus whose cards mothers exchange at school gates with a desperate trust. Teachers sell proprietary cures, from coloured cellophane to gymnastics to computer programs. A devoted, sympathetic department geared to dyslexia is now one of the best selling points of a private education.

I mentioned to Elliott that I have a son who is dyslexic in exactly the same way as I am, with pretty much the same IQ I had at his age. 'Ah, yes,' he says, 'there does seem to be a genetic link, particularly between fathers and sons.'

I asked Ali's permission before mentioning him here. He said it was fine, as long as I didn't make him look like an illiterate poster boy. He's now seventeen and struggling with exams. The provision for dyslexics is almost exactly the same as it was when I was at school – more work, extra reading, extra writing, one-to-ones with a woman with ethnic jewellery who speaks in a slow, loud voice.

Fairley House is a school that specialises in dyslexia and its associated learning difficulties. This is the gold standard for specialist help, and it needs to be: it's not cheap. They take children at the end of primary school to help them make the jump into secondary education. This is the great nightmare for parents; the competition for big school, both public and private, is fierce. Fairley House is a bright and jolly place in Pimlico, named for Gordon Hamilton-Fairley, the oncologist murdered by the IRA. I remember hearing the bomb that killed him. The school is noisy and energetic. Every wall, door and ceiling is covered in information – pictures, mobiles, labels. It's like being inside a hyperactive thirteen-year-old's scrapbook, a great, tie-dyed stampede of spangly encouragement and useful rubrics.

The headmistress might have stepped off one of her own walls, a lady with Day-Glo energy of the sort that seems to exist only in education and the more charismatic fundamentalist churches. She bobs down the school corridor like a cork in a millrace of children, shouting encouragement and cosy admonishments with a pantomime zeal. She has assigned me to shadow an attractive and winning lad called Zinzan. We go to his maths class with Millie, George and Lewis, taught by Mr Taylor, who's been bitten by the same dog that got the headmistress. We're learning percentages using packets of sweets. They try to teach everything with a practical example or a stick-in-the-head image; they learn pi using real pies. I sit on the little chair behind the desk, and the oddest thing begins to happen: I can feel myself regressing, the panic begins to constrict my chest. I can't follow what Mr Taylor is saying. I don't understand.

Millie leans across and helps me, not as a politeness to a grown-up who's older than her dad, but with the fellowship of the impaired; another word-blind, number-paralysed school sufferer. It all rushes back over me: everything falling off my brain, like hearing through double glazing, the fog of incomprehension, the panic of being left behind. I'd completely forgotten the loneliness of classrooms where it all makes sense to everyone else. I look down at the page and my handwriting belongs to a child. I get it all wrong. 'Never mind,' says Millie. No, never mind. This is the most salutary of lessons. I had utterly buried this feeling: being here in this place. To fail with the kindness of professionals willing you on, egging you to understand, just to grasp the simplest corner of a concept that is forever opaque and ghostly. I still can't do long division, or short division. I have no idea how grammar works. I can't name the parts of a sentence. And, do you know the weirdest thing? If I were Chinese I wouldn't have any of this. It seems there is no pictogram for dyslexia. If I were being taught in Finnish, it's unlikely I'd be dyslexic. This is an overwhelmingly English condition. It's the language, stupid, our irrational, fraught and contrary written tongue, that breeds misconceptions and mis-understandings that some of us never get into our thick heads. We can't deal with the memory cards, the exceptions to rules, the little charming eccentricities.

English was only recently regulated and systematised, when public schools had to turn out a large civil service and the mer-cantile class of clerks who all needed examining and filing. Before then, English was firstly a declaimed, sung, spoken, hot language. Not the chilly, starched memo-for-your-files, cc'd written one. But there's no going back on it. It won't return to the glorious free-for-all, extempore, idiosyncratic, phonic whoop of the seventeenth century. This is the way it is. And school's currency is forever going to be words and numbers. If you can't collect them and order them, it doesn't matter how many sweets you count or pies you make or colourful drawings or pasta pictures. You are never going to be rich here. And we just have to live with that. Get on with the rest of our lives. If you offered most parents, indeed, most dyslexics, the opportunity to spell like a Scrabble champion but that the price would be ugliness, they'd never take it. And, anyway, how much do the rest of you remember about schoolwork?

The galvanising headmistress asked me if I'd talk to a few of the children about my experience with dyslexia. Of course, I said, through a pasty grin. She led me into assembly. *You want me to take assembly?* 'Just a few words. They're all very excited you're here.' How long shall I talk? 'Oh, twenty or thirty minutes, then questions.' I stood in front of this sea of blameless little faces, knowing that behind each of them there was already a room full of low self-esteem, full of catalogues of failure, a great weight of parental concern, and I wondered again at the horrible obstacle course we make of other people's childhoods after we've f***ed up our own. And I caught sight of Zinzan, and I felt the anger, the hot fury for the wasted, tearful, silently worried, failed years of school, and I had a Spartacus moment. I started talking, rather too loudly. I told them this was their language, this English, this most marvellous and expressive cloak of meaning and imagination. This great, exclamatory, illuminating song, it belonged to anyone who found it in their mouths. There was no wrong way to say it, or write it, the language couldn't be compelled or herded, it couldn't be tonsured or pruned, pollarded or plaited, it was as hard as oaths and as subtle as rhyme. It couldn't be forced or bullied or policed by academics; it wasn't owned by those with flat accents; nobody had the right to tell them how to use it or what to say. There are no rules and nobody speaks incorrectly, because there is no correctly: no high court of syntax. And while everyone can speak with the language, nobody speaks for the language. Not grammars, not dictionaries. They just run along behind, picking up discarded usages. This English doesn't belong to examiners or teachers. All of you already own the greatest gift, the highest degree this country can bestow. It's on the tip of your tongue.

And then I caught sight of myself, standing like a declamatory tick-tack man, bellowing like a costermonger, and I stopped and stared at the faces staring at me with expressions of utter, dyslexic incomprehension. From the back of the room, a teacher coughed.

Nelson Mandela

The corridors of the InterContinental hotel smell of the uneaten, unchanged and unloved. The mezzanine floor is a miasma of exhausted, reconditioned air and scream-absorbing carpet. It's one of those constructions of bleak, utilitarian comfort that make you despair of human ingenuity. Here, past the press/business facilities, is a conference room – one of those large open spaces at a premium in cities, used for the amplification of grand, commercial lies and celebrations.

It's 10 a.m. and the room's been fitted up for a big day. Men in shorts and work boots, wearing T-shirts boasting past crusades and convictions, move about with the concerted, head-down purpose of an imminent, immovable deadline. They are the international freemasonry of fitters, riggers and roadies. Blokes who are never without a corkscrew, a light and four yards of gaffer tape.

Every public event, anywhere on the globe, is built by these leftover medieval artisans who step lively, yelling unintelligible single syllables, testing sound systems, putting up podiums, lighting interactive screens and constructing bullet-point display boards with an air of smiley cynicism. You just know that at the final trump, an army of these bantering blokes with 'Iron Maiden on the road!' hair will rise up and dismantle the world overnight.

Keeping out of their way are other men, in suits, with airport ties and multiple phones. They text pleading demands into Black-Berrys. In turn, they are circled by girls with high heels and fussed hair and get-off-me grins. This is the public-relations commissariat. They go with riggers the way vultures go with jackals, employed by customers who want to avoid relations with the public. To a man and woman they look wrung out and worried like sheep. They are employed to be wrung and worried, to suck up and absorb all the anxiety of the organised, money-go-round world. Today, they're overseeing the *mise-en-scène* for a photo call: a simple stage, a backdrop, a couple of cardboard posters saying something portentous, sentimental and forgettable. It might be a product launch, an employee-of-the-month award or the declaration of an invasion.

Actually, it's the stage for Nelson Mandela to have his ninetieth-birthday picture taken with a hundred folk he doesn't know, but who know him. More precisely, it's the stage for a hundred people to have their picture taken with Mandela.

Stephen from Budapest, an economic refugee drone, pushes a vacuum cleaner across a tennis court of nylon carpet. He wears the dull overalls of public invisibility. He's too old to be chasing dust in a foreign country, prematurely bald with sad eyes. He says he likes London, what he's seen of it. But he's tired and, no, he doesn't know what this event is.

Terry O'Neill, the chosen photographer for Mandela's birthday tour, is sitting on the far wall while his assistants set up the big-format camera and the synchronised, megawatt hose-you-down lights. They check the focus on a chair for the umpteenth time. We all stare at it. The chair is the centre of the room; the riggers and roadies regard it with a professional respect, as if it were the apotheosis of Meat Loaf. It's a plush, overstuffed chair, a Louis XXXIII chair, the sort of international chair used for filling up corners in big hotels.

'Go and see how it looks,' Terry tells me. It feels mildly sacrilegious to sit on the chair, like sitting on the throne while the monarch's having a pee. Already, this ugly piece of hotel furniture is imbued with the saintliness of Mandela, and he hasn't even sat on it yet. The assistant snaps the shutter at me, pretending to be the best person in the world, and Terry, pretending to be Bono beside me. He's better at it than I am, and rubs the Polaroid, like trying to get warmth into a corpse.

He looks at the chair and says: 'Change it. Change it for something simpler.' The chair's moment is over. It goes back to being just hotel furniture, a nearly-chair.

This is all displacement activity. The photographers are bored and nervous. There will only be a few seconds for each shot, no margin for error or interpretation or finesse. No space to tell them they've got something in their teeth. Around the edges of the room are the napkinned trestles of inhospitable hospitality – the Thermoses of stewed, lukewarm, coffee-style bitterness, the plates of biscuits you've never seen in a shop or in a home, that only exist in corporate hotels. Guarding them are girls from the distant heart of Europe, who stand in unflattering uniforms waiting for something big to turn up and rescue them from the biscuits.

Most people drift in and collect in the room's dark marches. Sleek, older men with carefully managed grey in their hair, in better suits, worn with sleeker shoes and silk ties chosen by a tie-choosing assistant. Each of these men has another man or two for their support and affirmation. These are the captains of consumption, the herders of money, the gents who move the First World and shake the Third. Blue-chip CEOs who sponsor and fund and finesse this occasion, this happening. They have come to be photographed with Mandela: a small memento, a religious image to be displayed discreetly on the huge desk or in the annual report, or above the bar in the den. You can tell they're not used to being kept waiting – they rather enjoy the hair-shirtness of it. It's sort of appropriate before meeting a saint. In the topsy-turvy world of charity and celebrity, these plutocrats who have chancellors and finance ministers on their speed dials come at the bottom of the cheek-pecking, arm-clasping, back-slapping order. The talent comes first, and they are being corralled in a separate holding room.

One of the PR ulcers whispers 'Bring on the celebrity' into his secret-squirrel radio, and through the big double doors they come, gambolling like spring bullocks, beaming and dazzled by each other, the occasion, the event, but mostly just by themselves for having got here to this room. What a relief to be excited and giggly, not to be surly and cool, to talk all at once. In one corner behind a hastily erected cordon for their own safety are the cast of some multicultural, Milk Tray-coloured, feel-glad and horny musical. These perky, pretty teenagers have been mainlining adrenaline and endorphins. They started out as nature's hyperactive show-offs, but now they're levitating and vibrating with excitement, tumescent with joy and hormones. They involuntarily bop into little routines, jigging and staggering with a manic, incoherent happiness. They're hazy about who Nelson Mandela is, but they all know Will Smith is awesome.

Slightly apart is an old black man in a suit, the arms too long. He is unmistakably African. He's brought the stillness with him; the guarded eyes, the private face, the quiet politeness. He is Mandela's driver and has been since the beginning – since Robben Island. He looks at the gaggle of humming talent – it's not the worst thing he's ever seen.

Behind him is an open door and slowly, like the entry of shadow puppets, a phalanx, a protective crèche of people, sidles across the light. In the centre, one shuffling silhouette is unmistakably the figure of Nelson Mandela.

Walking with a stick, supported on each side, the radiant tableau moves towards the arena. The pop stars and the dancers, the plutocrats and PRs and photographers and all their assistant managers, handlers and agents don't know that he's just there and Mandela doesn't yet know that they're just here. It's the lull between colliding worlds.

He comes into the room slowly, slowly, his damaged feet in big, comfy slippers, sagging in the trademark African shirt, and they erupt – whistle and clap and whoop, and generally can't believe it. It's like *The X Factor*.

Terry says: 'Let's get the group shot over first' – he doesn't know how long he can hold back the hyperventilating show bunnies. Mandela is ushered to sit in the middle, in the new star chair, helped by his formidable Afrikaans secretary, one of those terrifyingly admirable women only Africa produces. He looks up and around, like a child who's just woken in a strange room, and sees all the folk who have come to see him, and smiles this brilliant, beatific smile, a smile that could break your heart. It is the most conscience-tugging, soul-moving facial expression in the world, and he got it in jail. Go back and look at all the photographs of Mandela before the island, and he is another righteous black lawyer with the ebony, private face and the guarded eyes. But he comes out twenty-seven years later with this miraculous face, moulded and creased by injustice into a transcendent African mask, this expression that speaks every language. The stars fall in behind and around him, like confetti at an arranged marriage. Annie Lennox sits on his left, transported. The seat on his right is kept empty. Will Smith slips in behind him, flicking peace signs. The pack of drama-school kids squirm at his feet like Labrador puppies. Where you sit is important, not just because closeness is a blessing but because this picture will be cropped for the papers and social gossip magazines, and only those at the epicentre are going to get the publicity fix. The empty seat on the right is filled by the ample thighs of Leona Lewis, Simon Cowell's latest vibrato-rich crooner of the beyond-irony transfusion, 'Bleeding Love'.

'Smile. Look this way, smile,' the snappers call. 'Madiba, Madiba, over here. Madiba!' It's a familiar patronymic of respect, but in a cockney accent it sounds like mockery.

Mandela regards the camera only fleetingly, not ignoring it, just perhaps not entirely aware of it. His eyes wander around the room at all these people and all this attention, all this expectation, all this love. And he smiles the smile. Behind him Will Smith – who by happy coincidence is promoting his film *Hancock* – grins and leans forward with the Vs, and everyone else arranges their hands in the semaphore of pop eloquence, and their faces into that contortion of egotism and charity. The flashes flash, the moment is caught. Terry turns away and gives me a look that isn't in the camera, and I wonder who on earth thought a pop concert was an appropriate gift for a ninety-year-old-man with bad feet.

But, then, pop concerts seem to be our culture's response to most things – the catch-all celebrations, commemoration and commiseration of everything: the Queen's jubilee, famine, hurricanes, birthdays and small, messy wars.

And why here? Why does Mandela come to London for his

birthday? Simply because here he can raise money to combat AIDS. We could have sent him a cheque, he could have sat at home, but then these people wouldn't have had their photograph, and we wouldn't have had the pop concert.

Now it's one-to-one time. The entertainers sit next to him looking nervous, some hold his hand, put an arm round his neck. Beside me, one of Mandela's carers mutters, 'Don't touch him', with sadness and anger. But only I hear it.

Through all this, he sits quiescent and patient, listening without hearing, knowing without understanding, smiling the great warm smile. His fearsome secretary is fearsome on his behalf, moving people on, holding them back: 'No managers today, no hangers-on, just performers.'

When the talent's all done, the businessmen scuttle in, uncomfortable in their suits, fiddling with their tie knots like vestigial scrotums, taking Mandela's hand firmly and meaningfully, looking deep into the camera's blinking eye, as if sealing some moral deal.

Why do they want all this so badly? This picture with an old African whose deification by the West is such an indictment of all other Africans. We can't help adopting worthy people from the developing world – suspending criticism like debt to make them worthier, investing them with a Christmas tree of wholesome goodness and blameless simplicity. There is more than a stain of racism here, an echo of colonial assumption. We see a good man and promote him to an impossibly great man by virtue of his having come from a bad and frightening place.

Poor, dark, benighted Africa; a continent of corruption, violence, megalomania, ignorance, sickness and superstition. How much greater is Mandela in our eyes because he's risen from the heart of darkness rather than, say, Tewkesbury or Oslo. They hug him and get speechlessly lumpy because he inoculates us against the fears and prejudices about the Third World in general, but Africa in particular. In the process of worshipping him, he is allocated patronising characteristics – an innate, natural wisdom, an avuncular sympathy for children. Someone here said that Mandela was 'Gandhi for our generation'. This is a wishful, fairy-tale nonsense that denies him his history, his anger, his blackness, his Africanness. Mandela was a revolutionary. Far from a pacifist, he organised and led Spear of the Nation, the terrorist wing of the ANC. In adopting Mandela as a smiley face, T-shirt slogan, album-cover vision of happy otherworldliness, we take him from his real family: southern Africa. We make him the West's boy.

He is a real hero, he's an African hero. His struggle and his triumph are their struggle and triumph. We can't buy them with an AIDS donation and a song. He's called Madiba because of his black Africanness, not despite it. He should be at home with his family on his birthday. Africans venerate age. He has lived twice as long as most African men can expect to.

There is a votive quality about these images – the great and the powerful once had themselves painted with saints to fool God and the neighbours. There's also something less edifying, something of the game hunter's trophy shot.

And it's over. Mandela is helped to his feet, slowly, slowly. The performers and plutocrats crowd the exit, stabbing BlackBerrys, shouting into their phones for cars and lunch.

Mandela is handed his ivory stick, and hobbles painfully. This, then, is where the long road to freedom ends. He looks exhausted, beaten down by the adoration of strangers, tired by the demands of so much love.

This has not been an edifying occasion. It's nobody's fault – everybody had good intentions, or at least enough good intentions. But altogether it's been sad, dispiriting. Nobody comes out of the photo call looking good. Already the roadies are tearing down the evidence, packing up the metal boxes. The photographers look at their screens, feeding the images into the river of celebrity and curiosity.

As he gets to the door, for the briefest moment Mandela pauses and looks at the wall where, unnoticed, the coffee girl in her uniform of invisibility still stands guarding the biscuits. She smiles at him. And Mandela bathes her in the great, hot African sun of his grin, and there are tears in her eyes.

Fishing

Water is the earth's most skilful designer. Water and the tidal moon are our keenest architects. Nothing that comes from the sea is ugly. Everything is sculpted and smoothed into an ergonomic, rhythmically satisfying aesthetic. Every shell, fin, stone and scale, driftwood and all the flotsam of man's manufacture is eventually whittled and worn into a pleasing aquatic beauty. And there are ships, built by men but designed by the element they live in. However meagre or humble their journeys, water makes them ultimately sublime. All of them except *Emulator*.

The first sighting of this ship-shaped thing, crouching in the bowl of Scarborough's small harbour, tugs your breath. All boats, even the most mundane plastic pedalos, have an ergonomic purpose. But not this dog of a barque, this crook-backed, axe-bowed, rusting Quasimodo decorated with the cross of St George like an ocean-going scaffolders' van. It was first light, and it hunched over the other rocking fishing boats. They were all inshore line-fishing crabbers, part-time day boats. *Emulator* is made for sterner stuff.

We'd walked the half mile round Scarborough's long bay after a night in the Clifton Hotel. I'd lain awake in the garret tower that Wilfred Owen had slept in on his final recuperation, where he wrote some of his bleakest poetry before passing over the sea to die. Scarborough is a fine town, neat and purposeful. The penny arcades wink fitfully on the front, the fish and chip shops congeal in the chilly dawn, the cliffs hotch with seabirds. Its Victorian stucco grandeur tells of a richer past, when there were more Yorkshire tourists come for the bracing air and the sand, a break from mill and mine, when there were more ships, more sailors and fishermen, more fish.

Fish and fishing is the front line of environmental politics – an issue that stares back at you from the plate. Fish comes from that other place, the other dimension, the two-thirds of the planet that is the alien element – where we are not welcome, we can only skim and churn the surface. When you catch a fish and stare into that round black jelly eye, there is no spark of recognition, no empathy. But at least we know what to expect. The fish had not an inkling you even existed, no notion that the world wasn't endless wet.

The catching and consuming of fish is hooked to a lot of buzzy, feel-good, groovy goodery, labelled with ticks and green smiles, ports of origin – as if fish lived in fields – promises of sustainability, of fairness, of freshness. The marketing of conscience and guilt. It also comes with the bad temper of fishing limits and national waters, of quotas and trade agreements, of unions and civic decline, national pride and international obligation. Fish bring with them a lot more than omega-3.

A man loads ice through *Emulator*'s hatches, another is carrying supermarket bags. We shout hellos from the flagstones. The ice man says, 'So, you made it? Managed to get up? Step aboard.' There is no obvious way of stepping aboard – no gangplank, no break in the slim railing. You just leap nonchalantly and cling, hoping not to slither down the slick sides to be crushed between steel and stone.

Even hobbled in the harbour, it's difficult to get about. Ropes are tossed, the throb of diesel grows hectic, and *Emulator* elbows its way past the lighthouse and the edge of the still-snoring town, pointing its broken, blunt nose nor'east into the North Sea.

Why is it called *Emulator*? Who or what is it emulating, I ask Sean, the captain, a cropped, round-headed man with a gimlet stare and a pirate's earring. 'Fook knows. I think the owner likes names that begin with vowels or summat.' She's nearly thirty years old and Sean has been with her since she was launched, all his working life. He sits in the tiny wheelhouse, his feet up, a cup of coffee in the failsafe cup-of-coffee holder, in front of him what looks like an electronics repair shop: stacks of screens broadcasting streams of interference. There's radar and sonar and the local TV news. He is surrounded by a confusion of paper: lists, logs, notepads and man-muck. The grimy window grudgingly offers a thin view of the horizon, obscured by the deck, masts, derricks and strapped-on aerials, like some council house-nicking satellite. The edge of the water plays peekaboo with the wallowing bow.

There are three crew: Sean, Mark and Stephen. Mark is big, lumpy and coarse, with diligent hands and a face that looks like a frostbitten turnip. These two men are in their forties, the sea has been their life and the rest of their life has had to make way for it. And then there's Stephen, slouched and whippety, a boy in his twenties with the easy smile of a lad who's always had a lot of explaining to do. He boasts the worst set of drunken tattoos I've ever seen.

Already he has two families ashore, all girls. Women are his weakness. Women and beer. You get the sense that coming to sea is a relief. There's no beer and no women on boats. This is a very masculine place: fishing is perhaps the last occupation that has no women. I ask if there are any female fishermen. 'There's a wifey who puts the crab pots out with her husband, but lasses are bad luck on boats.'

The native wit and badinage of Yorkshire is a relentless, repetitive mockery. Every sentence begins with an ironic rhetorical question: 'You're seriously going to wear that?' 'You really think Macclesfield will win next year?' So when I ask about the diminishing fish stock, I get back the sneered 'Who do you believe? People who are out fishing all their lives, or a bunch of academic civil servants looking at computer screens? There's no shortage of fish.'

Fishing and fish stocks is one of the areas of ecology and the environment where the activists in suits are diametrically opposed to the working men who make their living from fish. As a rule, environmental campaigners support and back indigenous food producers, but not in the case of fish. And it's not just here. Around the world fishermen say there are plenty of fish, and marine experts say there aren't.

'We've always said that warming is changing where the fish go,' says Sean. 'Fishermen noticed ages before the fooking noddies. Look at sea bass. There's no quota on them at the moment because there's that many in the Channel.'

Mackerel seem to be following the colder water to the north, to Iceland and the Faroes, incensing Scandinavian and British fishermen. The land-bound experts say that fishermen have a vested interest in continuing to fish unsustainably. 'Who's got the fooking huge vested interest?' the three men bellow at once. 'Fooking ecology movement, Greenfookingpeace,' says Mark. 'That's huge business. The environment is a fook sight bigger than fooking fishing, I'll tell you. Not one of them would work for what I take home.'

The economics of the *Emulator* aren't going to make anyone rich. Leaving aside the depreciation of the boat, diesel is the biggest expense. Agricultural diesel is 50p a litre. The engines run all day. They use about 4,000 litres a week. On top of that, they have to pay for the ice, boxes, insurance and transport on land, and the ship's owner takes 50 per cent of any profit. What's left they split between them. Last time out they fished for seven days and made nothing. They're at sea for about half a year. This week they're in debt for the fuel. They need £8,000 worth of fish to make a wage. If you tot up the hours, it's not anywhere near the minimum. But out at sea, none of those rules count.

The galley is the only place to sit. It's so cramped, if you put a stamp on it you could post it home. There are five of us on board now, but only four of us can sit at a time, which is okay because someone needs to drive and watch for tankers. There's a filthy stove and a little sink with a plastic bowl full of slopping, turgid, lumpy water. This is the only tap on the ship. There's no shower, no water you'd want to drink without boiling. They drink only tea, coffee and Tesco's cola. There are five mugs that are never washed and when you see the state of the tea towel you're grateful. We sleep in the bowels of the boat, a little dark dungeon up the sharp end with pods in the walls like Davy Jones's catacomb. The human part of this ship is made as small and claustrophobic as possible. The greatest part of it is given over to the fish, to the catch. To the cash. The engine rumbles and caws constantly, without cease.

There is a bin, a small bucket that's emptied over the side, and there's a lavatory without a seat that would be impossible to sit on because it's jammed sideways into a cupboard with a broken porthole. The thought of maybe having to sit on it – or, worse, kneel in front of it in the humping swell – is too awful to contemplate. Overall, I'd have to say that this is the most assertively filthy environment I've been in since I was a student. The boat is a Norman Wisdom assault course of pratfalls, whacked heads, lost fingers, rope burn, slicing steel, crunching blocks and grinding gears, or just simply and silently tripping and disappearing overboard.

We chug into the North Sea. It is the most beautiful day, the water gently undulating, gunmetal blue. I spend a lot of time staring out to sea. It's better than staring at Mark in the galley. Everything land is, water isn't. It's fickle, ethereal, moody and restless, hissing and slapping, whispering and booming. Its colour changes constantly from this cold blue to salmon silver, verdigris, golden, polished pewter, gull-grey leaden, like oil on steel. The English and Scots have fished in these cold metal waters stretching up to Iceland and Norway for two thousand years. The sea is calm, the wind a tugging breeze. The ugly, fat boat makes the most of it and rolls and yaws like a sickening diva. I'm relieved to find that I don't seem to be prone to seasickness.

We arrive at the fishing grounds, fifty miles from the coast. We are trawling for flatfish, bottom feeders, so the bed needs to be sandy. A huge reel at the stern unravels the stinking net of blue and green nylon. It trails into the water like toilet paper caught in a fat girl's knickers. It works like a shopping bag. At its edges are a pair of heavy iron plates called the doors. They sink the net and keep its mouth open. On its bottom edge are rubber rings that churn up the sand and mud, confusing the fish, which are drawn into the back of the net, called the cod-end. *Emulator* draws for fish for four hours. The crew get some rest, drink tea, man the bridge. Seabirds follow in our wake, hanging over the boat, wings catching the stiffening breeze, like thieving gulls following a tractor as we plough the water. There are pretty and delicate kittiwakes, herring gulls and gannets, a thieving skewer, but mostly they are fulmars, beautiful grey and white birds with dark eyes and strange tubular nostrils. Their name comes from the Norse for foul gull – they spit rancid oil as a defence.

The net is drawn in by a winch to a series of musical calls and instructions. Ropes hurl through tackle, hawsers sing at head height in fits of spray, chains clank and everywhere is in the way. These men's jobs are so familiar that they synchronise with a feverish elegance. The net is pulled like a purse, heavy and flickering with the pale head of small dabs. It is lifted to the fish hopper, where Stephen crawls in and tugs a series of sodden slip knots. The cod mouth opens and the hundredweight of fish fall as he struggles to back out of the little hatch.

From the hopper comes a conveyor slide. The three men in yellow slick overalls stand side by side. The fish slip out in a confusion of slime and tails, gaping mouthed. Each man has a small knife, continually stropped; with rubber gloves they grasp a fish and dig and disembowel each one. I had a go at gutting. A plaice took me two or three minutes. It was slippery and tough.

Mark holds up a leviathan the size of a four-year-old child. 'Fooking look at this. This is the fooking fish those clever fookers says doesne fooking exist any more. It's fooking extinct.' It is a beautiful, gleaming, pale green cod. They catch quite a lot of them – not codling, but big, muscly, full-grown cod.

There are whiting and orange-spotted plaice, and little dabs and lemon sole. There are big, oval, knobbly turbot and round, smooth brill. There are enormous halibut and fearsome gape-mouthed monkfish. There are jellyfish and lumpfish, starfish and an anemone they call tits, because it looks like udders. There is an octopus they stick on the wall and watch slowly climb along the roof while asking it the football results. There is a solitary red mullet, but mostly there are haddock, thousands and thousands of them, with their great big surprised eye, the fried fish of choice north of the border.

At my rough estimate, two-thirds of the catch goes back to the deep as corpses. Very little lives in the net. The fish are crushed and suffocated. They madly eat each other in the confusion and are drowned. Worst are the monkfish. Their wide saw-toothed mouths gape and scoop up mud until their gills are choked solid. Morbidly, they are buried alive with earth underwater. 'What do you think of this then?' says Sean.

'All this fish chucked back?' He answers his own question. 'We fooking hate it.' He searches for the word. 'It's wrong.' In front of each of the men is a wooden ruler with incised lines. This is the minimum length required for each species. Too small and they go over the side. The EU quota system means all fishing boats are catching far more than they are allowed to sell, and are then dumping much of it.

In the case of the haddock, large fish get a better price than small ones. They know they're going to catch their quota, so they only keep the premium ones. It's the same with whiting. It's immoral, it's insane, and that's not the half of it. The quota system, which is constantly being fiddled with and fine-tuned by men who have never been to sea and probably never eat fish with a face on, ascribes quotas to boats. You can scrap your boat, turn it into a bar or brothel, but keep the quota, which you can then sell.

Sean spends hours on the radio phone to his owner, trying to buy extra quota for fish he's already caught, or expecting to catch. So there is a secondary market in fishing quota that is traded, and the oddest people, such as investment funds, end up owning it. It's even rumoured that Manchester United owns quota.

Well-meaning environmentalists with plans and graphs and pie charts have come up with the worst possible outcome: a system, organised with a monstrous bureaucracy, where most fish are killed and thrown away for their own good. The most money is made by those who buy and sell paper quotas and never see a fish. And the cost of all this is borne by these three men and by the consumer. It is beyond the dreams of a flabbergasted Kafka, and everybody knows it is indefensible and it is sinful. And nobody knows how to stop it.

Except, of course, the Norwegians have done it. They insist that every fish caught must be landed. Instead of setting a quota for the numbers caught, they regulate the number of days boats go to sea. But what would the Norwegians know? They only have the longest coastline in Europe and are the richest people in the world.

The catch is cleaned, washed, packed into boxes with ice and stored in the refrigerated belly of the boat. We have dinner. We eat frozen burgers and chips; we have fry-ups and cold shepherd's pie. Beneath our feet are boxes of the most wonderful fresh fish from the finest cold water fishery in the world. Finally, reluctantly, they agree to batter and fry some haddock, and I cook some gurnard fillets.

Fishermen don't eat fish, and they don't swim, and they don't drink water. If you have to stick your rubber finger up the vent of a thousand plaice, you don't necessarily want to put one in your mouth. None of them like cod. 'You should see the fooking worms they get.' We sleep for a couple of hours. My pod smells sweetly of other men's night sweats and toe jam.

The *Emulator* trawls four times a day. I try to wake up for each catch. On the second day the net catches on something on the seabed and they lose the cod-end – that's £1,000 of net. They have to stay up to sew another one on, as the boat heaves and plunges in 20-ft waves. Then they dredge up tons of mud. It's hard and it's dispiriting. That night the moon is huge and clear, the sea platinum and jet.

On the third day there are a hundred boxes of fish – monk and premium green cod, flat and haddock – and they decide to turn back to Scarborough to send them to market by road to Grimsby. It's another expense, but the prices should be better there. The fish are unloaded on to the dock. The prices are fixed. They have yet to make a profit. The *Emulator* will turn round and go back for another three days, but without me.

We are an island. That geography is our defining characteristic.

Our legends and creation myths are all of seafaring people. There was saltwater in our veins, and the men who went down to the sea had a special place in our pantheon. Yet through treaties, neglect and embarrassment, through a natural desire to belong, to join in, we have relegated the sea to a damp patch. An inconvenience, an environmental black spot.

While we worry in an abstract, comfy way about the estimated, second-guessed numbers and provenance of fish, we ignore the endangered and vanishing farers who go out in boats, in the sea and the wind. Men who are formed and sculpted into a remarkable breed, whom we are conspiring to eradicate. And as we do so, we drain the salt from our veins.

For days after we left the *Emulator* I could feel the phantom sea shift under my feet, and if I closed my eyes I could see myself surrounded by the soaring fulmars, which seemed to lift the boat until it was flying with them, and I remembered Mark's farewell. 'What you going to write about us, then? You going to be nice? Actually, I don't give a fook. Write what you fooking like. We won't be fooking reading it. It'll only go to wrap fish in.'

Food, Inc.

There's a moment in the documentary *Food, Inc.* where a mother whose child has died from food poisoning and who now lobbies for safer food and accountability is asked what she feeds her family. She pauses and replies: 'I can't tell you. I would be open to a lawsuit.'

And you look at it and you say, what? You're going to get sued by a dead fish? The salmonella is going to do you for slander? Well, yes, that's exactly what she meant. Thirteen American states have 'veggie libel laws' where food manufacturers can sue for defamation which, being a food critic, I find worrying.

Food, Inc. is a good and important film but not for the reasons you may think. The charity premiere in London was full of ladies who don't lunch; gastro-neurotics who wanted a sort of Jamie, Monty and Hugh reverie about thatch and dew, along with a hand-wringing hippie rant against Mr McGregor and the fat controllers who run supermarkets. The goodie bags on our seats contained stuff from organic shops and flyers from Ethical Pizza. That may be what they all imagined they saw but it's not what this film's really about. As the director, Robert Kenner, says: 'I gradually realised that while I set out to make a film about food, I was now making a film about unchecked corporate power.'

While working on *Food, Inc.*, he attended a hearing on whether cloned meat should be labelled. An industry representative spoke against it in these words: 'I don't think it's in the consumers' interest to know. It would be too confusing for them.' Too confusing? More confusing than a law that prevents a mother saying what food her son ate before he died? No, maybe not that confusing. But close.

There is, of course, a huge difference between American and

European farming. Start with the slaughterhouse. The protocols are a constant contention between the EU and the American Department of Agriculture. American cows go to their burger covered in their own and each other's faeces. Faeces are the commonest contagion for a whole spectrum of food poisoning, so the meat is chemically cleaned post-mortem. Here, animals have to go to the Elysian Fields with their bottoms wiped, and although we have plenty of agri-businesses in Europe – there are beet fields in East Anglia that have two time zones and herds of cows in Germany that could invade Poland – still this continent is more diverse in the crops grown, the food made and the size of farms than anywhere else in the world. Europe's mixed farming is mostly down to the much-ridiculed common agricultural policy, which has protected small producers by creating vast lakes and mountains of comestibles to maintain prices. Europe has also kept large numbers of localised markets that are still emblematic of local culture and its countries still cherish the Appellation Contrôlée system that enforces the locality and manufacture of prepared food, from Roquefort and Parma ham to Champagne and Melton Mowbray pies. As a continent we also care a lot more about the aesthetics of food: in short, we're more epicurean about it, where Americans are egalitarian. (Just four firms produce 80 per cent of the beef in the United States: it may not be the best, but it's almost certainly what the guy next door is eating.)

So food is in many ways very different in America and we Europeans could be forgiven for smiling patronisingly when *Food, Inc.* highlights the desperate state of America's health: the epidemics of obesity, the 20 per cent diabetes, all self-inflicted from a refined diet of processed carbohydrate and fat, all knock-on effects from the dominance of the American food processing industries.

But, Kenner says, we shouldn't be complacent about our superiority, because Big Farma is set to take over the world. It is already a fact in Latin America; Brazil has ginormous farms that may put American growers out of business. Malaysia has planted forests of palm oil, the vegetable lard that is the third devil ingredient after soya protein and corn syrup. China's agriculture is industrialising rapidly, not just to feed its enormous population but also to offer it a diet that is more Western, with increased consumption of dairy products and meat.

Or, as Kenner says: 'My line of the day is "Coming to a supermarket near you", because you're going to be flooded with this stuff.'

The part of *Food, Inc.* that everyone should see and understand is about what happens when the source of most of the nation's food is controlled by a handful of anonymous interlocking companies that are joined at the wallet and the boardroom to government. America's history of deregulation and the promotion of free enterprise and the unquestioned belief in the holy goodness of capitalism have trumped all other considerations. So you've got to a position where indeed you can be sued for saying the burger tastes vile. It's an infringement of somebody's right to a business – as was proved when a bunch of Texas beef producers sued Oprah for saying there might be mad cow disease in the national herd: they lost, but only because Oprah could afford to defend herself.

American food manufacturers are as secretive as arms dealers. They say it's to protect trade secrets. In fact it's the old truth that nobody will eat a sausage that they saw being made. Mass food manufacturing doesn't look remotely like cooking or the picture of picket fence and homely red farm on the packet. For Uncle Ben, read Scientist Sam. In America there is a lobbied belief that huge food conglomerates are best left to regulate themselves, that the fairest policeman is the free market. This works only if the market really is free and you can make informed choices. The picket-fence fantasy of food, carefully maintained by both industrial manufacturers and organic distributors, means there is little real information or understanding of where our dinner comes from and how it's made.

There are good historical reasons for this: the great rise in proprietary processed and branded ingredients came in the nineteenth century, with the move of populations to cities. And although they offered convenience, that wasn't the original selling point. Branded food wasn't always cheaper; it was often sold at a premium because it was considered safer. The industrial processes we complain about are what first attracted Victorian housewives. Packet food was sterile, controlled and predictable. The joy of branded ingredients was in their consistency and purity. You see that in all the early advertisements that emphasise the safety of ingredients, that they could be offered to infants and invalids. The great success of modern mass production has been to eradicate adulteration and serious food poisoning. The spectacle of the poor woman who lost her child in *Food, Inc.* strikes us as so sad because it's so rare: 150 years ago, before branded food, she wouldn't have made it into the story because it would have been so commonplace.

Anyone who has travelled to India knows that vomiting, diarrhoea, fevers and worse are constant concerns. That's what eating everywhere was like before processed food. The fact that we so completely trust the volume and ingredients in packets of food is a great thing; the fact that we can feed sixty million people three times a day without poisoning them is an even greater thing and is the triumph of the past century.

Then something went wrong. As food processing got more efficient, efficiency for efficiency's sake took over. The process became more important than the product. Commercially, food couldn't be allowed to rot, so its ability to rot was surgically, scientifically removed. The formulae for the lo-fat, lo-carb foods needed to make the obese feel happier robbed the foods of their flavours. So flavour in ever more tempting combinations had to be artificially added, with the help of marvellously complicated formulae. The flavourings and coatings tasted good and if they were as addictive as mother's milk, that's because they were designed that way. Designed what way, exactly? Please don't ask. Secret. Commercial in confidence.

To make real choices about our daily bread, we need to be told and shown everything, not leave it to self-regulation and the market. Food labelling is too obtuse and partial. British food manufacturers recently successfully rejected an easily understandable system for denoting the sugar, fat and salt content in processed food. They said it was misleading, implying that knowing nothing was simpler and preferable.

We should know far more about all our foods and their processes. Every schoolchild should be taken round a slaughterhouse. They should have to spend a day picking organic cabbages in October. Ideally everyone who wants to eat meat should kill a chicken and pluck it. Gut a fish. Vegetarians should harvest soft fruit, make their own polenta. Food is a bloody and backbreaking business. We get through a gobsmacking amount of it every day and we need more information, because information is power and power moves markets. This applies equally to the organic, wholefood, hunky-dory cottage industry: the marketing of happy livestock and Hardyesque farmers, the unsubstantiated wishful PR of health claims and the bogus homeopathy of their value-added, live-longer smugness is no less mendacious than the happy families of mass-produced industrial food.

Personally, I think your type 2 diabetes is your choice. Enjoy. As is your weight, what you eat, when and where you eat it. All I insist on is that I don't have to watch you doing it and that I can eat something else. We want to maintain a continent that grows everything from lingonberries on the fjords to figs in the Cyclades. Where we can eat a grouse in Inverness and the minute spawn of sardines in Sicily. Where the loonies who produce a thousand types of cheese can have their madness and skill protected. And where you can get panforte in Siena and HobNobs in Tesco.

We need to grow up about where our food comes from and what goes into it, to stop being squeamish and believing fairy stories. There should be government, preferably multinational government, rules to protect producers and consumers, to maintain trust and standards, to support markets and the pay of those who make, pick, pack and slit the throats of your breakfast. We need to be informed and it's too important to be left to business, the market and faddists.

Chickens

'Gently but firmly, that's the way, just hold her underneath. Get your finger between her legs. She likes to feel secure. Now, hold her close, so she's safe. And just look at her.' The little brown hen shuffles and ruffles a moment at being disturbed, and settles into my palm. The weight is very satisfying, a compact solidity. Under the beautiful and intricate feathers, there is a crouching dinosaur. That round eye, bright as a lost sequin, black as oil, looks back at me and I am suffused with a feeling of calm. A sort of giddy happiness, a silent chuckle. The hen nests in my hand, her head syncopating from side to side, and somehow she's spinning away tension and worry. There's just me and this little hen, muttering clucks, talking to herself, the two of us calm together. Just for the moment, we're okay, we're doing fine.

The man who is standing with me says: 'There's nothing quite like holding a hen.' He's right. There is something deeply satisfying about it. It's unexpected, unlikely and a little embarrassing, but it is virtually impossible to hold a hen and not smile. This chap is a judge at the bantam show. We are in a room crowded with stacks of hens and cockerels and their gentle-fingered fanciers. 'You know,' he adds, 'men and chickens is perhaps the oldest symbiotic relationship in the world. Maybe as old as man and dogs.' For over 10,000 years chickens have lived under our wing, and we under theirs.

Newbury is an unlikely place to find a poultry show. A town principally famous for a race course and a bypass, it eminently merits the bypass. In the low rise of industrial warehouses and playing fields on the outskirts of town, there's the leisure centre, crowded with Sunday families coming to swim. The place smells of chlorine, and echoes to the squeals and yells of splashing, crop-

73

haired lads and tattooed parents. Fat girls in tight costumes slob about, sucking their towels. It's about as far from rural husbandry as you could imagine. But then, through an anonymous door, you're into the back room, possibly a ball-game court. Here are the wonders of feathers and beaks, tail and claw: a battery of vanity. The crates piled one on top of the other create aisles, a fox's supermarket that smells of ammonia and fresh hay.

I start to walk, and with a rising vulpine panic am dazzled, then confused, then incapacitated by the vast, common-or-garden, exotic, numbing variety and diversity that defies utility or ornament. The immense ingenuity and post-Darwinian cosmic Tourette's of chickens. The stark, feathered bonkersness of these birds. Men in sheds have accessorised hens with a carnival of wattles, hats, tails, spats, bald patches and party frocks. I'm accompanied by various experts, but I'm beggared for questions. All I can think to ask is 'Why? Why does that one look like it's going to Ascot? Why has that one got moon boots? Why has that one got a head that looks like a clown's scrotum? And that one's got no face at all! Why did anyone start on any of it? How did a four-minute breakfast end up as this God-defying creation? This shattering cock-a-doodle-doo of genetic expressionism?'

'Best to take your time,' says a kindly gent, 'there's a lot to take in at first.' All around me are bright starlit eyes that click back and forth, shivering in their wattles as the hens regard me. They are our oldest friends, but still they look at us with an intense curiosity. Every time a chicken sees something, it is with an expression of droll surprise, as if all of life were an incomprehensible folly, an inexplicable show of colour, light, movement and worms.

Let's begin at the beginning. Nobody knows exactly where the first chickens were domesticated – India, China, Thailand, Vietnam – somewhere around 10,000 years ago, which is to say at the birth of farming. The wild bird is a red jungle fowl, *Gallus gallus* (the French made it their national bird because of the similarity to Gaul, and because they still behave like chickens). It is a member of the pheasant family.

Very, very few animals ever become domesticated. A mere handful. It isn't simply a question of humans catching and breeding them into a state of acquiescence until they become useful; we have tried for thousands of years to domesticate cheetahs and deer without success. And it isn't a question of the animals hanging around until we get to love them. Rats and mice would be sharing our beds if that were the case. There needs to be a mutual benefit.

Jungle fowl are essentially flightless. They creep around in the bush, looking vain and laughably aggressive. They were the KFC of the Asian food chain. Because they nest on the ground, they need to lay lots of eggs, and it was the eggs that first made them useful to humans. In ancient Egypt chickens were called the egg-a-day bird. In hunter-gatherer societies, eggs are rare, so the jungle fowl exchanged its eggs for protection. We are big omnivores, and a hatched chicken tastes good, too. But in species terms, to get domesticated is winning the lottery. It's the smart move. There may well be twenty-five million chickens killed in America every day, but there are probably over thirty billion in the world. That's not bad for a nervous, vain groundling from Asia. So calling any of these chickens rare is laughable. But the variations in them are.

Commercial egg-laying, nugget and curry mass-produced chickens are white mongrels with numbers, not names. They have very little to do with these amazing exotic and stylish creatures that come with heritage and history, such as the Dorkings with their extra toe, the chicken that was brought here by the Romans. Or the beautiful Hamburgs, in their variety of colours, that once travelled the world with the Vikings and whose bones are found in every Norse camp, and who stayed on in the north of England to be bred for sustenance and pleasure and fearsome competition by Lancashire miners, who'd show them in pubs. Every country has its chicken whose qualities and plumage reflect the land and the people who keep them.

Commercial chicken production and backyards parted company a hundred years ago. It was the Victorians who really took to breeding fancy hens. They went with the newly suburban classes who wished to have some romantic link to the bucolic life of their parents. Chickens are both practical and ornamental. They tell people you are here to stay, you're putting down roots. There is a Victorian watercolour look to them. The sight of hens takes you back to children's books, kitchen gardens and the smell of baking. They also coincided with a desire to eugenically improve everything. The Victorians started clubs and societies and brought their natural orderliness to labelling and measuring. They came up with the small bantam version of hens that was aesthetically in scale with smaller gardens and allotments and the miniature grandeur of the burgeoning middle class. And, like everything that came in clubs and societies, there were rules and regulations and elected officers who governed everything from the colour of a wattle to the curl of a feather. There are still hundreds of bantam clubs and societies, run with the strict authority of the Lawn Tennis Association or the Collective of British Sex Workers.

The British Belgian Bantam Club is one of the largest. There are two general varieties of Belgian bantam, and I could explain them to you, but you wouldn't thank me. Bantam is one of the few words to sidle into English from Java. It is the name of a port town fought over by the East India Company and the Dutch that was said to be the home of miniature hens. Chicken-keeping increased hugely during both world wars as eggs were rationed. My grandmother couldn't look at a fresh egg without commenting on the foul, or perhaps de-fowled, nature of the powdered variety.

The judging of bantams is one of the most arcane and obtusely complex mysteries I've ever been privy to. It's like someone shifting a curtain and giving you a glimpse of another dimension. It makes football refereeing something you could do in shorts with a whistle. I asked a judge to tell me what he was looking for, and within thirty seconds I realised I was not seeing what he was seeing. I was staring with an illiterate, coarse clumsiness. What he saw was the hyperrealism of tiny defects and minute perfection, and then something else, something metaphysical. 'This one is not proud enough. Look at him – he needs a fierce vanity. She should be a geisha, elegant and shy. This, here, should look like a teacup.' A teacup? 'A teacup.' And slowly, as if by magical, hypnotic suggestion, the little thing transformed into a teacup, like the Mad Hatter's tea party.

The birds are looked at standing, then held in the hand. They need to be amenable to strangers, and they have to have, somehow in their tiny heads, an awareness of their own inimitable internal teacup and fierce vanity.

Depending on each individual breed, there are hundreds and hundreds of faults a judge must check for. Here is a mere soupçon of the litany of orthodox poultry no-nos: fishtail points on a single comb, thumb marks on a single comb, flyaway single comb, white on red earlobes, red on white earlobes, wiry neck feathers, twisted tail feathers, bent breastbone, roach back, wry tail, squirrel tail, knock knees, bow legs, stalk legs, duckfoot, bumblefoot, cocks without spurs, hens with spurs, parrot beaks (the manual adds: 'Kill all affected birds'); and that's before the individual stipulations of each breed – the set of a wing, the colour of an iris, hard or soft feathers. The professional tricks for cosmetic improvement wrought on these fowl are as obsessive as the cosmetics for the chorus of the Moulin Rouge. Not a feather out of place. Earlobes that have been Tipp-Exed and not a parrot beak to be seen. The judging is a mercurial calling, done with insouciance and the stone face of a Korean traffic policemen. At last there emerges, as with entrants in a race for Pope, a row of finalists. Britain's Next Top Bantam. The cages reveal the immense variety of breeds, from the martial-looking game hens to the boudoir accessory Cochins.

Chickens are genetically adaptable, which has added to their success around humans. It is as if they have understood that, dowdy and featherless as we are, we crave variety and innovation in others. So hens have evolved, allowed us to meddle in their deepest DNA. Making changes of colour and shape. They have put up with the absurdities and difficulties of mops on their heads and feathers between their toes, while inside still maintaining the psychic Knorr cube of essential chickenness, the essence of their flock.

If judging chickens is difficult, it is as naught compared with judging eggs. When I was told there was a competition for eggs

I admit I thought it was a joke. But they don't joke about domestic fowl here. An old Merlin of a judge attempted to show me the rudiments of egg classification. With hands the size of breakfast trays and fingers like toasted Hovis, he gently lifted an egg and held it to his nose, and explained what was wrong. It was its shoulders. Well, who knew that eggs had shoulders that could go wrong? This one was too wide at the top, this one too pointy. These were too round, these too uneven. This, he said, was a nice egg, a gold-medal egg. And this one, he whispered, had been polished, a red-card offence. These had straw marks. It was like obstetrics divination. But there was more. On the table next to the eggs there were plates of broken eggs. Here yolks were compared and contrasted: this one too flat, too pale, here the albumen didn't hold together, this one was fertilised. It was the scourge of Herod, the cracking of the innocents.

At the end of the room there was a double row of cages. An avian orphanage. A place for the unwanted, the surplus, the less than. Hens and cockerels which had failed to live up to the exalted standards expected of them. The joy of hens is that they can happily produce two or more broods a year, so quantity is prodigious but quality fugitive. Showing and breeding is cruelly eugenic: there is little space for sentiment in the constant war against hollow pea combs.

I am entranced by a pair of hens. They have a classic chicken shape, with small red wattles and combs. Their white feathers are outlined in black, as if someone had gone round each one with a thin felt tip pen. They are Silver Laced Wyandotte, an American breed that originated in New York in the 1870s. They are utterly captivating and £14 for the pair. I feel my heart race, and that slight light-headedness you get before making a life-changing decision, before you do something inappropriate and impetuous. I sauntered, in a rushing sort of way, to find the man who was bartering the hens, and I flung money at him. He was surprised, unused to such financial keenness. Bantams are a parsimonious and careful hobby, home-made and home-bred. I didn't even try to bargain. He was a bit disappointed about that.

'Very nice, the Wyandotte,' said a passing expert. 'Good starting hens, dual-purpose, eggs and table bird. Nice temperament. They don't fly much, you won't be fishing them out of trees. But you haven't done the hard bit yet.' Oh dear, what's that? Food? Water? Vet? De-guanoing the cloaca with a warm Q-tip? 'No, mate. Finding a box to get them home in. Boxes round here . . .' Don't tell me, they're like hen's teeth.

I noticed that the men who breed, keep, judge and play God with chickens in turn grow to subtly resemble them. Their many different shapes and sizes, from gangly thirteen-year-old-boys to ancient, dumpy taxi drivers, take on by osmosis by the constant handling a certain zoomorphic fowlness. They cock their heads and ruffle themselves, they pick things up with a precise curiosity and then drop them. And they like being around each other. Bantam men, I'm discovering, are by nature and breeding happy enough and charming, submerged in their hobby, entranced for life by their birds. Contented in their little flocks of communities and societies, they spend their weekends migrating to church halls and leisure centres, and long evenings in front of the telly with a hen on their laps, coiffing tail feathers, applying flour paste to earlobes. They, you would imagine, share a calling that is wholly blameless. Their expertise and patience, their absorption is enviable. The bantam is a good thing. It is difficult to imagine a better thing.

There is, though, just the one problem. An old Essex cabbie tells me he's thinking of giving it up. He's been sued six times by neighbours. 'I've spent God knows how many thousands on the sheds; missus never gets a holiday. People don't like the crowing, I had the council round with recorders and microphones, court orders, lawyers. I fought for my birds for years. But I'm getting on.' It's a constant refrain, the crowing of cockerels disturbs second-home owners, who come to the country for peace and quiet. They take out nuisance orders against church bells and livestock, and turn chickens into early soup. The country is becoming a retirement utility, another society with rules and regulations, a library of green hush. But this noise, Chanticleer's morning clarion, has woken us for ten millennia. It is a warning and a reminder, a votive welcome to the day's work, to breakfast, to our shared communities. And, most important, it tells us we are not alone on earth, that we travel in company.

And in exchange for boiled eggs and roast chicken, we owe these marvellously adaptable, homely birds our protection. Hen husbandry is growing. You don't need much expertise. It's not expensive. You can eat your mistakes. And it's a bellwether for hard times. When people are frightened, they run to hens. When times are hard, when we feel insecure, hard done by and frit by the future, we go back to our oldest mates and hug a hen.

I take my Wyandottes home to my tiny garden in Chelsea. They settle in and scratch about, and mutter to each other. My twins feed them kitchen scraps and squat on their heels, watching. They cluck at the dog with a crescendo of matronly hysteria, and they seem not to want to lay. But I don't mind. They continue to captivate me. In the evenings I go and sit with them, and each time I hold one and stroke its neck, I am overcome with that childlike calm that burbles away worry and the knotted problems of modernity. I make the connection with this worthwhile and simple little feathered dinosaur.

There isn't a happy ending, I'm afraid. Softly treading on eggshells, my partner said: 'You know we can't keep them. You travel so much and there's the dog and the foxes and the rats. And they're another thing. We don't need any more things', and, she adds, as if to make it better, 'we do owe Arun and Elizabeth a wedding present.'

So they went, and now they scratch on Elizabeth Hurley's farm. Far better for them, really, I suppose. But I miss them still. There is a bantam-shaped hole in my chest. As they went, I cleared out the hay from their box and ... you're ahead of me.

One pale egg. Not too broad at the shoulder, nicely rounded, finished to a gentle point, good overall symmetry, no marks from straw. A pretty good egg. I boiled it and shared it with the twins. There's not much to go round in a bantam's egg, but with soldiers, we agreed, it was probably the best egg in the world.

Towton

Get on to the B1217 – the Ferrybridge–Tadcaster road – just after the M1 joins the A1M, and you've crossed that unmapped line where the north stops being grim and begins to be bracing. Go through Saxton, past the Crooked Billet pub, and on your left you'll see rising farmland, green corn and copses – and old landscape, untroubled by poets or painters or the hyperbole of tourist boards, but handsome, still and hushed. The road is straight; it knows where it's going, hurrying along, averting its gaze. Through the tonsured hedge you might just notice a big old holly tree on the side of the road. It seems out of place.

Get out of the car, adjust to the hissing silence and step behind the tree. Hidden from the road you'll find a gothic stone cross of some age. Nobody knows who put it here or where it's from. For centuries it lay in the ditch. A date recently inscribed on its base, 28 March 1462, is wrong. It should be the next day: the 29th, Sunday. The movable feast – Palm Sunday.

This oddly lurking crucifix is the only memorial on the site of the largest, longest, bloodiest and most murderous battle ever fought in Britain – Towton. Bloodiest not just by a few hundred, but by thousands. Its closest home-grown mortal rival is Marston Moor, fought two hundred years later with a quarter of the casualties.

By all contemporary accounts, allowing for medieval exaggeration, on this one Sunday between 20,000 and 30,000 men died. Just so that you grasp the magnitude, that's a more grievous massacre of British men than on the first day of the Somme. Without machine guns or shells, young blokes hacked, bludgeoned and trampled, suffocated and drowned. An astonishing 1 per cent of the English population died in this field. The equivalent today would be 600,000.

Walk in the margin of the corn as it is ruffled by the blustering wind. Above, the thick mauve, mordant clouds curdle and thud like bruises, bowling patches of sunlight across the rise and fall of the land. In the distance is a single stunted tree, flattened by the south wind. It marks the corner of this sombre, elegiac place. It would be impossible to walk here and not feel the dread underfoot – the echo of desperate events vibrating just behind the hearing. This is a sad, sad, dumbly eloquent deathscape.

Back down the road at the Crooked Billet, in the car park you'll find a caravan on bricks that is the headquarters of the Towton Society. The pub is happy to have them here; the council has given them temporary permission. Most weekends this is a visitors' centre, if there's someone to volunteer to open up.

I'm met by a band of enthusiasts: an amateur historian, an archaeologist, a metal detector, a supermarket manager, a chemical engineer, teachers, a printer, a computer technician, a schoolboy and his dad. They are a particularly ordinary English gaggle – the sort of men and occasional woman you'll find in huts and garages or rummaging in car boots and boxes on any weekend. Keen but defensive, proud and embarrassed, inhabiting that mocked attic of England's hobbyists, aware that their interest tiptoes across the line between leisure activity and loopy obsession, they are instantly attractive. Enthusiasm is always likeable. English enthusiasm, so shy and rare, is particularly winning. The men are beginning to wiggle into leggings and jerkins of boiled wool and linen, belting on purses and daggers, stringing bows, filling quivers from the boots of Japanese 4x4s, slipping back across the centuries with apologetic grins. I'm handed a skull. It wears the mocking expression common to all skulls and has long forgotten the fear and agony of its traumatic wound: a double-handed hammer blow to the back of its helmeted head so fearful it split the base of the bone and disengaged it from the spine.

The chances are you've never heard of Towton. The most fatal day in all of English military history has been lost, left to be ploughed under by the seasons of seed time and harvest. It is as if there was a conspiracy never to mention it. There are surprisingly few contemporary accounts of the battle, and they are sparse, though all agree on the overwhelming size and mortality.

The reason Towton hasn't come down the ages to us may be in part that it was in the middle of the Wars of the Roses, that complex internecine bout of patrician bombast, a hissy fit that stuttered and smouldered through the exhausted fag end of the Middle Ages like a gang feud. The Wars of the Roses have no heroes; there are no good guys and precious little romance. They're as complicated and brain-aching as Russian novels and pigeon-breeding. To begin with every protagonist has at least three names – family, county and title. Their wives and mothers are just as bad, and almost everyone is called Henry or Edward at some point in their lives, and it's all about heredity and family trees. There are feuds and alliances that have precious little to do with the commonweal of peasants and citizens.

The Wars of the Roses aren't taught as history in schools any more, only as literature, as Shakespeare's great canon of regicide and revenge that can be seen as our nation's *Iliad*. And though Harry Hotspur, Warwick the Kingmaker, John of Gaunt and Bolingbroke pass across the stage bawling stentorian English, still bloody Towton is absent, silent as a mass grave. Briefly, just so you get a feel for the threads that come together to weave the shroud of Towton, here are the basics. The Wars of the Roses kick off in 1455, though they're not called the Wars of the Roses (the Victorians made that up). It begins with the eight sons of Edward III, possibly the best king we ever had. One of them's called Lionel – I thought I'd mention that, because I'd have liked us to have a King Lionel. Edward started the Hundred Years War, and his eldest son was the Black Prince.

The problems, the pushing and shoving in the royal queue, arise from here. It's a power struggle between Plantagenets, except they don't call themselves that. They think of themselves as Angevins, descended from Jeffrey of Anjou, whose symbolic flower is the yellow broom, the Latin for which, *Planta genista*, gave us Plantagenet.

After a bit of argy-bargy, happy slapping, black dungeon work and a couple of on-your-toes to the Continent, we get Henry V – cocky sod and, more important, lucky sod – who wins Agincourt but unluckily is then killed by the shits while his son is still a nipper.

Henry VI is a sorry excuse for a monarch. Even by the standards of the inbred, pathetically inept medieval court, Hal Six should never have been put anywhere near a throne. It was said he would have been better suited to sainthood. Obsessively religious and miserable, he probably suffered from catatonic schizophrenia, inherited from his grandfather, the French king. He was incapable of governing a truculent and bitter nation. And he had that other curse of medieval monarchs: a ruthless, scheming and vindictive wife, who produced a very suspect heir, considering Henry had never shown anything other than disgust and incomprehension at the idea of hiding the pink sceptre. For long periods he would retreat into vegetative states. England had a cabbage as a king. That's the Lancastrians.

On the York side we have Edward, Earl of March, who is everything the fairy tale demands: 6ft tall, handsome, dynamic, smart, sensual and brutal. After his father was executed and his head displayed on Micklegate Bar with a mocking paper crown, Edward had himself tentatively proclaimed Edward IV, and the sickly Plantagenet Henry went north to raise an army.

York and Lancaster imply that these wars were a northern spat between round vowels. In fact, they weren't geographically specific; though they were, roughly, North vs South. Edward marched north with his supporters. One of the reasons Towton had such a bloody cast of thousands was that it was one of the few British battles that had two legitimised kings fighting each other. Both Edward and Henry used the decaying system of hierarchical obligation to raise their forces.

By the time Edward had got to Pontefract, Henry and the Lancastrians had moved from York to this broad ridge of farmland.

At the dawn of Palm Sunday – the day Christ entered Jerusalem – Edward's army arrived on the rising land above Towton to find the Lancastrian hosts awaiting him. Across a valley, on a ridge, their flanks protected by the River Cock and woodland, things didn't look too good for Edward's Yorkists. If you were a betting man – and he was – you'd put your house on Henry taking the day, rested, fed, with more men. Half the Yorkist army, captained by the Duke of Norfolk, still hadn't arrived, was out there to the south, trudging the muddy arteries of England. And it was snowing – great howling, razoring gusts of snow.

Medieval English battles, like the dirges that commemorate them, tend to follow a set course. The aristocracy dismount; they fight on foot. There are mounted prickers roaming around the rear of the army to discourage the deserters. It is the English way to slug it out, toe to toe, get stuck in, show iron faith. They stand with their men, except for Henry, who is too frail and dotty – he's back in York telling his rosary, chewing his nails, being nagged by the missus.

The armies face each other, an arrow's length apart, perhaps 300 yards. The archers step forward, communion wafers still stuck to the roofs of their mouths, muttering prayers to St Sebastian, patron saint of archers. The order 'Knock, draw, loose' sends a hissing curtain of iron-tipped splinters high into the white air.

English archers have attained a mythic status down the ages because of the showy underdog victories at Crécy and Agincourt. They were nation-specific – only the English and the Welsh took on the discipline, the plebeian odium and the round loathing that came with a bow. None of the continental countries deigned to partake, preferring to be nobly kebabbed. They relied on specialist Genoese crossbowmen – the Polish plumbers of medieval battlefields. Not even the bellicose Scots and Irish could be bothered with bows, but when used in sufficient numbers and with discipline, the longbow was the lethal arbiter of battlefields for three hundred years.

It was slowly replaced by gunpowder. Any terrified peasant could point and pull a trigger, but it took a lifetime of aching, deforming practice to muscle up the 100lb of tug needed to draw a yew bow to dispatch a cloth yard of willow-shafted, goose-feathered, bodkin-tipped arrow 200 yards through plate, through chain, through leather and linen and prayers, into a man's gizzard. The longbow was the most lethally efficient dealer of death on European battlefields until the invention of rifling and the Gatling gun.

The archers stepped forward and together chucked up what they call the 'arrow storm'. An English archer could fire fifteen to twenty arrows in a minute – that's what made the opening moments of battle so horrific. The eclipse of arrows would have crossed high in the frozen air, and in that moment Edward and the House of York had their touch of luck. The thick, stinging curtain of snow slashed the faces of the Lancastrian line, making it difficult to aim or judge distance, pushing their arrows short. And it carried the arrows of York further and deeper into the Lancastrian line. God howled and cracked for Edward that morning, searing the cheeks and freezing the eyes of Lancaster.

The metal detectors have found the long, broad trench of bodkin points, showing where the first appalling fusillade was loosed. Emptying their own quivers, they began firing back the arrows wasted by their enemies. There may have been half a million arrows fired in ten minutes that day – the largest longbow shafting in history.

Organised ranks of men standing under an arrow storm can do one of three things. They can take it, the steepling hysteria, the terror, the incessant keening of the goose feathers, the thud and grunt, the screaming and pleading, the smell of shit and vomit and split gut; they can stand with their skin prickling in mortal expectation. Or they can retreat – get out of the rain, give ground, lose form and purpose, and run. Or they can attack – move forward, confront the butcher, the bloody, unmanly, unarmoured, jeering peasant bowmen. This is what Lancaster did.

Heads down, slipping and sliding down the frozen incline, they moved across the short valley and crabbed up the other side. All the while the arrows came, flatter and harder. A glum statistic of medieval battles is that the host forced to move first usually loses. But Lancaster had the advantage of numbers; they were on home ground.

As they approached, Edward shouted above the wind to his men that there was to be no quarter given, no ransoming of fat earls and mercantile knights. This battle had been a long time coming. There was a black litany of insults and humiliations, of murder and summary execution, a debt to be underwritten in blood and tears. As the army crossed the valley, there will have been the harbinger noise, the crack and boom of early firearms. York's Burgundian mercenaries detonate their pieces. The oldest bullet in the world has been found in this valley.

So the two armies, screaming obscenities or just howling like mad dogs, slithered together and joined one of the most hellish experiences of human ingenuity: a medieval battle in the snow.

At the front line there is little room for swashbuckling or dainty footwork. This is a match of thud and stab. The weapons of choice are daggers and maces. Men with iron sallets buckled to the backs of their necks, so they can't be yanked forward to offer a spine stab, stare wide-eyed through slits, straining and flailing with short, maddened blows and ache-tensed muscles into the faces of men inches in front of them.

There was a lot of armour about in 1461. Most men would have had some form of head protection and bits of plate, but the most common protection was a stab vest made from layers of linen sewn together that might deaden the blow, absorb a spent point or a fisted poniard. But this wasn't about killing the opponent. It was about putting the man in front of you down – on the ground. He'd be dead in seconds.

The most common injuries are to the head and neck, and death must often have come by way of suffocation – the air squeezed from your body under the weight of men behind you, jammed in the mangle of battle. The pressure and the impetus came from the army that wasn't yet fighting, shoving and heaving.

Lancaster begins to get the best of it. The battle line expands into a vale now called Bloody Meadow. Most medieval battles have an allotted time. Perhaps because the armies at Towton were uncharacteristically large, and perhaps because for so many of the men this was not their first fight, Towton went on way beyond its span into extra time, gasping and heaving, sick with gore, men expiring of dehydration. On into the afternoon, Edward ever more desperate as his army gave, inch by inch, across the plain. And then, up the B1217, came the banner of the white boar – Norfolk, with the rump of the army. Edward's relief must have been seismic. They wade into the Lancastrian flank. It's the turning point: the line shudders and stalls. And then the movement is back, Lancastrians catch their heels on the bodies of their own dead. The line falters, bends, bunches and breaks. In moments, an army unravels into a rabble, and the rabble runs. And it's time for lunch.

Back at the Crooked Billet we sit in the snug. Some of the Towton Society are dressed in the burgundy and blue of the House of York, with its badge not of a rose but of a sun in splendour; some are kitted in the no less risible leisurewear of Argos. We eat roast beef as tough and tasty as an archer's glove and Yorkshire puddings the size of breastplates. It should seem odd, but it isn't. The rest of the pub barely gives them a second glance. And they talk with glee about this place, this patch of earth, this battle, and the clotted, internecine politics of the Roses. It's easy to mock re-enactors, dressing up and empathising like clairvoyants. We are taught that history comes in books, not fields, to be seen like a court case, with facts and evidence, to be measured against precedent and doubt, to be unemotional, reasonable and forensic. But that's not how it was.

There is another history here. A story handed down that has grown fluent and smooth and rhetorical, that expands and shrinks with the needs of the moment. It is a story of belonging, the events that stitch us into this landscape and in turn sew this landscape into a country. It is the tapestry of us. These are people who can still raise lumps of emotion over the misrepresentation of Richard III, which may well be mildly bonkers but is also endearing and as valid and important as anything done in a university library.

After lunch we troop back to walk the rout of Towton. The wind is up; the clouds spit gusting drizzle. Behind us is Ferrybridge and the massive Drax Power Station. In front, caught in a shaft of sunlight, is York Minster, whose towers were still being built when Towton was fought. We step through the corn that grasps at our legs, sighing and whispering. The retreat was where the real killing happened, the slaughter that put Towton in a league of its own, over and above the Somme.

The Lancastrians ran. The army of York, the fresh men from Norfolk and the prickers on their horses, harried them, whooping with relief and the anger that comes after fear. This was the moment when they made their bounty, the coins and rings and rosaries, the badges and lockets and hidden purses that would pay for the farm, for the cow, for the wife. They moved down into the valley of the River Cock and thousands drowned, their linen jerkins soaking up the frozen water, pulling the desperate men under.

We follow up the old London Road. Before the A1, this rutted, overgrown track was the aorta of the nation. We get to the river, now little more than a stream, dodging rocks and fallen logs. Here, hidden in a swaying copse of ash trees, was the Bridge of Bodies, built of Lancastrian dead to form a dam, the spume running with crimson gore. This was the final horror of Towton. We stare on to the dark water in silence.

'You know, this is the bit I can't imagine,' says the printer, 'what it must have felt like to be hunted down, hundreds of miles from home, to have been through that day, to be wounded, terrified, desperate – what was that like?' And we fall into silence again.

And then, because we've been talking of many things, he says he's got a son all set to join the army, keen as a greyhound for some soldiering. Standing in this awful, overgrown secret morgue, he says he's proud but terribly worried – it frightens him, the thought of his boy. And there, in those words and in that silence, is the thing that history does when you meet it halfway. It bends in on itself and folds the run of years to touch the present, not with a cold hand but with the warm breath of a moment ago.

It snowed all that Palm Sunday. The thick snow deadened the noise of dying whimpers and cawing crows, the shocked and exhausted soldiers too stupefied or disgusted to pursue the rout, the carters and baggage-train servants, the prostitutes and local peasants scuttling up the ridge to harvest the dead, fires being lit for porridge and to mull wine, the breath of the living pluming in the crepuscular white light like small, ardent prayers of gratitude.

Towton gave Edward the throne for a time. Henry fled to Scotland, his wife to France. Ultimately he was imprisoned in the Tower, and finally, ten years after Towton, murdered, possibly by starvation, a means that avoided the sin of regicide. The House of Lancaster died with him. Edward snuffed it in 1483 – of indulgence, obesity and a cold. He left his young sons in the care of his brother Richard. Bad choice. The house of York perished at Bosworth, making way for the Tudors and the New Age.

Towton was the last great explosion of the dark and vicious Middle Ages. It comes at the end of the bleakest of centuries; the war with France, the civil war, the Black Death. It was the last time the old Saxon–Norman system of obligation would be used to such catastrophic effect.

The dead of Towton are buried all over here, in mounds and trenches, in pits, in Saxon churchyards and the deserted hamlet of Lead. They are both history and landscape. They make up the most perfectly preserved great battlefield in the country. If Towton were a grand house, it would be nannied by dozens of quangos and charities, patronised by posh interior decorators, fey historians, titled ladies, Anglophile Americans and the Prince of Wales. But it isn't. It's kept by the quiet, respectful community and by this small band, this happy breed of marvellously eccentric enthusiasts, who, as we walk through the corn, I see are the yeomen of England walking back through our history, through Cobbett and Dickens, through Shakespeare to Chaucer and down the years to Domesday. They honour this blessed land, this earth of majesty, this seat of Mars.

The Guinea Pig Club

'Have you ever met a Guinea Pig before?' asked a capable lady, as she put her hand on the door. 'No? Well, nothing to worry about. They're extremely nice, very friendly. I'm sure they'll put you completely at your ease. It's just the hands. When you shake hands ... well, they haven't got any. Haven't got many fingers. Just be prepared. Some people find it unnerving.'

The elliptical wing of a Spitfire was unsuitable for a fuel tank, so they placed them in front of the cockpit behind the Merlin engine. The Hurricane's wings did contain fuel tanks, and they were protected, except where the root of the wing met the fuselage, under the pilot. If the tank was hit, burning aircraft fuel would be drawn into the cockpit. Within two or three seconds, the plane would be virtually unflyable, the flames so intense, blown with such Bunsen force that they were invisible. Amid the struggle for control of their mortally injured machines, with the anxiety, the adrenaline, the screaming engine and the rising fear, the first moment the pilot would realise that his cockpit had become a kiln was when the dashboard melted in front of his eyes and the skin hung from his fingers like rags. Every metal object became a searing grill; bailing out a terrifying struggle to escape a medieval witch's hell. If the windscreen slid back, great gusts of flame would be flung into the pilot's face.

In 1940, there were four hundred burns injuries to RAF pilots; thirty of them were fighter pilots from the Battle of Britain, which, in August, was at its pivotal, precipitous moment of indecision. The loss of aircraft was critical, the loss of pilots calamitous. The gossamer-fine net of defence of the nation was rent, the heartbreakingly young and inexperienced fliers were spun ragged by the free-ranging Luftwaffe. The engineered brilliance of the

Spitfire and the Hurricane went some way to mitigate their lack of training and inexperience, but the Hurricane in particular was prone to become a flaming meteorite. It took a great deal of courage simply to get into one. Even if the pilot survived being shot down, the chances of him flying again within months, even if his burns were minor, were slim.

Before the war, each of the services was given its own hospital. The RAF's was a small suburban one, the Queen Victoria Hospital in East Grinstead. The experience of the Great War implied that there would be few flying casualties compared to the other services. In East Grinstead, the burnt fliers found a surgeon called Archibald McIndoe. Wars are, by their tumultuous nature, times where men meet their defining moments. The point where they rise to a brilliance that in other times might have passed them by in the peaceful night. Nobody met a more admirable destiny than McIndoe did at East Grinstead.

The capable lady opened the door. The room hummed with the familiar noise of dinner. Round tables full of people in black tie and women wearing occasion hairdos. It might have been the annual general meeting of a golf club or a Rotarian dinner dance. The only thing that told that this wasn't a work do or garden society was the handful of RAF cadets, in their unimpeachably ugly uniforms and huge boots, selling raffle tickets. That and the discreet brooches bearing a small, fat, winged rodent in a flying helmet worn by many of the old men – the Guinea Pigs, as they call themselves, because they were all experiments. Nobody had ever treated burn injuries like theirs. Nobody knew where to start. There are no German Guinea Pigs because German airmen simply died of their burns. Their medicine was three decades behind ours, and they didn't know that what initially kills is dehydration. The body sends all its liquids to the burn sites, which is why they weep. They cry, and then you die.

This will be the last time the Guinea Pigs all get together. This is their final annual dinner. It is the end of a long story. After this, they'll wind up the club, have a service of remembrance with Prince Philip, and decide what to do with the current account.

Now they are all in their eighties and nineties, and they'll go their own quiet ways after a lifetime of mutual support and friendship. The club has been their pride and protection, linking each of them, like the traces of a parachute, back to those desperate separate moments of destiny that threw them out to be flaming torches above the South Downs, or bright pinpricks in the explosive dark over Europe.

McIndoe was a New Zealander who had a genius for surgery. As a young man he studied surgery at the Mayo Clinic in America, and was offered a full-time position there, but he had the promise of a job in London with an eminent surgeon. When he got here, it fell through. He had an uncle who treated disfigured soldiers from the Great War, and so worked with him as a stopgap, ending up a young man with untested but extraordinary talent at a little provincial hospital, waiting for something to turn up and test him. The mighty Merlin engine and the war obliged. Nobody expected burns. The injuries of the First World War had mainly been the blast; the great, thudding blows of high explosives, the ripping iron that squashed and shattered. The treatment was little more than fleshy engineering and camouflaging prosthetics.

Since the inception of military flying, burning has always been a particular private horror of the airmen. They tend to get burnt in particular places, the exposed skin of the hands, face and neck, legs above the flying boots, and groins. Eyelids seared off, lips and noses burnt like crackling, the dreadful death of being cooked as you fall thousands of feet to the welcome oblivion of earth. Pilots have been known to fling themselves from cockpits without parachutes, preferring the silence of the wind and the unfelt impact. Being burnt alive is a horror that could debilitate aircrews, particularly in bombers, where the casualties equalled those of officers in the First World War. During the height of the bombing campaign, there was about a one in four chance of finishing your thirty tours. Would you leave the house for those odds? But you have a house because young men did. The death that waited for them was rarely quick or painless. Bomber crews had medical kits that contained tubes of cream for burns and lots of morphine. Having morphine on board was as much for the morale of the rest of the crew as for the burn victim.

McIndoe invented the modern scale of plastic surgery and reconstructive facial work. He gave young men back their eyelids and their noses, carefully grafted and replaced their faces, mended their fractured jigsaw skulls, and covered the stumps of their hands over sometimes dozens of operations – all the time working from the experience of one operation to the next. He developed the extraordinary pedicle graft – a trunk of skin that was attached from an undamaged part of the body to the injured part, such as the nose, to give the graft a healthy blood supply so that new skin could grow. He performed, if not miracles, then things that had never been done before. But he also saw that surgery was only half of it. He had to pull the young men back from the depression, self-pity and the despair of nihilism. Apart from the appalling and constant pain, these young men had to look at themselves in mirrors and see all their youth melted into horror-story drawings. And they were fantastically young. It's always difficult to remember how desperately unprepared they must have been. Look at the nervous confidence, the faux-arrogant faces on *University Challenge*, and then imagine thousands of them, with fuzzy, soft moustaches and awkward pipes, and then think of taking a blow-torch to their faces and futures. McIndoe understood that the battle was to give them back hope and confidence, when the RAF thought the battle was to get them back into Lancasters. He was relentless in character building, going to extraordinary lengths to build a sense of *esprit de corps* among the young patients, joshing and encouraging them. He employed only the best nurses, most of whom were beautiful. Sex and seduction became a large part of the recuperation at East Grinstead. Someone said, pointedly, that you could barely open a cupboard in the hospital without an airman covered in bandages and a nurse covered in very little tumbling out.

McIndoe wrote thousands of letters to fight for his patients' right to a decent life. He fought the War Office and the RAF, and, later, employers. The whole of East Grinstead became part of their reintroduction to the world. Burnt men would be taken out to pubs and shops and for walks. Nobody stared. Nobody gasped or whispered behind their backs. Many of the Guinea Pigs made their homes here, and many married their nurses. Then, after the war, McIndoe fought to give them civilian jobs. One man went to work as an engineer. 'I kept my hands in my pockets at the interview,' he said. 'I'd been there three weeks before they realised I didn't have any fingers above my second knuckle.' Of all the young men McIndoe treated, not one committed suicide.

In the ballroom, I looked round the table, trying to pick out the Guinea Pigs. It's difficult – old men get old faces. But here there's a truncated ear or a taut eye. The smooth, papery skin of a burns graft looks rather becoming when it's aged. They don't look horrifying or bizarre. Each has a comfortable appearance, a sense of faces that have been lived in with a knowing ease. And because of their flying helmets, most of them kept their hair follicles, and have incredible amounts of thick hair. Even before you know who they are and why they're here, there is an aura of beauty about them. That's not wishful romance or sentimental pity, it's the simple truth. They have a look that is winning and enviable; a singular, handsome directness. And, astonishingly, they all look decades younger than their real age, as if in their final furlong God has at last given them back that portion of their youth that was stolen from them by the flames.

After the horrible hotel catering and the prosaic announcements and thanks, they mill about with the banter of men who have known each other a long time. They talk easily about the hospital and their treatments, about McIndoe and the nurses, about the war and about flying. Their stories are polished smooth with modesty, understatement and repetition. The crooked smiles and little shrugs hide crypts of pain and valour. It is as if they have made a pact to tell their lives as unremarkably as possible: 'I worked for the Electricity Board.' 'Then we moved to Bolton.' 'I was shot down over the Ruhr.' 'I watched my hand melt.' What is ultimately most moving and most valiant about all of them is this blissful ordinariness. Having been given new faces and a new start against the odds, having looked once, briefly, into the burning light of oblivion, they have made a precious, glittering ordinariness of the gift of life. They got jobs, they got married, had families and caravans. Their daughters married, their sons were a worry, they have grandchildren, they retired to gardens and charity work. They keep in touch, they look out for each other. The great victory of these men is that, with their broken hands and fractured heads and glass eyes, they fashioned for themselves the most precious, elegant object in a free society – a quiet life of small joys.

A nice man who'd crash-landed his Spitfire and lost both his legs and his face, and was so badly burnt that the man who pulled him from the cockpit got the bravery medal, who later started a limbless servicemen's charity and is now in his eighties but doesn't look a year over sixty, and whose children, it turned out, were at school with me, asked if I'd write something for him. Something about the boys who are coming back wounded from Afghanistan and Iraq. 'They have the most terrible injuries – things we would never have survived. But they don't have what we had. They don't have each other, and a dedicated hospital.' Many of the Guinea Pigs said the same thing to me. They are deeply upset at how injured servicemen are treated. To them, it's personal.

Someone began playing the piano, and they huddled round, clutching their pints, singing 'Roll Out the Barrel' like a scene from an old war movie. Their families stood back and watched them with that very English 'Oh, he's off again' pride.

Acts of bravery are generally that – an action. A moment. But the bravery of these men has been lifelong and sustained. And their great valour has been to make it look so unexceptional. They are the best of us, but only because we make sure they got the best from us. McIndoe said in 1944: 'We are the trustees of each other. We do well to remember that the privilege of dying for one's country is not equal to the privilege of living for it.'

The Space Race

You really had to be there to understand, to fully appreciate, quite how astronomically underwhelming man's first step on the moon actually was. Think the millennium bug without the sense of doom. Think Mother Teresa's funeral but without the laughs. Neil Armstrong finally getting out of the silver Portakabin, gingerly setting his big wellies in the dust, like an old woman getting off a train, and saying: 'One small step for man, one giant leap for mankind.' A line of such wincing, vapid, flabby faux profundity. The overwrought result of a committee of earth-bound suits looking out of the window, overcome by portentousness, it sounds like the blurb for a film poster, or the motto on a charity's letterhead, or a jingle for a breakfast cereal.

At the time, it didn't sound like that at all. It sounded like 'Smurarshheashsshhhhstepancindggganeeeepinde'. Back in the studio, James Burke, a man who at the time was more famous than the astronauts but, like them, seems to have spun out of orbit, had to repeat what they'd said. So what we actually heard was spaceman's first words from Shepherd's Bush. We'd waited for this giant leap for hours. The television set had been a grey fizz all night. Nothing happened relentlessly, building expectation to an anaesthetic torpor, until they blew the hatch on the greatest anticlimax of the twentieth century (if you don't count Brigitte Bardot's film career).

Still, it was the high point of a race that promised us the moon, but provided only reflected light. It doesn't really surprise me that most American kids believe the moon landing was a covert operation carried out in a hangar in Texas with all the shadows pointing the wrong way. A good conspiracy theory is always so much more entertaining than what actually happened. In fact, everything that happened in the fifty years of the space race was nothing like as exciting as what happened in *Star Wars*, or *The Right Stuff*, or even *The Jetsons*. Space never lived up to its billing. I am a child of the space age. Space and nuclear war were the abiding rhythm of my childhood. Rockets were going to get us one way or the other. It all started with Yuri Gagarin, which was exciting, mainly because I was young and he sounded like the Little Prince. Then there was John Glenn, and that, too, was quite exciting. We were living in a grey time of round-pin plugs and Bakelite switches. I listened to the martial music and the static from the thin edge of the atmosphere on a wireless set the size of a pygmy's coffin that glowed with glass valves – it was technology from silent films.

Science fiction was hitting its golden age, and space was an easy sell. I can remember the exact moment when it all went wrong and crashed back to earth. It was when the Chinese got in on the space thing. Made in China was a byword for shoddy, for something that fell apart in your hands and gave you an electric shock. Not wishing to be left out and to assert their place as the third way to megalomania, the *Red Book* merchants catapulted a satellite into the never-never. All it did was send back a little tune, called 'The East Is Red', which sounded prophetically like a ringtone. We could find it on our transistor radios as a satellite passed overhead. It was a silly, crappy little ditty, and I knew that the space race wasn't about men becoming gods in the wide blue yonder: it was about international brand management and market share on earth. Space wasn't the final frontier. It was a bigger billboard.

The soundtrack was very important. The Russians had those great men's choirs, the mournful sound of superhuman effort and suffering, as if their cosmonauts were pulled into space by workers hauling on ropes. In the West, we had 'Telstar' by the Tornados, the greatest instrumental pop song ever, and Holst, and 'Fanfare for the Common Man', a piece of wartime workers' encouragement knocked out by Aaron Copland. But the soundtrack of the big black was nailed by *2001: A Space Odyssey*, with 'Thus

Spake Zarathustra' and the floating counterpoint of the Blue Danube waltz.

All great endeavours trail an aesthetic, a look, like a comet's train. It isn't conscious or planned. It's the collective style of popular reaction. The early 1960s grew out of science fiction, flying saucers, cosmological geometry, and was exploited by people who wanted to sell things to children: sweets, cereal, duvet covers. Having taken on the polished chrome fins and neon of 1950s America, it somehow failed to move on. Almost as soon as space travel achieved a look, it dissolved into kitsch – *Star Trek*'s tight polyester T-shirts and ankle boots. Just as policemen and doctors unconsciously grow to imitate the actors on *Z Cars* or *ER*, so the travellers in space became parodies of their cheap children's programme doppelgängers.

The kitsch of space achieved its cartoon-cliché nadir with Carl Sagan, the polo-necked romantic lead for easy science. Sagan was the *Reader's Digest* Einstein, a popular salesman for the space race. Like the men in the cigarette advertisements, he oozed wannabe lifestyle. Then he came up with the time capsule. In retrospect, it's almost impossible to explain how much serious thought and energy went into this most absurd and hubristic of exercises. The brief was to send an invitation to passing extraterrestrials. It contained all sorts of human bits and pieces. Everyone had an opinion on what should go: Bibles and Korans, photos of old people, aborigines and Balinese dancers, bits of Mozart and the Beatles. It ended up like the montages they play on rolling news channels when they've run out of adverts. Someone pointed out that aliens possibly didn't speak English, so they added universal mathematics, which all Martians were said to understand, and a map of how to get back to Florida.

The largest fuss was made of the images of a man and a woman, etched into indestructible kryptonite. It was the communal compound image of us – unless you were black, of course. The heated argument was about their nakedness. Should Mr and Mrs Earth have genitals and pubic hair? They're still up there representing us as a depilated Barbie and Ken. And we knew that space was not about up there at all – it was all about down here and our weird, tortured view of ourselves. And not in a good way. Space exploration became a metaphor for the vain, ego-ridden vanity of government and power. It trailed along in its shadow the collateral of spying, nuclear deterrents and Star Wars, and it gave us the GPS, a speaking map in your car; not so much infinity and beyond, more how to get to Leeds avoiding toll roads. When the Cold War finished, the point of the space race collapsed. Nobody went back to the moon – there was nothing they wanted or needed on the moon, except poetry and mythology. In a very human way, they just left some junk up there, and a bit of a corporate eulogy signed by Richard Nixon. It wasn't grand or brave or intrepid; it was ugly and stupid and laughable. The space race wasn't like Columbus or Magellan or Cook, bringing back something useful or explaining something important. It was pointless and wasteful.

The space race left us with the space stations; a zero-gravity gypsy trailer park, a rotting, dangerous caravan rolling around the world being looked after by bored third-rate security guards with physics O levels and bags full of piss. The experiments that were supposed to be its *raison d'être* are mostly school projects: can mustard and cress grow in space?

Kaliningrad on the Baltic coast has given space more travellers than any other place on earth. It boasts dozens of Soviet memorials to the daring adventures of the travellers to a distant darkness. But the statues are chipped, filthy and overgrown. Kaliningrad is one of the most polluted and miserable places in Europe. The space race was a joke at its expense. In Moscow, the museum of cosmology – where you can see Yuri Gagarin's Sputnik, no bigger than a 1950s cocktail cabinet, and copies of the rockets that sent dogs into space before they'd worked out how to bring them back – is now empty except for snakes of uninterested school kids. This is old Communist Russia. Nobody wants anything with CCCP on it. The space race isn't a symbol of power and bombast. It's an embarrassment, and that is the great truth about the space programme: it was the future that got overtaken by the present. The rockets, the magnificent noise and power and fury that was meant to symbolise our energy to go on and up, now look like old, wasteful carbon technology. The future isn't going to be in exploding ever-greater amounts of fossil fuel. The dream that space exploration would find new worlds for man to colonise looks like running away.

All that new science that was promised, which was going to spin off the space race like presents from a Christmas tree, turned out to be Teflon and pens that write upside down. The massive leap forward of the space age was computing – and that had nothing to do with Houston or Cape Canaveral. It was invented in garden sheds in California. The science of propelling large lumps of metal containing two foil-wrapped geography teachers through gravity is as obsolete as the technology of steamrollers. It was never as beautiful or inspiring as astrophysics. This is where the future of space travel really is. It's in going without moving. The unnecessary bit of the space programme turned out to be the animal, vegetable and mineral components. It's the maths that's going places. The final frontier is not out there beyond the Milky Way. The planet we need to get to is our own. The excitement is on Earth. The heroes children want to be aren't spacemen. They want to save dolphins and live with penguins.

The one lasting aesthetically beautiful thing that did come from the whole guzzling, ugly space business was that photograph of the blue planet: astonishing and moving and vulnerable, our great group photo. And, ironically, that image did more than anything to galvanise the nascent ecology movement. We needed to get out of the world to look back and see what was important and where the fight for the future really lay.

When the extraterrestrials get round to opening the junky metal box we sent them, what they'll find on the inside is probably not Carl Sagan's sexless couple, but a dead dog.

Poetry

One of the most satisfying things about words is their black and whiteness, the neat, austere simplicity of their process. Letters on a page are so direct, so literal. The connection between writer and reader is intimate, personal and immediate: a moment of thought held, suspended in a few marks, then reinvigorated. It has remained the same since cuneiform was pressed into wet clay with a reed. Words on a page have no backstage, no sleight of hand, nowhere to hide the workings. Words are what they say they are. You read a sentence and you can see how it was made; you can trace the thought. You know how it's done – just as long as it's prose.

With poetry, however, the rules don't apply. It's a fish of a very different colour. On the face of it, it looks the same; the letters, the words are familiar. But it isn't what it appears. By some internal magic, poetry hovers above the page, over the words. It happens outside the black and white lines, as if the writing were clairvoyant, calling spirit meanings, voices from beyond.

Here we are, about to appoint a new poet laureate. And poets are ducking for cover, hands over their faces, Birkenstocks flapping, sidling out of the limelight like stage managers suddenly asked to audition for *Hamlet*. There are those who ask if we really need a poet laureate at all, paid with a butt of sack, clasped to the heraldic bosom of the Establishment, forced to be toasted at all those plastic dinners and stand in receiving lines, expected to trot out easily yapped pompty-pom doggerel for royal births, the Olympics and the launch of nuclear submarines. The poet laureate is an Aunt Sally, to be shied at by all the couplets of philistinism and ponce-bashing that the press like to indulge in.

Yet poets are not naturally showmen. Poetry is by nature and convention a secret art. Poems are coded messages for your eyes only, left under pillows, behind whisky bottles, tied to roses, written in water. There are no regular poetry reviews in cultural magazines, or poetry programmes on telly. Nobody is televising their awards live. Poets fall a long way behind actors and musicians, artists and novelists for celebrity. I expect Seamus Heaney and Wendy Cope could stroll hand in hand through most branches of Waterstone's unmolested. Poems sell few and far, for little or less.

This reticence, this unfashionable shyness, belies the truth of verse: that most of us are gaffed, flayed, stitched up and stuffed by poems. We're marked out and buoyed up by them. Even if we haven't read a new one for a decade, still there are verses that are the most precious and dear cultural amulets we own, hidden in the dead letterboxes of our hearts. Ask anyone what's right at the centre of their personal culture and it will be poetry. Snatches, lines of verse, we take them to our end. A poem is a thing that transcends its construction.

I write a great many words a day. I organise them with as much care as I can manage, I handle them with respect and pleasure, I enjoy their weight and effervescence, I pile them up and lay them in patterns. I love them with a gay abandon and defer to them with a lion tamer's wariness. They are the tools of my trade. I reckon I can make a craftsmanlike job of most wordy things, from a shopping list to a eulogy. But I have no idea, not the faintest inkling, of how a poem is made. Of course, I've tried. I've chopped the lines out. I've counted the syllables and I've counted them back again. I've stretched internal rhymes and made silk similes out of sow's metaphors, but it's not poetry. It remains resolutely page-bound: prosaic, poetish pastiche.

The hardest thing after writing poetry is writing about poetry, as you must already have noticed. It makes the author sound either pretentiously airy-fairy or thuggish. For a start, nobody really even knows what poetry is. It effortlessly jumps the fences put up to corral and protect it. The *OED* offers 'imaginative or creative literature in general, fable, fiction' which doesn't begin to cover it, then begs the question by offering 'the art or mark of a poet'.

And again 'composition in verse, or some comparable patterned arrangement of language'. The word 'poet' got its first recorded use in English in the fourteenth century with Chaucer. It came from the Norman French and, before that, Latin and Greek for 'the maker'. People have written books defining what poetry is and isn't, but they only tell you the mechanics. It's like eviscerating a swallow to understand flight. I asked an editor what poetry was. She said, 'It's that which can't be edited.' You couldn't make a poem from any of those descriptions, yet poetry is as plain and recognisable as a motorway sign.

You know poetry the instant you see it; the first line tells you. Yet it has no rules. It can rhyme or not. It can have as many rhythms as a Brazilian ballroom, lines of any length, as much or as little punctuation as it feels like. But poems can also be as rigorous as mathematics and as capricious as sixteen-year-olds. Poetry exists outside grammar and it can tie itself in more manners and etiquette than a Japanese dominatrix, but it is unequivocally real and solid, the most monumentally profound and intimately touching declaration in the world, and it can have any number of subtly different meanings. A woman once wrote to Dylan Thomas saying that she loved his poetry, but was worried that her understanding of it was not what he'd intended. Thomas replied that a poem was like a city: it had many entrances. Poetry is the apex of culture, the spire of civilisations. It is the scalpel of emotions and the anvil of thought. It whispers and it bellows the unsayable with mere words.

How does it manage that? You can't teach being a poet, you can't train to be one. I was once a judge in a poetry competition, and I can't tell you how many people who aren't poets write it. I have yet to hear a convincing explanation of where poetry comes from and how it arrives, but I do know it is the highest calling of a cerebral, emotional, aesthetic existence. Poetry, along with drumming and dancing, is probably the most ancient of all our arts. There was rhythm and rhyme before written language. Its meter resonates from our own heartbeats to make stories. Before somebody wrote down Homer's *Iliad*, it was memorised and repeated. Poems lit up the memory of our collective past, told us who we were and where we came from, and they still do.

People who never read poetry still reach for it at the precipitous points of their lives. At moments of great happiness and terrible sadness, those emotional places where prose is leaden with its own wordiness, only poetry will do. There will invariably be verse at funerals and weddings, at war memorials and the desperate pleading for love. There is poetry for the unrequited and the inconsolable, for the ecstatic and the erotic. There is always poetry. We tell poems to God and call them prayers. The more I write prose, the more I read poetry. The more poetry I read, the greater and deeper its mystery, why it works in such fantastic profusion, from Victorian epics to haiku. (Which, incidentally, I've never got the point of: aren't they just limericks that don't make you laugh?) When I was fifteen, I went on a family holiday to Mallorca. Walking on the olive steps in Deià, we met a stranger in a black toreador's hat with silver and turquoise rings on his long fingers, and a torrent of white hair. He had Geronimo's profile.

We said hello. That night, he came to dinner at our pension. He shook my hand. It was Robert Graves. I was thunderstruck with awe. He was everything I wanted a poet to be.

A few years later, at the dregs of a garden party in All Souls, Oxford, there was a sudden thunderstorm and a man in horn-rimmed glasses, a scruffy overcoat and a forgettable hat asked me if I'd like to share his umbrella. We were walking the same way. He wanted to know which college I was at. I said I wasn't from round here: I was at the Slade, in London. We went into the chapel in Magdalen and walked in silence. I asked him quietly what he did. He said, 'I'm the librarian at Hull.' And he, too, was exactly what I wanted a poet to look like.

In my life, we have had a particularly rich period of poets: Auden, Graves, Masefield, Larkin, Thomas, Day-Lewis, Spender, Betjeman, Heaney, Hughes, Logue, the recently deceased Adrian Mitchell. They have written between the lines on every facet of our lives, from the landscape to Edwardian plumbing. The poetry of our times is a fairer record of our concerns and hopes and our collective life than film or television or painting. Now we're talking about a new poet laureate, perhaps getting rid of the post altogether, making it a quango, a teaching job for encouraging lyricism among the depraved and deprived. And that would be a terrible waste, to discard this post through a cool cultural reticence, a liberal embarrassment.

The role goes back, in one form or another, 10,000 years in England, to before English was a language. There have been some very good poets and some exceedingly bad ones. The people who have turned it down are as illustrious as those who have taken it up. But there has never been a time, since the distant campfires of our ancestors, when we haven't needed a poet. A laureate stands as a lightning rod for us all. The point is not necessarily their poetry; dirge or doggerel, it's all poetry. It maintains a connection with the lyrical beat at the heart of the tribe.

Turner

The auditions for this year's Turner Prize are performed with a yawningly predictable exuberance down the central halls of the old Tate. Some think that attaching the name of Britain's greatest painter to this fine-art version of *Big Brother* is a travesty and an insult. But Turner himself might not have minded. He was fiercely competitive, with a canny eye for a commercial opportunity. Just down the corridor you can see a work exhibited in 1818. *The Field of Waterloo* is an unlikely painting. Even if you're familiar with Turner you probably haven't seen this 9ftx6ft canvas, his entry to a national competition to commemorate the defeat of Napoleon three years after the event.

He chose the battlefield at night. The dead are pressed together like human brawn, a rough pâté of uniforms and limbs that flows over the limpid rise and fall of the landscape. Turner actually went and sketched the battlefield and marked his notes with the numbers of the composting dead who are illuminated by a white flare in the centre of the picture, fired to frighten off scavengers, robbers and ghosts. The picture is spectacularly mordant and inappropriate for a jingoistic nation pumped up with martial grandiloquence. It's an anti-war picture that treats the French and the English as equal in death. It didn't go down well, and in truth it isn't a triumph. Turner wasn't very good at painting people – they always look like puppets propped up in a landscape, often with their faces turned away from our gaze. Not because he couldn't paint or draw: it's as if he were shy, not entirely comfortable with company.

Beside *Waterloo* is another strange picture, *The Exile and the Rock Limpet*. Why Napoleon (who appears to have been made out of a peg by gypsies) should be gazing so rapturously at a small bivalve in a ruddy sunset has never been successfully explained. Very little about Turner is exactly what it appears. We see him as the pre-eminently English artist, a virtual Shakespeare. He is presented to us as archetypally English as a National Trust tearoom; John Bull with an oily rag. We think of Turner as the tourist board stepfather of impressionism, a painter of marine nostalgia and fuzzy landscapes, because that's mostly what we're shown. But he was also from another English tradition – of radicalism, a nonconforming, awkward mysticism. When he died in 1851, Turner left £140,000 – about £11 million in today's money. He'd done well for himself. He never married and he left the bulk of his work to the nation. One condition for the bequest was that two of his pictures be hung each side of a Claude in the National Gallery in perpetuity. This was a homage to the master of classical landscapes, and also posthumous one-upmanship. The other condition was that the rest of the collection be shown in a gallery devoted to it.

In the late 1980s a grudgingly grateful nation got round to knocking up the Clore wing of the Tate. Walk around it with the Japanese students snapping each other on their mobile phones and the gloomy pensioners looking for free warmth and culture, and it is both inappropriate and insubstantial. Built during a barren and parsimonious moment of national self-doubt and municipal small-mindedness, the galleries are cramped and mean, the ceiling too low, the proportions huddled. Turner's vitally complex canvases pace the walls like beautiful athletes queuing in a social services drop-in centre.

I came here when it opened, with my father, who blessed me with his passion for Turner. I remember the huge disappointment when we saw the Clore wing. It was like looking at fireworks through a letterbox. That a rich First World country could build this as a temple to its pre-eminent artist beggars both belief and pride. Beyond aesthetics and appropriateness, the Clore Gallery is just far, far too small. Turner's bequest was vast: 300 oil paintings, of which only half are ever on show, and about 30,000 images on paper – drawings, sketchbooks, watercolours – of which 70 or so make it to the public galleries. But they all belong to us, and anyone can go and see them at Tate Britain if they make an appointment. In fairness, the staff will bend over backwards to show you. And if you're lucky you'll find Ian Warrell there – a Turner expert and quietly inspiring curator.

You might do worse than start with *The Rivers of France*, a series of watercolours Turner made for engravers to turn into book illustrations, which was a very lucrative business. He illustrated *Childe Harold* – the epic poem that made Bryon wake up with a start and discover himself famous. Turner was part of the new wave of radical Romantics, not wafty proto-hippies but gothic-horror-story, godless, republican revolutionaries, and the first modern celebrities. Byron and Turner were the two poles that held up my dad's cultural tepee; they are the first inkling of the modern world. In his lifetime, Turner was more famous and respected as a watercolourist than as an oil painter. English water-colour painting flourished with a brief luminous brilliance through the nineteenth century before declining into amateur retirement therapy. And Turner is its miraculous apotheosis. His touch is the purest, clearest evidence of genius I've ever seen. It's both delicately tentative and yet utterly assured. The marks on the paper are like fencing with a feather.

The range of his technical vocabulary is astonishing, aeons ahead and beyond any of his contemporaries, predecessors or descendants. He even kept his thumbnail sharp for scraping and incising the paper. The best way to see the watercolours is close, without glass; the power, brilliance and intimacy make your head burn and your eyes shimmer. People have been known to forget to breathe, to lose the sensation of their limbs, to weep without noticing. Turner's mentor, John Ruskin, spoke of the intelligence of Turner's eye. He had this way of seeing that was both inspir-ationally lyrical and intellectual. He also had a naturally aesthetic dexterity, a thoughtlessly beautiful hand – and you don't find more than a dozen of them in a century in any discipline.

Turner drew constantly. He sketched on anything with a relent-less inquiry, making everything from exacting topographical and architectural notes for working up later to bored doodles at official dinners. To turn the pages of his slight, home-made notebooks is to be as close as you can be to the working and thought of an artist from another age – and then there's the smell of them. The marvellous sweet, spicy, sleepy smell of old paper. The splash of wine, the thumbprints and the little notes. Turner kept and collated all his notebooks. They were important to him: a stream of consciousness, a therapy, a flash-card diary. Often he drew barely looking at the paper: beautiful lines, light and fluid, sinewy, exploring marks. The watercolour books chase sunsets and clouds across the pages, tie down fields and trees and mountains. There are books of bell towers and just of cows.

Turner was an inveterate traveller, never so much an English painter as a pan-European one. The palette of colours in the sketchbooks is spare, earthy and moody. He seemed to have had a particular fondness for red. You can trace the splashes and dabs right across his art, a Morse code that snags and warms the eye, like little flashes of a winter robin, or drops of blood.

I was talking of these things to Ian Warrell when he mentioned that they had Turner's death mask in the gallery – would I like to see it? Gently it was lifted out of its box and tissue like an Ascot hat. I looked down at the angular, sunken face, those old restless eyes, hollow and finally closed, pursed mouth sans teeth, and the strangest gothic, mystical thing happened: it became my father. Since my dad died, I suppose I'd been thinking about him, having that familial conversation in my head, but this was just the image of him as he lay dying, and it was a shock, though not a sad one.

Turner was born in 1775 in Covent Garden, where his dad was a barber. A cockney. And Turner spoke with a broad London accent all his life. His mother was a nutter, in and out of asylums. His dad encouraged him to paint, sent him to drawing classes, and, when the boy started making good with his watercolours and engravings, he gave up the barber's shop and went to run his son's studio, looking after business. Turner & Son. His working-classness was important to Turner. Art was his trade, the family business, and he went at it with a working-class resolve, ambition and pride. You've got to understand the bequest in those terms. There was never a knighthood for Turner; he didn't get on at court, he didn't fit in – then or now.

He was deeply affected by his father's death in 1829 and his work changed. Not so much darker as louder, faster and more personal. It's as if something had snapped, some restraint. In the gallery is the painting *Death on a Pale Horse*. You wouldn't necessarily recognise it as a Turner; it could almost be a Goya. Death as a skeleton reaches out from the back of his apocalyptic steed. It's angry, sad and frightening, and it's rarely shown. It might have been lost for ever if, during the Second World War, Kenneth Clark, the young director of the National Gallery, hadn't been called down to see some old rolls of canvas being cleared out of the basement. They turned out to be about seventy Turners.

Even before his death, people tried to mould Turner into being a particular sort of artist. Principally the man who would be his mentor and substitute dad, the critic John Ruskin. Ruskin saw his genius, but not for what it was. He wanted him to be a romantic, eye-saturating national treasure. He didn't appreciate or like the more extreme, unknowable, darker painting, and was disturbed at the hints of eroticism. But after his father had gone, Turner painted more and more just for himself, accumulating the work that would be his memorial, his gift to the nation. These are the expressionist observations of atmosphere and emotion. It becomes impossible to tell how finished these canvases are. Turner just stops and it's as though every brush stroke is held down by the tension of its relationship with every other stroke; as if one more mark would topple the whole picture into chaos.

There is, in what must be one of the finest rooms of paintings anywhere in the world, a picture called *Snow Storm – Steam-Boat off a Harbour's Mouth*. I watched its great vortex of weather churn about with Ian and said it was perhaps as perfect a picture as had ever been painted in England. He said yes, it probably was. But did I know that its full title goes on to claim that Turner actually had himself tied to a mast in the storm to know what it felt like, and that a critic had sniffed that the picture was merely soapsuds in whitewash?

Back in the reserve collection, Ian fetched a set of notebooks. These are the very last that Turner made, on a trip to northern France. The marks scatter and tumble across the pages, making images of raw power and pathos that are beyond artifice or beauty or heritage or ego. Sketches that were never meant to be seen, the rhythmic jerks and peaks of a cardiac monitor that say: 'I'm here ... The eye witnesses, my hand records.'

'No more than a hundred people have seen these since Turner died,' said Ian. The paper smelt of sandalwood, tobacco, incense and black earth.

The Fourth Plinth

(July 2009: Antony Gormley's *One & Other*)

When I got to Trafalgar Square, there was a gorilla on the plinth. Obviously not a real gorilla. A real gorilla wouldn't have stayed on the plinth; the safety net wouldn't have kept anyone safe from a real gorilla. A gorilla wouldn't have been art; it would have been a disaster movie. Unless it was a stuffed gorilla. Then it would have been a Damien Hirst. No, this was a man in a gorilla suit. A gorilla suit that didn't fit. He couldn't do it up at the back. Imagine being too fat for your gorilla suit. 'Sorry, sir, that's the biggest gorilla we do.' Or perhaps he had no one to do it up for him.

The gorilla *manqué* (a phrase I don't expect I'll ever have the pleasure of writing again) stood on the plinth and threw things. A pair of Italians didn't seem to mind one bit being splatted in the back by a banana. They had, after all, come to England, and what do you come to England for if not zany humour and eccentricity? Up the road, they were changing the guard: a couple of dozen synchronised men wearing bears on their heads – and that's really a great deal more comically obtuse than a solitary nylon great ape.

So what was I supposed to think about the monkey man? Was he a miniature King Kong? Was he mocking the idea of memorial greatness? Was he an allegory of extinction and loss? Or was he a drunk fiancé from a stag night, who'd been put up here by his mates? Was there a Jane waiting at some desperate altar?

A specially adapted JCB cherry picker beep-beeped across the square to replace him with a lady in orange carrying a bunch of red roses. The monkey picked up his used banana skins, the JCB conductor in his high-vis jacket prodded out one of those long picky-uppy things, and, clambering in, the gorilla wished the lady in orange good luck. He sat in the JCB looking endangered. His hour on the plinth was over. Now it was back to being a supply teacher, or a groom. Or the doorman at the Rainforest Café.

The orange lady stepped on to the plinth and shouted 'Hello' into the wind. Her orangeness had a Buddhist hippie thing going for it; orange is the unwearable colour of universal peaceful protest. An artist wouldn't perhaps have chosen deep red roses to go with it, and I noticed she had sturdy, safety-first knickers on.

This is the sort of thing you must think about when you're going to be standing on a plinth in Trafalgar Square. When Antony Gormley's great democratised lottery project started, I watched the local television reporter ask him with that sneery, chummy, man-of-the-people common-sense incredulity that local TV reporters wallow in: 'This isn't really art at all, is it?' To which Gormley replied, with a straight bat: 'Why does it matter to you?'

In the thin crowd under the plinth, I heard people ask much the same thing. Is this art? Or, to put it another way, this isn't art, is it? It's the wrong question. The right question is, why does it matter to you? And that, in part, is what *One & Other* addresses. I should disclose here that Antony and his wife Vicken and I were all at college together. Well, not 'together' as such, but at the same time. And I think he is intensely clever, and talented, though not quite as clever and talented as he thinks he is. I also think that what he does is beautiful and profound, and memorable, which is the triple, the trinity of creativity.

This project seems to be a natural extension of one of his first works, *Field*. What is depressing about the art question is that art itself has been answering it for more than 120 years. It has been modern art's primary concern, and for people who have Andy Warhol prints in their loos to still be asking, 'Is it art?', as if that were an intelligent question, is immensely depressing. You just haven't been concentrating, have you?

The day after the plinth performance began, the memorial for the 7/7 bomb victims was inaugurated. No smug young TV reporter or watching banker asked, 'Is this art', but it plainly fulfils all the criteria. It was made by an artist, it's unique, it has an aesthetic, and no practical application, and it looks very like a lot of other things that are art, but it's a memorial, and therefore excused art. But if it were deconsecrated, if its memorial duties were taken elsewhere, would it then become art, and would it be worse as art than as a memorial? Look at Trafalgar Square, at the other creations here. No one asks if Nelson is art, but if someone put a gorilla suit on him they would.

'Is it art?' is a question asked by the culturally insecure, those who need to know that the bag they carry their opinions and prejudices in is a real Louis Vuitton. Here is a simple rule: art isn't anything. The purpose of art isn't to be art; it's to move, to be inspiring, depressing, exciting, to manipulate, to realise feelings and thoughts that are too subtle and deep to put names to. It could also make you laugh, comfort you, distress you and give you a stiffy.

On the other hand, the purpose of wallpaper is to paper walls. Don't mistake craft for art. Art may use craft, but that's not what makes it art. The proof of art is the same as the proof of pudding: it's in the consumption. You've got to feel it to know it. And if you want to know if something is art, look at the way other people feel it. We view art differently from the way we look at anything else. There are four sorts of art: good art and bad art, successful art and unsuccessful art. Successful art is not necessarily good art, and unsuccessful is not necessarily bad.

The woman in orange shouts at us groundlings. She is here to draw attention to female genital mutilation. Aha, of course: the big knickers. She pulls on a T-shirt that says 'Mali', and shouts: 'This is for the three million women who will be cut this year in Mali.' She takes out a curved pruning knife and, with a symbolic flick of the wrist, beheads a rose and flings the petals into the wind. Whether the girls of Mali would think a rose petal a good swap for labia and clitoris, no one asks. She then takes off her T-shirt and shouts: 'Who would like Mali? And throws it to a fat American in a baseball hat, who gives it to his wife.

It was funny. Who'd have thought you could get a laugh out of female circumcision? She has a lot of Africa to get through, and lots of roses to behead. The crowd are hungry for clitoridectomy T-shirts, wave their hands for T-shirts. (The T-shirt is the crossover between culture and politics; the personal pull-on billboard of conviction.)

Nicholas Penny, the director of the National Gallery and a man who I would bet a Poussin doesn't own a T-shirt boasting anything more than a polo player, took the opportunity of the interest in Trafalgar Square last week to say that he'd like the busy road put back outside the National Gallery, as a cordon sanitaire, a ha-ha, between high art and hoi polloi. Hee hee.

We are, he sighed, ruining the classical loveliness of the square. There are so many events here, so noisy, so smelly, so many people climbing on the lions and the pediments. This is, of course, the problem with classical monumental cityscaping: it makes people look so uncouth, de trop; we are merely human litter – and that, in no small measure, is the point of building monumental cityscapes.

This place is supposed to make you feel small. Its grandeur and its scale are a fist to the populus and two fingers to the French. The Georgians demolished Nash's square, which in its turn had replaced a medieval market of shops and streets. This square was made as a stone seal of civic imperium to convince a burgeoning, displaced and quarrelsome population of its duty, to remind citizens of the great and the noble, who had created their empire and their riches.

Can you name the men who share the square with Gormley? This is the arty version of naming the seven dwarfs or the Marx Brothers. Of course, swottily, I can. Henry Havelock, hero of the Siege of Lucknow; died before he ever got home, of the shits. General Napier, a man who was disliked in life but not as much as his statue has been disliked in death. He captured Sindh, and probably never sent the apocryphal telegram ('*Peccavi*'). George IV, sculpted by Chantrey, he of the bequest; and, behind him, busts of first sea lords: Jellicoe, Beatty and Cunningham. Behind them, in front of the National Gallery, James II, the worst king we ever had, dressed absurdly as Julius Caesar and sculpted by Grinling Gibbons, and George Washington, given to the people of Britain by the Commonwealth of Virginia; having sworn he'd never set foot in England again, he stands on imported, republican, Yankee dirt. And to the south, on an island, facing Admiralty Arch, is the best statue in the square, arguably the best statue in London, certainly the finest equestrian one: Charles I, by Le Sueur. He surveys Whitehall, where he lost his head, Westminster, and up to the palace.

No one would dare ask any of these stern bronze grandees if they were art. They are here to inspire the ancient, civic duty of pride, excellence, self-sacrifice and gratitude. But mostly, they're here to remind you of your place. Which is on the ground. This is the first great failing of having living people on a plinth. The living don't belong. They are too small. Monuments are big, because that's how we show achievement. The great and the heroic are bigger than human, because they've achieved more. On Gormley's plinth, humans seem even more insignificant. For a start, they're difficult to see, cut off at the waist by the elevation. They don't offer you a sense of diversity, or the nobility of the ordinary man. They don't have a communist heroism. It just shows you how very, very ordinary we are.

And the art the lottery winners make of themselves is gauche and clichéd. Watching the webcam, you see a succession of people awkwardly broadcasting worthy causes, doing party turns, auditioning simple dichotomies or visual puns. It's been pointed out that there is more than an element of reality TV about this process. That's not necessarily a bad thing, but it is a rather small and sterile accomplishment. What the constant stream of lottery winners proves is that art is not made by chance, or by the ordinary, but by people who are extraordinary. Art is not what you've seen before; it is something you've never imagined. And only very few manage to make it. The rest of us pastiche and plagiarise.

The woman collects her rose stems, to be replaced by a man who begins to read the Old Testament. He clears the small crowd before he finishes the first verse, and he underlines the truth: not about God, but about this plinth. It isn't a plinth; it's a pulpit, a complaint line, a soapbox, for windblown agitprop. You need to be dead to fill a plinth. You need only a grievance for a pulpit. This is Speakers' Corner come to Trafalgar Square, which is what marchers have been doing for a century.

So, individually, this is unsuccessful bad art, but for Gormley it's probably unsuccessful good art. And, in the nature of art, the piece becomes very good indeed when there's nobody there. An empty plinth with the ridiculous, nannying and ugly wings of a safety net, the beeping JCB, the guards with high-vis jackets, the permanent Portakabin containing a sitting room for minders, PRs and organisers, says something about the timidity of our society, the obsession with danger, the constant worry about chance and bad luck, the feeling that we need to be protected from everything and every possibility. That we might fall from the plinth and hurt ourselves.

We are failing to live up to the square. Havelock didn't need a safety net, nor Napier; even Charles met his fall with nothing more than an extra vest, so as not to shiver. Nelson, way up there, on his pillar, doesn't need a risk assessment or a safety harness, and he has only one eye and one arm. As ever, Gormley has created something contemporary and important: a memorial to health and safety.

Old Age

I want you to do something for me. Think of it as a game, a quiz, a trick. Go and find an old person – one who's not related to you or a neighbour. Just a random, strange old person, a lurking crusty. It doesn't matter what sex – sex really doesn't matter to old people. They don't do or have or belong to sex any more, they're just old. Old is the third sex: girls, boys and the aged. So, look at this old person, stare at them, get really close. Don't be frightened – they won't hurt you. They're not contagious; they're more frightened of you than you are of them. Right, here's the game bit. Can you tell me how old they actually are? Look carefully at that face, at the wrinkles, the crêpey, sunken cheeks, the frail, eroded jaw, the thin folds of wattle. Count the archipelagos of age spots, examine the wind-coloured hair patted into the habit of a lifetime. Look into the fretted, damp eyes, their lids sagging like ragged bedroom curtains, and add up the years. Pick a number, like guessing the weight of a cake or the height of a steeple. You'll see it's much more difficult than it looks.

You can discern the years between sixteen and twenty. You know a twenty-one-year-old from a twenty-eight-year-old, but I bet you can't mark a decade between sixty and ninety. You can't read the gradations and patinas. Not that old people hide them; you can't tell because you don't look. And you don't look because you don't care. Really, who cares how old the old are? Old is a destination. There is nothing after old. Just nothing. Now, just one more thing: take another look at your old person and tell me, what was it that determined that they were old? What made you think they weren't just young with a lived-in face and a hangover? If you can't tell what age old is, how do you know when they've got there? Do you think they just wake up one morning to discover

119

they're past everything but care and caring? Old is not a number. It's not a date. It's simply the absence of youth, the absence of attraction, interest, new friends, society. The absence of conviviality, warmth, choice, or surprise, or life.

We have a problem with old age, a huge problem. If we arbitrarily cut the birthday cake at sixty-five, then that makes the old 16 per cent of the population, which will rise to 22 per cent by 2031. The old use up more than 40 per cent of the National Health budget. But the old aren't the problem – it's the rest of us. It's you and I that have the problem. It's our collective refusal to look at the old, to be in a room with them, to ask them into our lives. The great terror of our age is age. We would rather consign the old to a netherworld, a waiting room where they are out of mind and out of sight. The fear is plainly not of the old: it is that we will become them. The old are the zombies at the end of your own home horror movies.

St Leonards-on-Sea was built by an old man. James Burton bought a lump of farmland on the coast and conceived a new town, a town of bracing gentility. This collection of gleaming, po-faced streets, the promenades of probity, the municipal gardens for civic reflection, became journey's end for the retired civil servants of empire and the imperial military, a final move for the widowed spouses of industrial engineers and provincial department store magnates, the rheumatic and the consumptive, the dun-achieving tricked down here to the sea's reflected glister that bounced off the white cliff stucco guesthouses and sedate residential hotels.

They came to play vicious bridge and smiley bowls, formed exclusive societies, had tea dances and charabanc outings, and filled stuffy rooms with Benares brass, Burmese teak, Turkey rugs and careful china. They hung gilt-framed views of Table Mountain and dead boys in khaki, and dusted the parsimonious riches of adventurous lives lived with a gingerish prudence.

St Leonards was, from the start, mildly risible, a crepuscular community twinned with the letters page, the Conservative party and the crematorium. But it was also a reward, a just desert, a symbol of a life lived with standards, with napkins and polished shoes. And if you had to be old, it was a good place to be old in at a time when being old was an achievement. But those old black and white granny ghosts should see it now.

The steely Channel still dowses the front with a squinting brightness, but the streets are gap-toothed, the shops boarded up or given over to charity. In the pub, the motes of wasted time dance in the light over yellow-eyed men in tracksuits, who measure the day in toothpick roll-ups. There is nothing genteel about St Leonards. Like the rest of the south coast, it has been given over to the long-term useless, the invalidity addicted, the flotsam of refugees and carelessly relocated. But they haven't displaced the old. They're still here, the indigenous community, but hiding. St Leonards has one of the highest populations of aged in the country.

On the sixth floor of a caretakered block, an old man sits quietly in his front room surrounded by pottery, china, wood, cats, none living. He has an untouched leatherette-bound edition of Dickens, and above the mantel a print of eighteenth-century huntsmen quaffing in front of a roaring fire. Their conviviality mocks his stifling solitude. The room has the smell of exhausted air. A clock strikes a cacophonous quarter that would infuriate anyone who had something else to listen to. Here the time doesn't go quietly. Everything harks to an absent woman. Her knick-knacks and mementos, the holiday souvenirs, the jolly vanities now fight for space and memory with the detritus of communal care: crutches, bottles of pills, easy-grip utensils. This man has diabetes, a heart condition, swollen ankles, but that's not what ails him. He's old and alone. His tracksuit bottoms are stained. Food is delivered every two days by a nice agency worker from the Philippines who does a bit of shopping for him. I am here with the district nurse, who wants to check his blood is not too sweet. She asks how he is; the question is rhetorical. He has a bottle of gin and the telly. Once he lived in Malta, once he was a private detective, once he kept real cats, once he had a wife and friends. He's not uncared for; he has the tablets and the tinctures, and a string in the corner that, if pulled, will summon a man in the call centre, who will phone to ask what the matter is and, if nobody answers, will send an ambulance. We as a caring society will fend off his creeping death, insulate his awful loneliness for as long as possible. We just can't supply him with anything worth living for. In another small flat along the seafront, another man sits in another chair that seems to have grown around him like a fungus. He sits with his back to the bright sea view. The room has hardly any other furniture. There is naught for comfort. In the corner is a glass cabinet containing a collection of china princesses. 'They're nice,' I say. 'Did you collect them?'

'Do you want to buy them?' he replies.

This man also has diabetes, and depression, and an ulcer on his leg that won't heal. He's had it for years. They think the best cure is to cut off the limb. He doesn't use it much anyway. He worked on the railways at Paddington, met all sorts – royalty, stars. Every day was different. He had a wife. She died. He had a son and a daughter. They don't see him or call. He wants to die. The loneliness, the sadness, has made living a mortal sickness. I ask him how old he is: sixty-nine. Only sixty-nine. He could reasonably expect to live like this, minus a limb or two, for another fifteen or twenty years.

These two chaps are not exceptional. There are people like them in every street, in every block of flats, above every parade of shops, in every dripping-laurel cul-de-sac, up communal stairs and down muddy lanes. The old sit in mushroom chairs, never further than two feet from a radiator, a phone and the TV. They don't go out much because out is frightening, panicky, hostile for the old. Outside is a country they don't belong to any more, where they're no longer included. Just think how few old people you notice, how relatively few there are among us, bustling and dodging in the streets, shops and restaurants. You will see none after dark. The old live like Transylvanians, terrified of the young, the swift and supple, loud and late, irritable young. Even when they do venture out among us we don't look at them, we don't see them; they cling to the wall, curl up like dead leaves in bus shelters, press themselves into corners.

I have become haunted by the absence of the old. Ever since the death of my father three years ago, I have got into the habit of asking middle-aged friends about their parents. There is a common narrative to their answers. They list the deficiencies, the problems, the conditions, the failings, the diminutions, usually with a tired fondness and a growing hum of exasperation. I sat next to a woman at dinner recently who told me how wonderful her father was because he'd died so well, so quietly and quickly, ne'er a fuss. And then with a sigh, 'Now my mother, she's always complaining, miserable, I think she's scared of letting go.' It wasn't said carelessly or without a decorous dab of concern, but mostly it was with annoyance.

You hear it, too, among the professionals who care for the old, reciting illnesses and shortages. You hear it in the media, where old age is a collection of problems. The old are slow and cold, brittle and cancerous, breathless, toothless, sexless, forgetful. And, most newsworthily, they're victims – of bugs, of councillors and chancellors, or welfare and weather. They're also the victims of grief and pity and comedians. To be old is to be stalked by taxes and frost, flights of stairs, and, finally, God. To be old is to vanish behind the sum of incurable, piteous conditions.

For many, the final furlong of a life is spent immobile in a chair, in a bright room in what's euphemistically called a 'home'. It isn't a home, just as Battersea Dogs Home isn't a home. It's a hospice for those who've been put out of a home. These villas standing back from the road in the outskirts of provincial towns, discreet as brothels, hidden behind leylandii, with bland, forgettable names, are run by opaque, care-dispensing companies that are the shallow end of healthcare.

It is estimated that a quarter of all nursing homes fall below care guidelines, which are themselves set disgustingly close to the earth. If you walk up the steps of an old people's home, holding the rail to steady yourself through the swinging doors into the little reception area with its pot plants and notice boards pinned with safety warnings and activity sheets, be under no illusion. If you ever leave, it will be in an ambulance or a hearse. You are here until you decide to let go, and the sooner and the quieter and the neater you can manage that, the better. Residential people's homes get less care and attention than prisons. They don't have to rehabilitate anyone. Every inmate is on a life sentence. These bright, wipe-down, neon-lit, disinfected rooms, smelling of fish, piss and Cif, are death row for the blameless.

I'm sent to be shown round a residential home in Putney. This is top of the range – they're proud of this one. Very nice, very busy and efficient. The directors and the PRs and the housekeepers who come to meet me all have the gimlet, spearmint keenness of folk on a no-nonsense, long-distance goodness mission. The walls are collaged with old record sleeves, Perry Como and the Carpenters, Jimmy Shand and Cliff. The doors and lifts work with security swipe cards; the rooms are full of inmates, 'guests', who sit for the most part in a ruminative stasis. A circle of old men sit together, none acknowledging the presence of the others. Their rheumy eyes swim, tufts of missed stubble prickle whitely. Only their fingers are restless, worrying a hem or blindly searching for something lost and forgotten. One holds a large teddy bear with a blue-knuckled hand, like a prize from a long-decamped funfair.

In another room three hunched old ladies watch *Oklahoma!*. 'I'm just a girl who can't say no.' In another, there's a church service. We sing 'Praise My Soul the King of Heaven'. In another room there is painting by numbers. The place is a hamster wheel of activity, singsongs and seated exercise, all purposeless. There is nothing left to learn, nothing to be fit for, nobody to give the paintings to, no more skills needed, no new tunes and no new verses. This is merely collective time-whittling.

Visitors often comment how similar old people's homes are to infant schools. There is a sort of neatness, a return full circle to the innocence of toddlers. It's a comfort to believe that the destination of life is to end up where you started – in nappies, being fed mush, drinking from a sippy cup with a matey, loud kindness that excludes dignity or respect. It's rarely mentioned, though, because it's a sensitive subject, that almost all the staff in care homes are imported from nations that have a far greater veneration for age than our own. As one Filipino cleaner said to me, 'You don't want to live with your old, and you're too guilty to even feed them.'

These homes are the final resort. When you fail at basic one-room, single-bar life, this is where you come. The government will make you sell everything you own to get here. Nearly all 'guests' have some form of dementia. This is the great unspeakable plague of our medically privileged times: dying from the inside out. Outside hospital, dementia isn't even classed as a medical problem: it's a concern of social workers. If it were medical, local authorities would have a statutory obligation to treat it.

In an acute old people's ward in a central London teaching hospital, almost all the beds are taken up with Alzheimer's patients being treated for their related conditions: the broken limbs, the burns, the cancers, the failing organs of tired, forgetful bodies. I ask their consultant, who specialises in geriatric medicine, if the treatment patients get is relative to the amount of outside support they have from their families. She grips her clipboard protectively and stares hard into my face, looking for reassurance or a reason to answer. Finally she says: 'Yes, of course. If a frail old person, probably with multiple conditions and a limited prognosis, is brought in, we think about where they're going to go after we've treated the most chronic condition. Who is going to look after them if they go back to live on their own? Yes, the quality of life is . . .' she searches for a word. 'If there's not much quality, we may well not do procedures that demand a lot of aftercare. We'll just make them comfortable. We're not talking about killing people, or even letting them die, just not prolonging unhappy, lonely lives.'

Now that thoughtful reply won't come as a surprise to anyone working with geriatrics or in the health service, but it might come as a bit of a shock to anyone whose granny is on a ward that's just too far away to conveniently visit. As a society we run old people's care like a donkey sanctuary. Perhaps that's okay – we're very nice to donkeys.

I ask the consultant if she'd leave her parents to the state. 'No,' she said without hesitation. 'They came from a very tight community – they didn't put the old out on the ice floes. I'd go home and take care of them.' And would you be happy to be treated in an NHS home yourself? 'No. It's not that I think they're bad – I think staff do their best. But it's not something you'd look forward to.'

Not one of the healthcare or social services personnel I spoke to said they would want to end up in their own care. They all said they thought the service they offered was exceptional in its diligence, that the staff were devoted, that everything that could be done given budget, staffing, red tape, directives, etc, etc, was done. But they'd rather die at home.

All life ends in failure. However much you've laid aside for the package tour of an afterlife, it ends in failure: heart failure, failing eyes and limbs, the failure of bladders and balance, the failure of memory and hope. But it should also be a long moment of success – the pleasure of a race well run, the pride in a family born, nurtured and fledged, a validatory break on the bench to remember times transcended and misfortunes overcome or stoically subdued.

We are one of the very few cultures in all the world, down all the ages, that don't treat age as an achievement in and of itself. There are no old people's homes in Africa, because the old live with their families and in their communities. They earn honorific titles – white hair and a stick are owed respect. There is a polite assumption of wisdom in experience. But we are terrified by the loss of youth. We kick against the clock, like infants trying to put off bedtime. We dress younger than we are, talk younger, stretch, freeze and stitch our sagging bodies to fool those younger than ourselves, and our genes, as if a cocktail of lentils, beetroot juice, positive thinking and hip-hop talk will make us thirty for ever, until we kick off in the middle of a dirty dream. We pray ardently without belief for a painless, switch-flick demise.

Ageing is so frightening in part because we treat the old so badly, and we treat them badly because we're so frightened of them. We ignore them and consign them to horrible solitude because we can't face the truth that some day someone will banish us. Most people in this country die weepingly lonely – cold, starved, and left in no doubt that they have overstayed their welcome. This is the greatest shame and horror of our society and our age.

The cure for this youth-tormented terror is blindingly simple. Reclaim the old. Include them in our lives. The antibiotic for loneliness is company. I wouldn't patronise the aged by claiming that everything they say is wise or steeped in the rare tincture of experience. They talk as much repetitive bollocks as the rest of us. But we never listen to them; we're deaf to the old. We assume they have nothing to tell us, nothing but loopy non sequiturs and circular complaints. Even when the news is about them, nobody asks an old person what they think. Young professionals para-phrase on their behalf.

You know, you really should spend an hour listening to someone who's lived twice as long as you, not as social philanthropy or goodness, but for your own sake, for the sake of your self-worth, to calm your speechless fears about ageing, and because you'll hear something funny and clever, touching and probably astonishing. Most old people are more interesting than most young people, simply because they're older. Experience may not bring wisdom, but it does make for some cracking stories. Every old person you ignore has lived through times and done things, seen stuff that you never will, and it's worth hearing about.

There is a towering, pitiful irony that the most popular use of the net, after watching fat Germans have shaky sex, is unravelling genealogy. We will spend hours picking through turgid ledgers and ancient lists to discover who we are, but can't bring ourselves to listen to the first-hand account of where we come from and what it was like.

We should, at the very least, ensure that nobody, none of our kin, compatriots, kith or countrymen, ever sits alone wishing for their own death because they know of nobody who wishes them to live. We will abate our own fears of ageing by ensuring that someone else isn't fearful and lonely. You get back what you give.

I look at the veneration of Harry Patch, the longest living Tommy from the Great War. He was the man who didn't just cheat death but transcended it – all those millions of deaths. People queued to see him, they nodded and committed to memory his whispered, papery thoughts. The great and the powerful stooped to shake his hand. He was a living memorial. When I was a boy, every old man I met had served in the Great War. Gardeners coughed up gas-ravaged lungs, publicans wore county regiment ties. The chap with the pinned-up sleeve who sold my dad a box of matches every morning at the train station had lost his arm at Loos.

Harry Patch wasn't a special case; as a young man he did what all young men did. He was exceptional because he beat the indifference of age: he lived long enough to come through the line and be reborn as interesting and wanted again.

FAR

Bombay

How often have you been stopped at a traffic light and thought, Damn, what I could really do with right now, this very minute, is a pink Barbie hairbrush and some skin-lightening ointment, or a plastic toy helicopter; a wrench set would be nice, or a yellow nylon teddy bear? You can get all of them at any intersection in Bombay. There is a world of commercial long shots, dodging the murderous taxis and their equally lethal fumes. If you ever wonder what the bottom rung of capitalism's ladder looks like, it's a nine-year-old boy selling a 40-watt light bulb in four lanes of traffic in Bombay. (Don't call it Mumbai. Only CNN weather forecasters call it Mumbai.) Each sixteen-second pitch, pressed up against your window, is a small triumph of hope, hype and horoscopes over experience, health and safety.

For three decades, I'd been keeping a top-ten list of the weirdest free-market impulse buys I'd been offered at Bombay traffic lights. For a long time, the winner by a short head was a hatstand, a 6-ft, free-standing wooden hatstand, carried in the midday heat by a spindly man with a rag on his head and a big, hopeful, semi-demolished grin. Of course there are lots of things you could buy that you didn't know you wanted. You could get that dust-coloured little girl a fistful of rice and lentils for the listless brother on her hip. You could buy the legless lad dodging traffic a new wheel for his skateboard. You could stand to get the window-tapping, glass-smearing, imploring sea of ailing humanity a drink of clean water. You could change the world one scrofulous waif at a time, or you could buy yourself an issue of *Vogue*. A catty, ragged, cropped-haired gamine offered me a fresh *Vogue India*, and instantly, effort-lessly, leapfrogged the hatstand to reach the top of my surreal crossroads impulse list.

I've been coming to Bombay for thirty years. I first saw the Gateway of India rise out of the dawn from the deck of a Glasgow-built ferry chugging up the Arabian Sea from Goa and I knew instantly that I would love this city in sickness and in health for a lifetime. Have no doubts, banish all Western-sneering prejudice: this is one of the great cities of the world. If you want to know what nineteenth-century London or New York felt like while they were still vital, before they got scared and wanted peace and quiet, it must have been a bit like this. But Bombay is bigger. Much, much bigger. This is a metropolis with the throttle open. The aspiration hums like a turbine. You can feel the streets sweat, strain, and bulge like choking hot veins. The city grows up and out. It heaves at the edge of a great curve of shore. The once imposing civil servant's taste of the imperial British city is being elbowed aside by the steel and concrete yearning for power and purpose and riches.

Bombay is a flesh magnet, sucking in hundreds of thousands of bony, barefoot impresarios. For every new, smoked-glass banker tower that shoots out of the cracked pavement, there are miles of instant slum, packing-case sub-cities that hug the great edifice of commerce as if they were totem poles. The needy immigrants work their way into every flat surface, waiting for the opportunity to step up. The corrugated tin and rag huts are made with the packaging of consumption. A crate that once held an air conditioner is now a home to the family of a man who will dig holes in a hundred degrees so that his son will be able to work in a room with an air conditioner. The streets of all great mercantile cities aren't paved with gold; they're paved with beggars dreaming of gold.

The one thing Bombay doesn't need any more of is cars. Traffic reaches a fidgeting stasis first thing in the morning. It stays there as the day heats up, in great ribbons of slumped motors fraying along main roads. Indians drive with an ambivalent extempore gusto, unencumbered by the handicap of rules, training or insurance, but bolstered by a startling belief in reincarnation. There are no laws of the road, only the eternal and unknowable commandments of existence. And you honk. All horns are honked at all times. If you forget to honk your horn, the backs of the manically Sikh-driven lorries have HORN PLEASE, written in decorative script on their tailgates.

Out of Bombay's chaotic hustle has grown the vaunted, courted and cajoled fragile Indian middle class. Much is expected of the middle class. Nobody really knows how many of them there are. Some say there are 350 million. Some say only thirty million with paid-up membership dues. In a nation of more than 1.1 billion, barely a sliver in the pie chart of reincarnation. But you know them when you see them. They have the worried and harassed, overnourished look of the rest of us, and they suffer from all our acquisitive ambitions. They want stuff. Their wives want more stuff. Their kids feel entitled to stuff. Their aunts and their cousins, whom they count by the dozens, demand stuff. Then there's the neighbours' stuff to be kept up with. And stuff doesn't just happen. They're in debt, right up to the little red dots between their eyes. India's emergent middle class is learning the first lesson of the international credit caste: that you will be held hostage by the very consumer economy you create, and the bigger it gets, the harder you work, the higher the ransom.

Bombay is enjoying a status boom, unmatched anywhere in the world. There are Italian restaurants, wine bars and nightclubs. There's charity, and there are openings of things that don't need opening. There are guest lists and blacklists, fashion, flirtation and casual infidelity. (But they still don't kiss on-screen.) There are reams and reams of gossip, and a compulsive appetite for young, empty, Westernised celebrity. I read one young starlet's interview about her first TV soap role. 'What did you think when you first saw yourself on-screen?' she was asked, with an exclamation point. 'Oh, I was amazed by what a really good actress I was!' Faux humility, understatement and self-deprecation are refreshingly not natural Indian vices. Status and snobbery are. One of the quickest and easiest, takeaway, ready-made status symbols is a car. India's roads were once a jam of egalitarian Ambassadors, indigenous copies of a pre-war, British Morris

Oxford made in Calcutta with drum brakes that work as brakes about as well as they work as drums. Actually, they tried to replace them with modern disc brakes, but having one car in a million that can stop efficiently is to invite mayhem and mutilation, so they thought better of it. When no one can stop, everyone's safer. It was a very Indian solution. But they're all gone now, the Ambassadors, finally made obsolete by avarice. And now it's Japanese and Korean imports, and the home-grown Tata Motors, which is producing the first, true 'people's car' since the Volkswagen, a $2,500 family runabout that's going to mobilise the nation, to the ire of Western environmentalists, who'd rather see families piled high on bicycles.

As a model for India's New Deal dream, cars are a simple metaphor of success. So when they told me there was a vintage car rally in Bombay, I had to see. Owning an old car is one of those comfy signposts of affluence. It ticks both boxes: expensive and impractical. Vintage is macho. And, best, you can flaunt it to the neighbours without needing to have them in the house.

The rally here is run by the VCCCI, the Vintage & Classic Car Club of India. The club is not just about cars. It's the story of two men, very different men, who, in their own way, represent the two passing faces of Bombay. Mr Pranial Bhogilal founded the VCCCI. Mr Nitin Dhossa now runs it and is responsible for the rally. They don't speak.

Mr Dhossa is not an easy man to talk to, mainly because he's a difficult man to get hold of. I suspect not being available is something of a professional habit. Both the London and New York offices of *Vanity Fair* made concerted and determined efforts to arrange an interview, even just to confirm the date of the rally. Very occasionally, his phone was picked up by an irate woman, who pretended to be his secretary, but who I suspect is probably his mother-in-law. She would tell me that, like Elvis, Mr Dhossa had left the building. So I just turned up in Bombay and somehow got him to pick up his mobile.

Naturally, predictably, he was a paragon of avuncular charm. We arranged to meet at the Cricket Club of India for the interview.

The gruesome Battle of Towton was fought in this Yorkshire valley in 1461.

Towton Society members, dressed in the burgundy and blue of the House of York, wade through the corn-covered battlefield.

Navigating the *tsingy* landscape.

Walking along the Avenue of Baobabs in Madagascar.

The sixteenth-century rural life that differentiates Albania from its European neighbours.

Under a statue in Durres, one of the oldest cities in Albania on the Adriatic coast.

Below: At the source of the River Danube, near Furtwangen, Germany.

The view of the Danube from Ulm Minster church, once the world's tallest building.

Cast-iron footwear in Budapest – a tribute to the Jews killed next to the Danube during 1944-45.

Opposite: By the Hallgrimskirkja, a Lutheran parish church in Reykjavik.

Left: The Arctic.

Below: Digging out tents in the storm.

Above: Haiti.

Christian survivors
pray outside a
collapsed building.

It's one of those closed, stuffily self-regarding institutions that make an Englishman abroad cringe with cultural embarrassment. It's been said that one of the reasons the British managed to rule India with such apparent ease and so few soldiers was that each nation found a kindred spirit in the more embarrassing character traits of the other. Both are shamefully partial to snobbery, class and clubs. The waiting list for the Cricket Club is longer than a natural lifespan – another reason for admiring reincarnation.

I walked in, and a secretary, sitting under a large painting of a defunct colonial, told me that Mr Dhossa was taking tea on the outfield of the cricket pitch. At that moment I was tapped on the shoulder and the man introduced himself as Mr Dhossa. A tall, tweedy gent with the neatly coiffed facial hair of a man who's both trying to tell you something and conceal something. He looked like the bursar of a small private school. 'Let's take tea.' He led me out to the pitch, which was large enough for professional matches and was surrounded by tiers of empty stands that could seat thousands. Instead of cricket, there were a number of wicker tables and chairs. At each, small groups or couples talked noisily and ate egg sandwiches as waiters ran between wickets. It was a bizarrely Lewis Carroll vision of a nostalgically familiar Victorian Sunday afternoon. 'Mint tea?' inquired Mr Dhossa as we sat down. And then, before I'd had a chance to reply, 'You must excuse me.' He stood up and went to sit at another table. Ten minutes later, he returned and explained that it was his cousins, who needed some small favour in the marriage line. He poured the lukewarm mint tea, oddly adding milk and sugar, and another gent silently joined us. 'This is Mr Gill,' said Mr Dhossa helpfully. 'He writes for an American paper – *Vanity*!' The gent looked politely blank, and Mr Dhossa's phone played a loud pop song. He apologised and took the call, which turned out to be from an interviewer with an Indian newspaper.

The gent and I sat in companionable silence, sipping our tepid toothpaste tea, watching the club members do passable imitations of the dull bits from E. M. Forster. I couldn't help overhearing that at the rally there was going to be a birthday celebration for a

1908 Wolseley, with a cake, and that it was going to be a great deal of fun. And that there would be prizes for best costume. Car owners were to be encouraged to dress up in the motley style of the years their cars were conceived. Mr Dhossa pronounced 'Oldsmobile' as two words, the second rhyming with 'nubile', which made it sound like a senior citizen's walker, and I got a fit of the giggles. After half an hour, he hung up. And with a look-what-I-have-to-put-up-with shrug, he said that it had been very nice to meet me, that I must come to his rally, that I might be able to get a ride in a car, and that he'd give me lunch. 'Good local food. Have you tried curry?' He handed me his card, which boasts eight numbers, e-mail addresses and websites, and is emblazoned with the logos of the British Automobile Association; Alliance Internationale de Tourisme, Genève, Switzerland; Federation of Indian Automobile Associations; and Fédération Internationale de l'Automobile, Paris, France; and still has room to tell me that Mr Dhossa is executive chairman. He is plainly a man with many, many revolving cogs, very few of them connecting.

The next morning I took a taxi through the claustrophobic traffic around the bay, and up into Malabar Hill, the old patrician neighbourhood. Opposite the governor's mansion there is a frankly and screamingly hideous vast red stone Victorian palace. This is Mr Bhogilal's city residence. I rang the bell. The metal security gates creaked, like something from *The Addams Family*. A functionary's face appeared and regarded me without interest. Inside, there was a dusty courtyard, surrounded by what looked like stables full of ancient and huge motor cars. It's difficult to overegg or hyperbolise the scale and bizarre caprice that were the leitmotif of nineteenth-century rich Indians. They make today's Arabs and Russians look pastel and timid. I was led into a reflection room that had marble walls with inlaid glass marquetry of a funereal exuberance. No one makes this stuff today, because no one would dare. Ornate occasional tables and mantels support bronze and gilt reproductions of late Renaissance and baroque sculptures, mostly of naked women in the throes of ecstasy, many also supporting lampshades at the same time. The wiring is all haphazard and temporary. Plugs and switches cling to surfaces and dangle provocatively. The furniture has frayed and chipped and sagged with well-bred exhaustion. In the centre of the room, apropos of nothing, there is a large marble bath. Crouching in the middle is an Italian sculpture of a boy trying to get a thorn out of his foot. Most strikingly, on the walls are hundreds of cheap gold frames containing greening photographs of motor cars. The house is silent and shuttered. Light seeps in where it can, and the dust plays in the slanted sunshine.

I waited for Mr Bhogilal, who didn't enter so much as appear, wraithlike. One moment I was alone with a lot of orgasmic bronze women, and the next, here was a pale man with a pleasingly round face and hopelessly sad eyes, framed in feathery white hair. He took my hand, rather than shook it, and then dropped it like a stale roll at a buffet. He sat next to me on an uncomfortable little sofa. He was wearing a long kurta pyjama. The shirt was made of the finest, frailest gossamer cream silk with a floral design printed in raised gold, like delicate icing. There were three buttons that were diamond studs, and on his soft hand was a diamond so big it would have guaranteed a backstage pass to a Saudi princess.

Mr Bhogilal didn't offer anything as bourgeois or common as charm. He exuded the sort of extinct courtly manners that make you feel like you're being slowly swaddled in the winding sheet of history. An elaborate gavotte of self-deprecation, flattery and insinuation, all delivered in an upper-class Indian accent which you rarely hear any more, a fluting imitation of the Duke of Devonshire. A flunky brought small, ice-cold silver cups of lychee juice, and we talked of cars. Mr Bhogilal has possibly, perhaps, probably, the largest collection of vintage, veteran and classic cars in the world, although he'd never be so vulgar as to actually count them. He collects them because his family has always had nice motor cars, and a chap's got to do something.

When India won independence, the rajas, who had, for some time, bought extravagant wheels as toys, had to get rid of them fast, partly as acts of egalitarian contrition, but mostly because they needed the cash. Mr Bhogilal, being neither contrite nor strapped, bought them. The rajas were famous for having their cars customised. Often they put large silver bells on the front, because Indian villagers were likely to be so terrified by the appearance of a roaring, honking monster that they'd simply freeze in their path. The bell was reminiscent of those worn by buffalo, so they'd understand the thing was merely a beast of burden and they'd skip out of its way. One nabob, having felt himself snubbed by a Rolls-Royce salesman, ordered six and had them turned into garbage trucks. The Rajputs of Rajasthan were particularly strict about their women, who were forbidden to talk to their chauffeurs, so their limousines had illuminated dashboards that had instructions which could be worked by switches in the back. TURN LEFT, GO TO THE TEMPLE, RETURN HOME. Mr Bhogilal tells me the story of two rajas in Berkeley Square, London, who walked into the Rolls-Royce showroom. This is a joke, and he tells it in the way that cautious men do, not to embarrass you with an outburst of uncontrollable laughter, but as a polite intimacy. The rajas look at the latest model and decide that they should acquire one each. Let me get them, says the first one. No, no, says the second. But I insist, repeats the first, you paid for lunch. Mr Bhogilal pauses and smiles, glad that I wasn't humiliated by glee. He pulls out a bright plastic child's photo album of the sort you can buy at any traffic light. In it are snaps of his cars. He refers to each by name and engine size with the quiet love of a headmaster showing off alumni. He particularly enjoys the Art Deco ones with fins and swooping bonnets. The Maybachs and Lagondas and Hotchkisses. And he likes to paint them hot Indian colours that sparkle like strippers' nail varnish. I ask politely – as politely as I can – what the Bhogilal fortune evolved from.

'Mills,' he says, in a voice like rustling tissue paper. 'Cotton mills, flour mills, sugar mills, steel mills ...' he sighs, exhausted by the thought of all those mills, and then manfully continues, 'chemicals, pharmaceuticals, property', and then gives up. 'Many things.' He waves a hand, dismissing the heavy thought of work. Most of the really titanic Indian fortunes come from cotton, and the opportunity offered by the interruption in European supply made by the American Civil War. 'I was chairman, but in a very amateur way,' he says, distancing himself from the practice of trade.

None of your cars are going to be in the rally tomorrow?

'I heard something was happening, but I have nothing to do with it now. Well, the sort of people involved, they get dressed up. I understand that there's a man who comes as Gandhi. He is a professional Mahatma, in a Rolls-Royce perhaps.' There is a wistful smile, apologising for almost forcing a laugh. 'And there are prizes for everyone.' He reaches out, and as if by some pre-arranged magic, a flunky appears with an envelope. 'The man who now calls himself the chairman or chief executive or something,' he says, 'he is not a man of character. Bluntly, I could only call him a crook. I found him. He did work for me. You understand there is much tedious administration. Running errands, he did that. When I found him, he was . . .' Bhogilal searches for the *mot juste*. 'He was . . . mud. I raised him up. I made him. He was mud.' And out of the envelope, he brings a neatly stapled sheaf of photocopied paper. It appears to be a signed confession from Mr Mud. It's dated 2003, and written on 100-rupee paper, an arcane Indian legal device for swearing affidavits. 'You can keep that copy,' says Mr Bhogilal. It's smudged and almost illegible. This is not the first time it's been copied, or, I suspect, passed on.

Having, with the utmost courtesy, damned and possibly slandered his former employee, Mr Bhogilal draws our meeting to a genteel close and shows me around some of his house. A dining room has a chandelier that is so huge it touches the table like a vast crystal breast hanging from the ceiling. We pass a bust of George VI. 'He visited us here, out in the courtyard.' A servant turns the key on some huge specimen of pre-war British engineering. 'Would you like to take it for a spin?' asks Mr Bhogilal. No, no, thank you awfully. I try to keep the anxiety out of my voice. The idea of leaping into Bombay's traffic at the wheel of this behemoth is terrifying. Mr Bhogilal nods apologetically, sorry to have put me in the position of having to rudely refuse a hospitable gift. At his feet, there is a sandy puppy. He stares at it and laughs quietly, sounding like a breeze passing through dried grass.

The rally itself is a predictable Indian confusion of good intentions failing to meet aptitude or expectation. A lot of old cars in varying degrees of decrepitude park up in a central square where the Bombay police band, in sticky nylon uniforms, oompah their way through pop classics. Their rendition of 'Like a Virgin' is particularly unexpected. There is a brace of the obligatory reality show model/actress/dancer/whatever starlets to wave flags and simper, and a few people turn up in costume, mostly as joke Englishmen with toy guns. Sadly, Gandhiji hasn't made it. Thousands of the new Bombay apprentice middle classes wander around in expensive jeans and sneakers, taking pictures on their mobile phones. Cars take all morning to drive off in clouds of smoke into the Sunday traffic, only to break down at regular and inconvenient intervals. The rich, sulky sons of hard-pressed fathers pose in shades and hair gel and skid off in Lamborghinis and, bizarrely, VW Beetles. The cars themselves are beside the point. Like the elaborate and beautiful models of gods at religious festivals, they are simply symbols of something greater. Something to come. The much-prayed-for reincarnation from consumed to consumer. That evening, as the lights shine around the bay, I pass a vast, silver Rolls-Royce with a bell, stalled in the middle of the road. A ragged boy stands on the running board, tapping the window, offering a feather duster, Christmas lights and last month's *Vogue*.

New York

Everyone recognises New York. From the sweaty jungles to the shivering tundras, we all know the look, the silhouette, the height and breadth of the city. This place is the most famous man-made vista in the whole world, and that's something. From abroad, we see it not just as America's greatest metropolis but as a defining image of the modern age. It's been modern for quite some time now. The durability of its modern promise is founded on the life that's lived in it. New York walks its walk and has its own particular strut and conceit. It's a city that has always felt and behaved the way it looks. Its architecture is an evocation of what it is to be in New York and to be modern. But that's changing. And it's changing by design.

This new architectural catwalk of 'high-design', 'high-concept' and 'high-priced' condo buildings doesn't only fail to fit the vernacular of New York, it looks like a clearance sale from Europe and the Middle East. The designs are the blueprints for the New New York, most of them foreign, international – like cheese and handbags – and they incite that residual cultural cringe: the cachet of being imported. What they all seem to have in common are their vast expanses of glass. Over in Europe, we're all a bit fed up with the answer to every urban architectural problem being a sheet of textured glass wrapped around steel. We've grown cynical about the metaphor of transparency, openness, harmony, and light. It's not like floating in the sky. It's like living in Pyrex. Like being the ingredients in some glutinous civic fruit cake. It's not that these new Manhattan buildings don't look very good. It's that they look lazily derivative, and they'll make New York look like every other grubbily transparent financial hub in the world.

'Real estate is being marketed like fashion,' an excitable young bedroom broker to the rich and famous told me in the back of his stretch limo. 'Architects are the new couturiers.' New New Yorkers – bankers, fund managers, moneyed elite – don't just want the right geographic address. They want the social comforts and personal confirmation that they're on Style Street. 'Your home should say something about you.' Loudly and in a foreign accent, presumably.

Take the Richard Meier buildings, the spare glass blocks in the West Village where 682-square-foot studios go for more than $1 million. Looking out over the Hudson, they squat like Papa Bear, Mama Bear and Baby Bear, waiting for some entitled Goldilocks to come home. They're striking because they're so unlikely. Like finding three zebras in your garden. But in a suburb of Berlin they would be as unexceptional and uninspiring as leather shorts and an oompah band. Inside, they're a precious design oxymoron, a mixture of minimalism and old seventies industrial functionalism. There are obtrusive pillars, and there's hardly anywhere to hang a picture, let alone your hat.

The basement swimming pool I saw looked so dystopianly depressing that I expected to see an inflatable fund manager floating face-down. You look at these buildings and all the other imported bendy glass and steel erections, with their tacky design features worn like second wives' engagement rings, and you wonder who the New New Yorkers think they are. Who's going to live here? Who are the new, insecure, design-anaemic rich?

'Lifestyle is the way a person distinguishes himself or herself. It is the artistry of living ... Nationality and class have been replaced by lifestyle.' Don't take my word for it. That's coming from Ian Schrager, the Buddha of disco, the Confucius of the dirty weekend. Consider that statement: heritage, achievement, geography and history are all passé. Over. What really matters is your thread count, your iPod menu and the table they give you. Schrager sent me the glossy self-published book of his gnomic thoughts in a box of Plexiglas wonder, complete with two DVDs. He sent it to my home in Chelsea. Chelsea, London. This tome of gravid aperçu was a brochure – though 'brochure' seems too mean a word – for a building at 40 Bond Street that is as yet unbuilt. Prices start at $3.35 million for a 1,269-square-foot one-bedroom.

'This is what I did with my nightclubs and hotels and I intend to do with people's homes.' Imagine that: coming home and finding a shrieking gay Cuban bouncer with a clipboard on the door; three peroxided trust fund brats with added silicone bits, all talking at once, locked in the bathroom; and a family from Idaho in town to see *The Producers* asleep in your bedroom.

On the façade of the new Schrager building there will be a fretwork squiggle made from aluminium. They're calling it a 'sculptural gate'. They're so pleased with the squiggle pattern, they've shaved it into the floors, stamped it on the walls, engraved it in the glass and put it on the cover of the brochure. They boast that it's an extrapolation from New York City street graffiti. So, after they clean up the street and move out the kids who do the graffiti, they offer you chic designer graffiti instead. No one seems to have noticed the irony of this, or indeed, seen the writing on the wall. New New York's design revolution is not meant for New Yorkers. It's built for New New Yorkers, and they have altogether more suburban, provincial insecurities and private desires.

The look book for hotelier André Balazs's 40 Mercer comes in the *de rigueur* box with an added hardback nursery story about Jacques and Jill, a pair of rat-like carry-on dogs who run away from their fashionable, svelte-but-dumb owners to set up home in a new apartment. If that weren't vomitous enough to make you throw up a Burberry check, the brochure comes with a bell. Now, who spends millions for an apartment on the strength of a fairy tale that goes ding-a-ling? The first thing that strikes you about all the promotional material for New New York is the corpulent waste, the embarrassing profligacy, the utter purple bollocks of it. This stream of smiley airhead literature for the property boom is everywhere, tumbling from the guts of papers and magazines, thudding into the mail, its tone orgasmically perky. The most ubiquitous word is 'unique'. Everything's 'unique', usually decorated and qualified with 'luxuriously', 'shamelessly', 'timelessly', or, my favourite, 'one-of-a-kind uniquely'.

The sales suite for 40 Mercer is in the Mercer hotel. The salesperson walks in with a humourless professional smile. She's not what I expect. Not one of those chain-saw-voiced, neurotically enthusiastic divorcees who have real estate instead of love. This one is the realtor from a Raymond Chandler novella. She gives me one long, slow-burn look, like a social actuary. In a beat, she seems to sum up my net worth, potential income, status, and I feel myself fall short. No – collapse short. Then she does what we in the Old World call 'French flirting'. Which is like regular, full-beam flirting, but done to show you what you're not going to get. Flirting with malice. She shows me her teeth, licks her lips, picks up the clipboard, flashes a wink of cleavage and we go to see the building.

It's hissing with rain. 40 Mercer is a skeletal box of girders and plasterboard. We chug up in a dripping service elevator to the penthouse (which could be mine for a mere $12.9 million) and step into a tangle of utility pipes, dangling cables and tortured rusting house guts. They're all angular, heavy and dirty. The flirt doll picks her way through and starts to paint imaginary pictures in the air like a geisha doing a dance. Her long, pale fingers point to brown metal, rubble and wet air, like a fairy godmother's wand. Construction workers wearing layered headgear of baseball caps, bandannas and hard hats watch her build castles on their time with a barely concealed carnal irritation. They mutter in proctological Spanish, fingering the triggers of their drills, plumping their baggy, damp crotches, and I can't help noticing that on the stair-well landings, wherever she stops, there is, just behind her head, a large graffitied penis, usually with a terse exclamation referring to Don, who apparently 'focks hos and takes it in the as'. Oddly, they don't put that in the brochure, but the place is infested with penises. Everywhere you look it's like a Neolithic fertility site.

The floor-to-ceiling windows are a popular design feature in most New New York buildings. In Europe, we're growing rather tired of living in hot and cold, steamed-up, hermetically sealed display cabinets. But in New York it's imported. 40 Mercer has big red and blue strips on its windows that I thought were protective shrink wrap.

'That's coming off, right?'

'They are a design feature of the artistic conception,' she says without moving her lips, like she's talking dirty to a tramp. 'On different floors, they're either red or blue.'

'But if I buy one of these apartments I can take them out, right? I don't have to have a red window in my living room.'

'Well, sir, for the conceptual integrity of the building, you're not allowed to remove them. You could, though, cover it up.'

'Hold on, I can spend a few million and then black out one of my own windows because some architect thinks primary stripes look cool from the street?'

'It is a unique feature of the building.'

Right. We leave. I watch her white shirt go transparent. A man passes and walks into a lamp post. I think he broke something. It's probably the best thing that has happened to her all day.

It's a strange and lonely calling, that of the lifestyle salesperson for New New York. They wander the empty corridors like the friendly undead. Or they sit in rented offices with the tarry coffee evaporating on the burner and a neatly laid-out collection of marble shards, exotic wood veneers, door handles, hinges, paint finishes, and 'artistic renderings' of unbuilt atriums and spa decks in the sky, their lives trickling away in the service of some second-hand Swiss concept of unique urban living. They are the curators of the museums to the timid future, a civilisation that hasn't moved in yet. One lady bravely staving off her personal future in a tiny office is as pleased to see me as a spaniel that's been locked in a cupboard. She eulogises the opulence and life-changing exuberance of a bathroom the size of an Amish wastebasket. 'Oh,' she sighs, 'you've got no idea what a steam shower can be until you've been pounded by five huge heads.' I smile a smile that I hope implies that indeed I do know but I won't tell.

All the undead realtors are desperate for you to know the oddest things. They all begin with the ceiling height. Now, I have never walked into a room and thought, Hmm, 11 feet high! A big man must live here! Then they tell you the provenance of the washing machines and the door fixtures. Again, I've never thought, Wow! These people really know their stuff! They understand the importance of a good hinge! And then there's the wood, more exotic than a fusion restaurant menu: bog-stained Irish elm, gnarled Honduran corset pine, smoked Austrian oak. Sounds lovely with a little horseradish cream throw pillow.

Salespeople haunt the empty apartment, spinning a life made of brushed steel and twelve shades of Indian marble. After a time, the repetition of this lifestyle blends all the apartments into one apartment. They all have minute, $100,000 kitchens that no one will ever toast more than a bagel in, which is just as well because there's nowhere to sit and eat anyway. There are hardly any dining rooms, or even living rooms. New New York style has a 'great room'. A place to plug in your laptop, prop up your flat screen, suck Starbucks and surf soapy Asian babes. The bedrooms are for solitary fear and chemical unconsciousness. They seem to contain just enough oxygen for a single night's sleep. These apartments don't have space for a family, or dogs with hair, or lives that involve more than passive absorbing of electronic stimuli and e-mails.

There's an overriding sense of impermanence. This is a fashion choice, and, like all fashion choices, it's transitory – it's pleasure and cachet swiftly usurped by the next fashion hit. No one will buy one of these gloomy spaces and say, 'I want to have kids here. I want to grow old and die here.' This is simply an investment opportunity with sleepover possibilities. It's a silent, screaming, locked-away loneliness. They're building apartments for people who don't have anyone to entertain and wouldn't know how if they did. Their box is not for lifestyle, but for storing an unexplored, unused life. In one glass-fronted living space, I met a vague, rich young man. Every surface, every facet of his existence, had been taken care of by the building's designer. 'Where are you going to hang your pictures?' I asked, and he pulled at a wall that slid open to reveal stacks of frames. 'This is my art collection. Neat, huh?'

Finally, there was 20 Pine Street, in the financial district. Not strictly a new build, but the conversion of a large old bank building. The developers enlisted Armani Casa to design the interiors. The sales suite is a vast stage set for Gordon Gekko to fight to the death with Daddy Warbucks, all done up in a reprise of Milan circa 1980. Imported, passé overstock passed off to the Americans, like selling beads and mirrors to Indians. I wasn't allowed to see the apartments in real time, but I was allowed to see the real-time brochures come to life in a glowing presentation on a number of large screens that described for me step-by-step – with wistful music and the comforting and dependable voice of an erectile dysfunction commercial – the sort of person I might become if I allowed myself the privilege and pleasure of owning one of these apartments.

The salesman chants the wonders of the lifestyle in store for me, ever more luxurious as you rise up the tower: the butlers, life managers and social trainers. There are clubs and caterers for every whim. So by the time I've reached the Elysium of the penthouse, I'll need to do nothing for myself. They will take care of every thread and surface. Mere money will turn me into a functioning social quadriplegic.

Whatever these New New York lifestyle brokers tell you about the sales and occupancy of these buildings, they're lying. They're not lying because they're wicked – they're lying because they want you to be happy. They want you to get aboard this vertical trailer park because they want you to have a cool, imported, classy, unique lifestyle. When lots and lots of people have one, the world will be a better place. All the salespeople believe the brochure. They know this is the map for born-again Gotham. In truth, there is a swamp of unsold apartments. I'm told that many of the ones that are spoken for are speculative investments. They'll stay empty for long weekends, through the summer and ski seasons. These blocks are constructed to be ghost towns echoing with the hum of unappreciated climate control. Their gyms will have Fox News silently terrifying the unexercised machines. Their entrance halls, with their slinky, ergonomic space, will doze as the elevators wink.

This building boom isn't a great expression of design and architectural excellence. It's a massive speculation to relieve bankers of their bonuses, and bankers' money is sterile. It buys peace and quiet and second-rate ideas. New York is a city that was built out of risk and danger, with much more poverty and failure than riches and success. Fund managers kill the thing they crave. They want to buy their way into excitement and that old promise of the New York vista, but they drive it out and make it extinct. The final, unpalatable zero-tolerance truth is that hedge fund managers, bankers, cynical architects and insecurity exploiting designers are far more damaging to the unstylised life of a city than all the junkies, prostitutes, panhandlers, urban cowboys, bag ladies, homeless and graffiti kids they replace.

2008 US Elections

I. Republican convention

So, hi there. Welcome to Pig's Eye, Minnesota. Funny old name. Funny old place. Minnesota. It's Indian for 'wrap up warm'. The Sioux used to say, 'we're going to Pig's Eye' and their mother would say, 'Minnesota'. And then, as so often happens, the religious right came along and spoilt everything. And changed Pig's Eye to St Paul and told everybody to go to bed at 7 p.m. and feel guilty.

St Paul is the state capital, although nobody knows that. Everyone thinks it's Minneapolis next door. They call them the Twin Cities and St Paul suffers from sibling envy. Minneapolis is bigger, louder and picks up loose women. Minneapolis used to be called All Saints, but to stick it back to the Catholics they renamed it Minneapolis, which is Indian for 'I'm not wearing any knickers'.

The Republicans chose St Paul for their convention because, like Colorado, Minnesota is a swing state. It doesn't swing very far and it doesn't swing very often and it doesn't swing in a way that is exciting. This is where the Swedes and Norwegians came to try to whittle Scandinavia out of the hem of Canada. Back home they grew to be the most liberal nations in the world. Here they grew silent and maudlin. There's a Minnesotan joke – only the one. It goes like this: there was an old Norwegian man who loved his wife so much he almost told her. That was so funny I almost laughed.

Minnesotans are hard, dour, diligent Calvinists with hand-made virtues, genetic stoicism and long underwear. They boast a state characteristic called 'Minnesotan nice' and they are. They have an unrelenting, unwavering, unvarying and unquestioning niceness.

The convention is a nice, lacklustre affair. It starts badly with an empty hall, cancelled on the first day in deference to Hurricane

Gustav. So we have to spend Monday finding out interesting things about Minnesota. The state mushroom is a morel. The state drink is milk. I'm not making this up. The state grain is wild rice. The state fish is the walleye. Its bird is the loon. Minnesota has the world's smallest carnivore, the least weasel, but no one's ever seen it. Each year the eleven prettiest farm girls are sculpted in butter and exhibited in a rotating fridge. I know – the excitement. St Paul doesn't quite boast – because boasting isn't very Minnesotan – the largest shopping mall in the world. A perky, peachy girl told me that if you spend just three minutes in every shop, it would take you three days to get round. If you spent three days in this mall, you'd need a straitjacket and intravenous opiate.

There was one thing that I quite liked. It was a T-shirt among the otherwise dull McCain memorabilia. On it was the face of Barack Obama superimposed on Mr Spock. The similarity's quite spooky, what with the prominent ears. Obama Vulcan is giving the *Star Trek* salute and saying 'Live long and prosper' which could be a quote from one of his speeches.

You see what they've done there? It underlines, exaggerates and emphasises his otherness. He's clever, but he's alien. Only half human. Half extraterrestrial. And the thing that stops Obama being just another skinny lawyer from Illinois is his blackness. The symbolism couldn't be any clearer if the face had been projected on to Al Jolson.

The elephant is the Republicans' totem animal and the pachyderm in this ice-hockey stadium is blackness. Nobody mentions it. It isn't in speeches or off-the-record background briefings, but it's just the constant humming theme, like a distant generator. The Republicans' bottom-line strategy, their last hope, is that, when all alone in a voting booth, enough Americans in enough states won't make a black man president. They're not racist. They've seen it on TV and in Hollywood. But in real life, the commander-in-chief has gotta be a white dude.

At this convention the Republicans have just thirty-six black delegates. That is perhaps the most shocking statistic of the whole election. That's less than 2 per cent of all delegates. Fewer than one per state and less than any other election for forty years.

Those are the interesting things that I found out on Monday and Tuesday. But on Wednesday everything changes. It all gets Technicolor with sprinkles on top and it comes back to the subject closest to Republican hearts: sex. Sex and the young. Hot, pro-creative sex.

Sarah Palin is making the keynote speech. She has flown in from Alaska with her family. The announcement that this obscure governor is going to be the vice-presidential nominee has propelled the convention into the biggest, kitschest reality show in the world. The relations and the speculation about paternity, mater-nity, fecundity, mendacity and the gestation period for Eskimos has led to a Gustav of schadenfreude that has overwhelmed the shallow blogs on the web. Sarah's womb is the black hole into which the best laid plans of the Republican party have disappeared.

Depending on how fundamentally hard right you are, Palin is either a godsend who speaks to the experience of ordinary small-town large-breasted American woman and sticks two fingers in the eyes of the coastal latte liberals. Or she's a hideously embarrassing mistake who will swamp the election in underclass redneck sexual incontinence and that everything is about damage limitation and trying not to think about what would happen if President McCain died and this was the First Family. Not so much from igloo to White House as igloo to White Trailer.

The convention does what it knows its heroes Teddy Roosevelt, Ronald Reagan and Arnold Schwarzenegger (in *Terminator*, not *Kindergarten Cop*) would have done: they charge. Mitt Romney and Mike Huckabee make vicious ankle-biting speeches. Rudy Giuliani gives the speech of his life, a sustained rant of spittle-flecked invective, innuendo and verbal cage fighting. Giuliani is Republican road rage. He is also a Republican road wreck: pro gay marriage and abortion, with a private life that would get bleeped off *Jerry Springer*. But he tees up Sarah's speech. (We all know her as Sarah, because this is so like morning agony television.) Entering with her family, she has a 'throw the snow-mobile keys into the fur hat' sled-dogging look to her. The naughty smirk of killer librarian. There's a whiff of baby oil and moose blood, a heady pheromone that rouses delegates to waggle their paunches at her.

She has been given a speech that is as well oiled and finely crafted as a synchronised beaver trap. It's very aggressive. It goes for the throat of liberals and Obama. It mocks and it ridicules. And some of it hits home. It's good for the room. They cheer to the echo. But outside, down the unforgiving prurient tube, I think she looks hard and calculating and a bit of a bitch. I can imagine people all over the country saying, I wouldn't want her for my mom. The first poll seems to indicate that she loses a vote for every one she wins.

At the centre of the week's fetid speculation on the blogosphere about Sarah is a baby. He's sweet and flaccid and beautifully behaved. And even if Sarah is not prepared to keep her family out of politics, at least Trig Palin is serenely keeping himself out. He's passed backwards and forwards through sisters and father and brothers and then on to Cindy McCain – a bizarre *Dynasty* character in mad woman's lime. People come up and pat him and coo at him and he just looks beatific and comforted. He is the eye of the storm. And it reminds me of a paraphrase of Hillary Clinton: it takes a whole Republican party to bring up a child.

Yet the most sustained excitement of the week isn't for Trig or Sarah or even McCain, or sticking it to Barack. It's for oil. For self-sufficiency. For cutting the umbilical pipeline with the eyeball-eating, terrorist-funding Middle East and the commie gangsters of Latin America and Russia. Let the world wallow in its own sump and turpitude. America needs to drill, drill for its dream. The marvellously priapic image of getting the bit between the loins had them chanting, then shouting, then roaring: 'Drill baby, drill baby, drill baby, drill.'

Thursday, the last day, belongs to McCain. This is when he accepts the nomination. Before he starts there are problems. The Republicans have used all their best speakers – Romney, Huckabee, Giuliani – to bolster the vice-presidential nominee. Today all we're offered are a couple of old mates you've never heard of and a millionaire Nascar owner who got evangelism along with money and delivers a buttock-clenching motivational speech as a bone for the religious right: 'Let God be your team's coach and play to his game plan.'

A couple of political cronies bang on about the military. The Republicans' lachrymose fondling of the services is weird. Any mention of boys in Iraq incites instant whoops and stomping cheers from the floor. It's the easiest, cheapest applause and it's at odds with the long American tradition of a citizens' militia, raised reluctantly, and of arms borne modestly.

Cindy McCain is sent to secure the podium for her man. She is another brilliantly weird woman, a second wife who started her affair with him just after he had separated from his first. She is the heiress of a beef fortune with cloudy origins. A short and selective film of her life reveals a woman who has modelled herself on Diana, Princess of Wales. There are photographs of her with black babies and Mother Teresa that look like Alison Jackson spoofs.

The hall never quite fills up. It has been a long and dreary week. Everybody's old. Dinner was at six. And it's getting close to bedtime. As McCain walks on to the stage to accept the ovation, he begins by thanking George Bush. There's a bit of a gasp. This is the first time the president has been mentioned. It's a reminder that all the things that Republicans claim they will change in Washington are a result of eight years of Republican government. The hard right is more comfortable being the opposition. It finds having to take responsibility for things full of awkward contradictions.

McCain stands in front of a great green screen that makes him look like the undead, which in so many ways he is. The years in captivity, the cancer and age have made a mess of him. He can't lift his arms above his shoulders. He walks like a man who's been bayoneted in the groin. He is a man who's been bayoneted in the groin. But most worrying is his head, which behaves like a rejected muppet. The expressions bear little relation to the words. His mouth can spring into a child's terrifying rictus grin at random intervals. One eye winks lasciviously as if it were out on the pull on its own and he has the voice of a cartoon character: reedy and softly sibilant, the tone of an anthropomorphic vole.

The speech is a calamity. He rambles and confuses sentence endings with beginnings, he punctuates tentatively and emphasises arbitrarily. There is no story, no thread, no interest. He loses contact with the audience who are distracted by a couple of angry war demonstrators. They chant 'USA, USA' into the gods like a losing football crowd. McCain blinks and grins and slaps. It's not good. When he actually gets to tell his own tough story of captivity, it's a ho-hum anticlimax. We've all heard it a dozen times already this week.

Finally, the desperate, bored crowd, who want to see the balloons, give him a standing ovation before he has finished, drowning out the last paragraphs. Even as he's thumbs-upping mates on the floor, the blogs are assassinating him: 'The worst acceptance speech since Jimmy Carter.'

Cindy's back on stage, elongated, polished and blonde, the apotheosis of Barbie. He is an abused puppet. And then they're joined by Palin, all too human. McCain seems to shrink between these two spectacular tabloid women. It has been Palin's convention, the pit bull Bovary. There is the brassy glow of nemesis about her, a delicious hint of salty revelations to come. Parts of the nation are addicted to soap opera drama and blue-collar tragedy and they will cling to her. She waves into the spotlight, naughty and manipulative and defiant.

Someone comments that Palin should drop McCain from the ticket. He stands there, stiff and twitching, with his skull grin, a good man, a decent, humane and committed man, fated by bad luck. It is his destiny to be in the wrong place at the wrong time, to fall from a great height into the hands of bad people. The balloons gently, mockingly carpet-bomb the stage.

II. Democrat convention

Denver is a great flat city on a plain. There is no discernible reason for building it here. It was constructed not so much from a spirit of pioneer grit, as are-we-there-yet whining. It was the sight of the Rockies to come that made the railway pause in Denver on the way from Chicago to California. There are still a worrying number of people dressed in dungarees and Casey Jones caps, looking like a get-together of the Waltons Appreciation Society. Colorado is home to the grey unisex ponytail, characterful, top-iaried moustache, un-ironic cowboy and Indian dressing up – and it's the state where tie never dyed.

There is no space pressure on Denver. It's spread like Marmite. Low aspects and expectations, as if it were trying to get away from itself. Cities are not the point of Colorado. The square-edged western state may not have real food or fashion or really much of a sense of humour – but they do have really real weather. They throw thunderous storms. Half of every local news bulletin is devoted to cloud. The weather is God's great big news. And the meteorologist is the only caster with a qualification.

The delegates arrive in town to a biblical plague of tornadoes. The TV screens are full of a little white house on the prairie lit by a beam of celestial light and behind it is a huge churning threatening black twister. Everybody knows it means something but they can't quite put their finger on it. For westerners, politics is really the great flat metaphor for the weather.

We're all here in Denver because Colorado is a marginal. As they put it, a coin-toss state. And the Democrats need it to be heads up, which it's only done three times since the war. This state encompasses many of the contradictory pressures and problems that toss the Democrats. It's both rural poor conservative and laid-back hippie liberal. It's environmentally anxious, keen for alternative power, but also desperate for blue-collar jobs and industry. It's driven by new ageism and held back by old-time nostalgia. They say it's the thinnest, or, rather, least fat, state and has the most cyclists. The girth quotient is increased considerably by the arrival of the Democrats. They wobble and sway in from across the continental United States and beyond, hyperventilating with enthusiasm, endorphins and the thin air of the Mile High City.

Great collections of party faithful are like any other sort of single-issue hobbyist: garden-shed weird. These are political Trekkies, Elvis Clinton fans, and the first thing you notice is that they wear their hearts on their sleeves, chests and buttocks. They are festooned in mission statements and feel-good puns: 'Obama is the new black'. Men clatter past swagged in buttons and badges like chain-mail curtains. The streets are beaming bright with a cacophony of competing T-shirts. There is no thought so banal that it can't be elevated by a breast, or so profound that it can't be made ridiculous by a beer gut. A chubby gaggle of Midwestern women roll past all wearing XXL that shouts, 'Yes we can' – Obama's message of hope. They look like a collection of ambulant fridge magnets. Yes, we can have fries with that.

The other people who are tipping the scales in Denver are the massive influx of police. This city is getting $50 million in federal aid for security and apparently it's all been spent on porky policemen. You remember the game Buckaroo, where you had to hang as many things as possible off a mule? Well, Homeland Security plays it with cops. They stand in sweating black huddles on street corners, bedecked with the accoutrements of containment and aggression, like malevolent Christmas trees. I watch one fat finest settle himself into a fast-food bucket seat and get trapped by his security belt.

The convention is being held in the Pepsi Center, home of the local basketball team, the Denver Nuggets, which only I seem to find a sniggeringly stupid name. It holds 20,000 liberal souls and the security is airport exhausting. It seems to both frustrate and galvanise the delegates as they're pushed and pulled by the gusset-faced bustin' bobbies. They can see that right here is the dividing line between left and right. It is the aspiration of Democrats to make a land that doesn't need a metal detector in every public door. What the Republicans want is better iris recognition technology and more arms-out pat-downs and cavity searches without a warrant. I particularly enjoy the security oxymorons who wear flak jackets with SECRET SERVICE printed on them in large white letters.

Outside in the beating heat a few special interest groups circle like abandoned pets. Extreme libertarians, or social democrats as we call them in Europe, complain sulkily about freedom of speech, when what they really mean is the failure of anyone to listen. There's a group of Iraqi veterans who patrol up and down the restaurant and shopping malls using their fingers as guns like nine-year-olds. 'This is street theatre,' one of them bellows, just in case. Trojan is giving away Magnum large condoms (do you think they were named after a large wooden animal inside which thousands of little men were hiding, ready to jump out and ruin your life?). They come with a pledge card that makes humping sound like a civic duty: 'Protecting and respecting ourselves and others.' There's a man who wants to tax meat on behalf of global warming and, after dark, the radical religious right emerge like the born-again undead with their hideous posters of mutilated foetuses and their banners condemning gays to the flames. The only time in the whole week I see anyone dead angry – but really angry – are the dozens of middle-aged black women confronted by these vicious divines.

The convention starts slowly. In the inattentive echoing hall Howard Dean (of the inappropriate yell) introduces the first speakers who are, for the most part, well-meaning, awestruck, grateful and instantly forgettable. Single-issue time-servers and survivors are given a grace moment in the spotlight. This convention falls into two halves: prime time and outside prime time. The national television exposure is the point. Why this thing happened. If it's outside the periphery of the glass eye, then it's irrelevant.

There are hundreds of makeshift little studios all over the room. They hang like precarious storks' nests from the tiers of seats. Hundreds of itinerant cameramen prowl the corridors and floor. Dozens of nervous men and small blonde women dab at their amber faces with damp sponges and compacts. You never know whether the chap with the intense eye contact and wires in his ear is secret service squirrel or Fox News. And they're either going to ask for an opinion or stick a finger up your bottom. There are hundreds of thousands of microphones. Every conventioneer has a camera. Everybody is recording everybody else. They're all commentators and viewers, participants and audience. The paper press sit hugger-mugger and irrelevant in an allocated gantry. They spend most of their time reading each other's political blogs on screen. Next to me, two porky, nerdy neocons from *The American Spectator* have fingers which fly over the keys with a deft familiarity that intimates an adolescence bereft of one-to-one nudity. I can't help noticing that one of them spends most of his time chatting on Second Life (a name that implies a lack of a primary one). His avatar is seven sizes thinner than he is. It must be said that we political journalists are not an attractive collection. We are trainspotters with malice.

The event has a strange, ghostly sense of unreality. You have to keep checking the banks of screens to see what is really happening outside this bubble. The floor fills up with the faithful who gather round banners proclaiming their state. The closer to the podium, and therefore the cameras, the more important are their votes, the tighter the races. Long gone is the time when conventioneers actually had a role in these proceedings. Despite all the trumpeting of democracy, their votes are irrelevant, their presence nothing more than light and movement. They are extras in an expensive telethon. And no longer do they wear celebratory boaters. Now they come in fancy dress. There are dozens of sequined Uncle Sams and home-made Ascot hats that look like elaborate birthday cakes with dioramas on them. I notice that Georgia has an excess of batty belles all looking like Miss Havisham Goes to the Notting Hill Carnival. But then I suspect Georgia is like that anyway. There are lost men wearing hideous white parkas that turn out to be Alaska's national dress. And the thousand women who all turned up in the same frock – the one worn by Michelle Obama on daytime television that she bought for $50. It looked great on the tall, fit, black woman. It's a cushion cover on a short, fat, white one. A bar mitzvah band plays eighties easy listening for the delegates and little intro music for the speakers. They get up and dance in the aisles. It is the law of crowds that only the physically spavined and rhythmically incoherent will bop with unconcerned gusto in public.

In the press gallery the good behaviour monitor who runs our lives asked me who I write for. And then, with a tone of stern disappointment, told me there's a dress code and I've fallen short. I was written a letter about it and please can I make an effort tomorrow. I dearly wanted to say, look down there. There are men dressed as Captain America. There are people in pink seersucker. But I didn't. I said sorry, and I'll come as Widow Twankey in the morning. She looked blank. 'Okay, sir, thank you for your attention.' I felt quite sprightly. I haven't been told how to dress for forty years. Next day she sidled past and said, *sotto voce*, 'You look very nice.'

This year, for the first time, women are in the majority of conventioneers: 24 per cent are black, 5 per cent Asian and Pacific Islanders, which is a good thing, even if the other 95 per cent have no idea where they come from (a clerk in my hotel looked at my driving licence and said: 'London, Switzerland, right?').

Everything kicks off with a tribute to Ted 'Zeppo' Kennedy. There is a sentimental video obituary broadcast on big screens. It's a nice touch. Let him see it before he actually croaks. And, as a big surprise, the man himself corporeally materialises on stage. The dancing delegates get frenzied with the soap opera poignancy of the moment. Ted is dying of brain cancer and they couldn't be happier. They hold up hundreds of placards saying 'Kennedy' and just for a moment it looks as if they are there to remind him who he is.

The climax of the night is Michelle Obama. She is introduced by her brother, a basketball coach of the Oregon State Beavers, which pathetically again only I find funny. But her speech is pretty brilliant – cogent, warm. She tells the story of her life and background, compellingly and clearly, with empathy and confidence. She brings on her daughters. Obama appears like magic, like the Wizard of Oz, via a video link. They are that rare thing, a happy complete black family with money. I think it's all rather lovely and, in the press gallery, I'm alone with this feeling.

It's difficult to decipher quite why Michelle is so loathed by right-wing hacks. She's black, a lawyer, a woman and taller than most chat-show anchors. I suppose that makes her the most scrotum-shrivelling apparition: a black chick with a dick and a writ.

Personal life stories of the Oprah type become the leitmotif of the conference. One after the other, every speaker gets up and begins by saying, with a cracking voice: 'I want to tell you a story about a woman who came to this country with nothing but a dream. During the day she folded anchovies. In the evening she ironed for lapdancers. She had nothing to live in but her dream. She brought up fifteen children. I am the youngest of those children and she put me through Harvard Law School by taking in taxidermy. There was always love in our home and road kill on the table.' Cumulatively, these stories sound like the York-shiremen's sketch from *Monty Python* as a twelve-step share. Each silky, coiffured and polished senator, congressman and governor outdoes the other with Stygian hardship. The effect is so cloyingly sentimental, it could give cynicism diabetes. But I am again the only one who finds the parade of Little Nell revelations hideously patronising. The implication being that if you don't wind up at least as an Ivy League lawyer, then your poverty wasn't bad enough and your dream isn't lavish and American enough. The only person who doesn't tell us about growing up in a bucket under the sink is Ted Kennedy, because we already know that he was born into patrician splendour paid for by illegal whisky-running during prohibition.

Three men suspected of trying to relive the Kennedy dream were arrested on the outskirts of Denver in a rented van, with a pair of rifles and a lot of methamphetamine. One was called Adolf, which does not help if you're in pursuit of the dream. This story looked exciting for a moment, until we were shown their mugshots on CNN, and then it was obvious that they were actually touring a stage version of *Home Alone*. The police say they can still tell the difference between a threat to Senator Obama's life and three stoned white supremacists with guns. Which is comforting.

The convention is so stage-managed, the script so finely

worded, the message so relentlessly repeated that instead of the loons in tinsel, which are by their nature uncontrollable, there are posters and banners that are handed out to the crowd, with appropriate words and phrases, to be waved at appropriate moments. They are T-shirt mottoes without the T-shirt and, when the delegates wave them, it's like one long Tourette's stammer. It removes any sense of spontaneity or, indeed, individual thought. It's all so mechanical, but we yearn for something to happen off-Autocue and for that we are relying on the Clintons.

In this soundbite circus they are Siegfried and Roy's great white tigers. Despite the years of domestication and careful training and men with guns, they're still wild animals and it could all go blissfully wrong. Hillary gets up and goes through the hoop of acclaiming Obama with a steely professionalism. She is admirable, if not loveable, and this speech is the best of her career, proving a salutary truth: that some politicians attain their true stature only in defeat.

Bill was something else. Something they don't teach at Harvard or behind the bike sheds. What Bill has, you have to be born with, and it's a gift beyond riches. He has political musk. He walks on the stage and it's like he's scent-marking. The ovation is thunderous and yearning. You can feel the dampness. The speech is fine: on paper it's no better than a B plus, but it's the way he tells them. The crowd doesn't hear what he's saying – they get something else, some aural pheromone. It's extraordinary to watch him work it, a syncopated, loose-limbed, baggy political Casanova, frotting them gently, killing them softly with his words. It's extraordinary and it's slightly pervy and grubby.

At the heart of this vast, expensive, micro-manipulated epic with its cast of thousands, there is an echoing minimalist pristine hole that is the place where the policies should be. Even for those of us used to the mood music of new Labour, this is utterly devoid of detail. A wish list for better tomorrows, universal healthcare, more jobs, cheaper, cleaner fuel, better schools, affordable housing, no war and a lot of new foreign friends is plangent, but it lacks any detail. Not just detail: there isn't even an outline. The plan is

... there is no plan. American politics has a built-in stasis of checks and balances. Changing anything is a long, slow, grinding affair. It's all in the nuts and the bolts. Detail is all. But what the Democrats are offering is that dream. Every speaker has the dream, passes on the dream, keeps the dream alive, invokes their children's names to feed the dream. They own part of the dream that is America. And it reminds me that this is the only country in the world where dreaming is supposed to be a good thing. When you wake to find it's all a dream, that's the end of the fairy tale. The end of the dream is where real life starts, where you go back to being a janitor and a waitress, where you clip coupons and pray you don't get cancer, and your kids get a charity scholarship. The absence of any new deal or cunning plan, or even the back of an envelope list, on how all this good stuff is going to be backed up, is worrying. Some might say reckless. Lots of America doesn't have a dream because it can't get to sleep because it's terrified about the mortgage. The next T-shirt after 'Yes we can' must simply ask, 'How?'

The convention goes through its first three acts like *Hamlet* without its prince. A drama without Obama. He makes spectral appearances on screens, always in shirtsleeves, offering brilliant homilies of Whitmanesque pathos and humanity. The rolling news channel pundits who spookily appear in threes, like the witches, offer fountains of advice, spells and premonitions. The expectation and speculation rise feverish and the Pepsi Center is just too small to contain the energy of the final act. The set must be huge, larger than any convention before – 84,000 people are invited to the Mile High football stadium. On the pitch they build a kitsch neo-classical façade that mimics the government buildings of Washington and, in particular, the Lincoln Memorial where, forty-five years ago to the day, Martin Luther King Jr delivered the most famous speech of the twentieth century. The auguries and destiny are begging for a transporting performance.

It doesn't begin well. At two o'clock in the afternoon there's a queue a mile or two hours long. Obama won't speak for another six. The show slowly unfolds with awful redneck music and Stevie

Wonder – who will now play any benefit or auction in the world – and there is a risibly Gilbert and Sullivanish line-up of generals, like a Miss World Domination contest. They wave coyly and want to work for world peace and with children and promise that Barack is their man. There are more personal stories of limbs and buddies left on the desert floor and then Al Gore races through his green speech like a fat man on thin ice.

And then, before we've had time to compose ourselves, Obama steps on to the stage, rangy, handsome and composed, a thin, dark knight come to reclaim Camelot. They cheer and cheer and cheer. The crowd grows into a single bellowing, adoring, rhythmic thing, echoingly fascist. But then why should the Nazis have all the good tunes?

Obama says thank you, over and over, aware of prime time ticking away. His speech is long and repetitive and disjointed, like someone remembering a shopping list and a poem at the same time. Perhaps it's an overdose of expectation, perhaps it's the pointed criticism of the Republicans, who say he's only a pretty wordsmith, a bearer of empty rhetoric. But the speech is under-whelming. It's fine. Better than fine: it's moving in parts. He lambasts John McCain, he promises the complete liberal goodie bag, he makes much of the dignity of work, and I can't help but notice the army of young volunteers who are exploited to run this whole performance and who probably pay for their own meals and travel.

There are occasional flashes of oratory and some transcendent insight: 'This election was never about me.' His fine churchy voice rises: 'It was always about you.' And the legions of the Obama'ed feel the truth of it. It is, indeed, all about them: 'Change doesn't come from Washington. You take change to Washington.' Inevitably, he remembers his family – but only the white half. Once, in passing, he mentions the man who gave him his talismanic blackness. Through the hush, out of the high stands, comes a long, eerie African ululation. The cry of Hamlet's father.

Madagascar

The high ground glisters and flashes like a pasha's ransom in the clear, shimmering heat; the sun catches the facets of crystal stones and splinters the light. This is all semi-precious rubble. A pixelated goblins' landscape of treasure, a gravel of uncountable finery. Quartz in all its geometric, prismatic brilliance splashes the day with the colours of a rhinestone trousseau; it's like the scorched end of an ancient rainbow. Outcrops of boulders have been worn by the wind to look like the spines of vast, extinct lizards, twisted and knotted into each other, an ossified orgy. Climbing them is difficult. We stumble and scrabble up the knuckle-slicing boulders with diamonds in the soles of our shoes.

This is an astonishing, comparison-defying place, the teasing imitation of unlimited wealth in a land of flawless eighteen-carat poverty. Tough, wiry men walk up these high ridges carrying axes and jemmies to mine amethysts and crystal eggs to sell for a pittance to hippie shops in the West as side-table whatnots and pendants of calm and luck. This place must have the best damn feng shui on the globe.

Beyond the spines of stone, the landscape stretches away into miles and miles of uncompromising plateau merging into shuffled peaks and ravines like the frown lines on an ancient face. It's inhospitable and magnificent. I squint across into this clear, sharp sunlight and the steadily steepling morning heat and my thoughts turn naturally to Haywards Heath.

The invisible mesh of connections that lace the world are rarely plain, never simple and invariably surprising. Of all the out-of-the-box, broad-brush ideas that launched the millennium, most lasted no longer than the fireworks, but one quietly ambitious wish turned out to be prophetic and has become symbolic of our belated reborn concerns for the fate of the world.

In 2000, Kew Gardens was given a heritage grant to collect and store 10 per cent of the world's seeds, rising to one-third at some time in the future, if the cash keeps coming. The problem is, they're actually going backwards, discovering more new species than they're collecting. It's shaming that so much of the world we're losing is meeting a nameless extinction – so they built a repository in Haywards Heath.

It looks not unlike a Bond villain's lair but with a gift shop – concrete and glass Nissen huts made to be act-of-man-and-God-resistant. Inside, in quiet laboratories, diligent scientists and voluntary pensioners sift through seeds and test them for fecundity before they're stored in a chilly, dry fertility clinic, prosaically in jam jars. So, do you go off to rainforests and pick up rare seeds and bring them back here, and pensioners give them a wash and a brush, then you put them in a larder, I ask? 'No,' says Paul Smith, head of the Millennium Seed Bank. 'We can't collect from the rainforests because the seeds are wet, and if they dry out, they die.' But you can keep them damp, I say, on blotting paper. 'No,' he replies with a measured politeness. 'Because then they germinate.' Ah, right, of course. Why are we going to Madagascar? 'I think I'll leave that to the seed collectors to explain,' he says, with a thin smile.

A man who knows Madagascar well told me that people who've never been to Africa before are blown away by it, and those who know Africa well are poleaxed by it. 'It's not remotely what you think. Forget everything your experience leads you to expect. It is utterly singular – one of one, and ever more will be so.'

Madagascar is the fourth biggest island in the world, larger than France, larger than California. It sits off the east coast of Africa the other side of the Mozambique Channel. It is also the world's oldest island, its humpy granite and marble backbone were ancient when the parvenu Himalayas were still speed bumps. Five hundred and fifty million years ago, it was at the centre of the supercontinent Gondwana – you can still see where the bump of Brazil once fitted into the Bight of Benin; where India connected with East Africa, and Australia attached to Antarctica to make one vast land mass before tectonic plates pulled the land apart, leaving Madagascar pristine and isolated in the Indian Ocean, free to develop in its own way. Unique is a word that is only memorable for its ubiquity and its grating qualification, but in the competitive geographical table of one-offs, Madagascar stands alone as a nature-made temple to the singular. It is the unique bumper Christmas assortment of uniqueness. Around 90 per cent of everything that lives here is endemic – it doesn't live anywhere else. Put into context, Britain has between thirty and forty indigenous trees (none of them endemic); Madagascar has at least 4,200. There are almost 12,000 plant species in Madagascar; it's not just peculiar species, it's whole genuses. There are eight endemic plant families, eighty different chameleons – half the species in the world – and most of the planet's orchids. It is the only place where you can see lemurs, the gentler local greengrocer pre-monkeys of the arboreal canopy who were made extinct everywhere else by the more aggressive out-of-town-hypermarket, shelf-stacker apes.

Madagascar is what's officially known as a biological hotspot, a self-contained reserve of unparalleled natural diversity, value and potential, and also a site of unrequited loss. There are, though, remarkably few indigenous animals. None of the super mammals from over the channel – no elephants, lions, giraffes, no big carnivores at all, no dogs, no rats, no ungulates or ruminants, no grazers or browsers, no antelopes or sheep or deer, nothing that's poisonous and, remarkably for Africa, very few things that have thorns. It was a place where the gentle greensward needed no deterrent, was born with the upper hand and grew in a bewildering clamorous profusion and diversity, unrivalled anywhere else in the world. This was five-star plant heaven, a bosky Elysium of exponential geotropic opportunity.

There are ten separate habitats here – from rainforest to arid, spiny forest by way of humid, semi-humid, damp, occasional showers and sunny intervals. For tens of millions of years, green was the only colour to be seen in Madagascar, until the winds and the currents and curiosity introduced a new, non-indigenous ubiquitous species. Man only arrived here a mere two thousand years ago and really only began to colonise 1,500 years back, so the world's oldest island is the most recently discovered by humans. Mind you, we've made up for lost time. Almost immediately we extinguished a number of lemurs. There used to be one the size of a gorilla, but most likely it was peaceful and foolishly trusting, and there was the mythical roc, the elephant bird, famous in fairy stories, the largest bird ever to peck the earth. Marco Polo claimed to have seen one called the *Aepyornis*, native to Madagascar but extinct for hundreds of years. It stood three metres tall and laid the largest eggs that tested the physics of a shell. They were thick enough to support their own glutinous content, but also thin enough to allow the chick to tap its way out.

Bizarrely, the men who came here didn't come from Africa. When Africans colonised everywhere else in the world, they missed out Madagascar. The first humans to set foot came the long way round from South East Asia and Indonesia, which is a bit like finding out that the Isle of Wight was populated by Greeks. Later, Bantu people from southern Africa did settle here, making a roughly homogenous, occasionally fractious mix of two continents. There are still straight-haired and curly-haired people.

The seed-hunting team spreads out across the hard ground. They look like ancient hunter-gatherers, keeping within shouting distance on the uneven rock. There are two teams: seed hunters and a mapping team who are compiling the first exhaustively definitive atlas of Madagascar's flora, minutely extrapolated from satellite images and painstakingly verified on the ground. It is a Domesday Book of the vanishing. This sort of eco-geography is the coolest, most compelling pool of green propaganda at the moment. Most ecological information is a great ball of statistics used diagrammatically like a pie crust over the globe. But this is real-time observed, down-to-earth and irrefutable.

Not much is growing up here. There's a small, pretty, yellow flower with a large knotty root that looks like an elephant's foot and so is called a pachypodium. There's a little herb that smells strongly of sweet turpentine and liquorice and is a distant relative of rosemary. They find an aloe – one of the hundreds of indigenous aloes. One aloe tends to look very much like another, unless you're an aloe detective, which luckily one of the collectors is. He's the author of the definitive guide to Madagascar's aloes, which I badly wanted to be called *Aloe, Aloe, Aloe*. Collecting seeds sounds easy: in fact, it's a Sisyphean pain. To begin with, they have to be ripe, and only an expert can tell – happily, we have one of them as well. And you have to be passing at just the right time, and then you have to collect three thousand of them.

Kew is well aware of its plant-napping history: intrepid, bearded men and hearty, deranged women plundering the virgin flora of the southern world, to fill the dank garden centres of Surrey. So this global seed project is only done in conjunction with indigenous botanical gardens, and they share the seeds: 1,500 each. The right to use them for commercial, medicinal purposes or as jewellery rests solely with the country of origin. This is important. There is no hint of pillage. This is about saving the planet, not exploiting it again; three thousand seeds isn't too bad if it's an orchid, which has hundreds of seeds in each pod, but it's a rupture if they're coconut. In fact, the largest seed in the world is the coco de mer, the nut that was brought back by sailors as a rude joke because it looks like beautiful genitalia and is now endangered.

Under a stunted tree by a river we come upon a gang of fierce men armed with spears. They've lit cooking fires and stabbed the entrails and tripes of a cow on their blades and are hanging them in the flames. They say they're a posse scouting for a larger group of vigilantes who are following; chasing bandits who have stolen the villagers' cattle. They will trail them through the high passes and across the plains, then fight and kill them. They grin and mime the demise of bandits. We wish them well and move on. Banditry is also endemic in Madagascar. Cattle-thieving is a way of life for some tribes, and cows are the only real wealth. They're eaten sparsely and kept for status. They arrived just after man and altered Madagascar's happy, green reverie.

That night we camp in a village. It's safer than being out in the open because bandits may be after cattle, but they're not averse to a little opportunistic robbery of a *vazaha*, the local term for a white man, who might be buying bulk crystals for health spas in Europe.

In general, Madagascar is pretty safe, the Malagasy are pretty friendly, except, as in so much of Africa, when it isn't and when they're not. The next day we drive across the central plateau of the island. This road is one of the country's main arteries. For 800 kilometres we travel what is not much more than a dried-up riverbed traversing mountains, curling and twisting back on itself, as if unsure of its own purpose or destination. In parts, drivers and herdsmen have gone off in search of smoother detours, cutting new roads, so the single track splits into three or four lanes, but will amble back together 100 yards or so further down the trail.

We travel in two Land Rovers full of people and kit. The drive takes fifteen hours and we never get above second gear. We pass only one truck and four lunatic Italians on motorbikes. There are villages of three-storey, brick-built houses with thatched roofs and rhythmically contoured steps of paddy with elaborate aqueducts and little canals. The people are dressed in bright nylon blankets, which seem to have come from car-boot sales. They used to wear woven shawls made from the wild silk of rainforest moths, but I expect Chinese nylon is cheaper. Some of the men sport mother-in-law wedding hats. Never having seen them on a mother-in-law, they think they're rather dashing.

Rice is the staple carbohydrate. The Malagasy have to eat it three times a day. At breakfast as a vile, sloppy porridge with shards of meat or fish, for lunch and dinner as a slightly firmer porridge with soggier lumps of meat or fish and chilli salsa that could remove nail varnish. Their capacity to stow rice is prodigious: they even drink the water it's boiled in. Of all the cuisines I've had to endure in Africa, Malagasy is effortlessly the worst. And this is one of the worst car journeys I've been on. It's not improved by the insistent and constant twanging of Malagasy pop music. The driver seems to need it to stay alert.

But we spine-jar and stutter across the roof of the island that is the most fascinating and huge landscape. It slowly curls past as a long, undulating steppe of grassland, with occasional clumps of imported gum and fir trees that have replaced the hillsides of indigenous forest. In the distance there is always a plume of smoke, the bright flickers of scrub fires.

For all the hours we drove, there was a constant warning plume, or leaning column, of mauve smoke – a malevolent marker of plunder and destruction. And then we passed through quarters that were seared charcoal-grey, the aloe scorched, trees blackened as if the flames had been in too much of a hurry to finish the job. The hot air of the car would be tinged with the sharp smell of fetid smoke. There is never anyone with the fires; there is hardly anyone up here at all. The little flames are like questing, grazing animals, the only inhabitants invading refugees; then suddenly we're in the middle of it, the fire dancing down the road, athletic and furious, searching the scrub for food, hissing and snapping, competitively leaping ahead, grabbing mouthfuls of green, belching and farting smoke and smut. A pack of flames: the leaves and branches twist and turn and shrivel.

This whole, huge landscape, the breadth of England, has been made by fire. There is no indigenous grassland in Madagascar; the soil is thin; it's the herdsmen who constantly immolate the earth, to eke out the grazing for the zebu, the hump-backed, pick-axe-horned cattle that are so intrinsic to Malagasy society that our local botanist couldn't believe they weren't indigenous. It is the zebus that have irrevocably eradicated so much of Madagascar's primordial landscape. But the Malagasy themselves seem to have a particular fascination with fires. They don't always light them for pasture; sometimes it's just to see them burn. There is a pyromaniac in all of them. As it gets dark, we come off the plateau and stop at a neon-lit truckers' café. Every lorry is manned by Chinese. Madagascar has huge resources of minerals and metal under its old skin. Until now the lack of infrastructure and the roads have made it uneconomic to mine. That was until China started eating the earth like a ravenous zebu. Now, ironically, it's the mining concessions that are protecting the forests, preventing the Malagasy from torching it.

We come to the western dry forest at Kirindy. To be frank, you need to be something of a specialist to get excited about arid forests in the dry season. It's a grey mess. A pale, dusty, dense confusion of tinder and, if you didn't know any better, you'd think it was dead. We walked through it and listened to the weebling cry of the male cuckoo roller as he called, plaintively, 'Shag me, shag me' to any available female. And then to a gap in the trees, where a clan of red-necked brown lemurs slip across the path.

The seed team find a hibiscus that they need. One of the tree climbers, an agile chap with knotted legs like strings of garlic in support tights, makes like a lemur and shins up the trunk and shakes it. Seeds fall like grey confetti, and we collect them in the twigs while the sweat bees cover us like Highland midges.

I found a beautiful orchid – white, with a delicate yellow centre. It's wild vanilla, but the seeds are unripe. Orchids are named after testicles. If you have a bollock removed, the operation is an orchidectomy. They're elegant, delicate, but somehow ballsy. That night we walk in the silent silver forest. It's an unnerving place. The paths are mottled with inky shadows, some of which turn out to be mouse lemurs. In the flashlight beam, their tiny pinprick eyes pierce the dark. Fifty feet ahead, a pair of larger eyes flash in the torchlight, and instead of running in the opposite direction, they begin to gingerly approach us. We stand, breathing in shallow, silent gasps. In the forest a night bird calls a shrieked alarm. The animal is about the size of a dog fox, but more lithe and sinuous, more like a big cat or a mongoose. It comes right up to us, right up to my feet, bold with curiosity. A beautiful otter-like face with the wide, deep, round eyes of a night hunter, a long body and an unfeasibly elegantly long tail that twitches warily. This is the fossa, the only carnivorous mammal in Madagascar. Indigenous and rare, a night hunter of lemurs and roosting birds. It sniffs with an epicurean delicacy, prowls around us and then saunters off through the forest, the trees' shadows striping its dark fur. It is an indelibly memorable meeting. Apart from having the most extravagant tail of all predators, the fossa is also said to have proportionately the longest penile bone of any mammal. Inside the pitch-black of my mosquito net, I drift to sleep listening to it hunt through the forest floor.

In a clearing there is a grave. A piece of ground the size of a double bed protected by a carved wooden fence. Although Madagascar is mostly Christian, Catholic and Protestant from French colonists and English missionaries, underneath, spiritually, the Malagasy are united by ancestor worship and the cult of ghosts. There are fearsome obligations to the dead. Many tribes exhume, wash or rewrap the dead at regular intervals. There are stories, perhaps apocryphal or legendary, of villagers having ritualistic sex with the dead, and of post-mortem cannibalism. The dead inform and direct the living. The ghostly world exists in parallel with the living one and then there are *fadys*, loosely translated as 'taboos', but both more or less than that. Some are as mild as superstitions; to transgress others can risk death or expulsion. There are *fadys* about the days of the week, colours and food; it's *fady* to hand an egg to someone. It's *fady* for children to mention parts of their father's body, or even to say his name out loud. It's *fady* to place your dung on top of anyone else's dung, so introducing the Malagasy to toilets was tricky. For some, twins are *fady* – one must be killed. The purpose and the value of the zebus is mostly that you take them with you in death. Funeral feasts can involve thousands of cattle and are a big source of collective protein. Zebu aren't just currency and social status, they're spiritual insurance.

Across two rivers, on terrifyingly insecure ferries, we get to the *tsingy*. In a country that runs superlatives ragged, the *tsingy* is a landscape so extreme, so unlikely, it can really only be described with heavy understatement. Soaring out of the jungle are a series of jagged, saw-toothed limestone pinnacles that look like a Gothic cathedral. The cliffs of sculptured stone form deep ravines and gullies, tunnels and caverns. They are virtually impassable except by death-wish climbers. But a couple of years ago a group of French mountaineers made a trail over and through the *tsingy*, bolting foot- and handholds into the rock, stretching hawsers and precipitous rope bridges over ravines.

If you're relatively fit and have comprehensive insurance, you can spend five hours in the intolerable heat traversing this astounding outward-bound adventure park. Being old and frail, fearful of heights, terrified of enclosed places, hysterically insecure and with no natural sense of balance, never having worked out whether I'm left- or right-footed, I loathed every moment, but I'd pay to do it again like a shot.

Scientifically, the *tsingy* is a rare view of comparative evolution. The gullies and ravines, with their spotlit shafts of sunshine that crawl along the walls, have grown to be pristine individual microhabitats. Within yards you can see two examples of flora that have not been in contact with each other for millennia. I traversed a pinnacle, swearing and pleading, and came upon a spindly tree that was blowing smoke from the end of each branch. Clouds of pollen were being puffed into the air. It was like a magic tree from a fairy story. There was no breeze, the air was still. I asked our man from Kew what it could have been. He said he didn't know. Actually, what he said is what all experts say, that he'd have to go and look it up, he wasn't absolutely sure, and had I been drinking enough water?

And then there are the baobabs. Baobabs are the most ... here we go again ... singularly bizarre and mesmerising trees in the world. There are eight varieties worldwide, six indigenous to Madagascar. One is shared with southern Africa and one is in Australia, a keepsake from Gondwana. When they burn the forests, baobabs are the only trees that remain, too big for the flames. The Malagasy call baobabs Queens of the Forest, and there is a *fady* protecting them. They stand lonely and magnificent in the blasted landscape. Nobody is sure how they're pollinated – perhaps it's by bats. There is a famous avenue of baobabs stretching along a dusty road beside a marshy lake full of lilies. It is the march of the baobabs. It's difficult to make something as prosaic as a clump of trees sound exciting, but this is nature's Angkor Wat. This is as impressive, tongue-tying and neck-prickling as any medieval cathedral. There is something melancholy about these great, red sentinels of the rooted world. They stand mute but expressive; they're hollow so nobody knows how old they are. If you need to believe that flora has a spiritual dimension, it's easy to imagine the baobabs have souls. The team from Kew says quietly that they don't find any baobab saplings, they have no children. Baobabs may already be the ghosts of the forest.

Hoarding seeds is one of the oldest instincts of civilisation. In times of fear, seeds are kept as practical talismans, a belief and trust in the future, a prayer that there will be a harvest. If you ask what the seed collection at Haywards Heath is for, they'll tell you airily and a little wistfully that it's insurance. If in the wild a plant fails, becomes critical or ceases to exist, here it is. Its life and fertility are held safe and we can revive them. Except the truth is, we probably can't. If a habitat vanishes with all its innumerable variables and enabling causes, then, with the best will in the world and all the seeds you can fit in your pocket, you can't put it back together. You can't manufacture a rainforest from scratch; the world isn't a herbaceous border. They can replenish and protect, but the seed bank is at best a vegetable catacomb. And it isn't insurance, it's a rebuke, an ark that reminds us of our sins. And although the scientists who run it with such ardour and care talk in the thick, dry Latin of empirical research, that is first and last an emotional endeavour. It is an animistic prayer of hope. A collection of seeds for the future; a hope that this bunker won't be the final harvest. And it isn't the collection that matters so much as the faith of the collectors. The hope against hope that we won't ultimately reap as we have sown.

In nine days in Madagascar, over two thousand second-gear miles in two Land Rovers, over two rivers, two teams comprising fifteen people collected just seven species of seeds.

Algeria

'Is this your first time in Algeria?' everyone I meet asks me. It's a polite inquiry, a courtesy veiling an admonishment, an accusation. 'Where were you? Why did you take so long?' And with a weedy smile I reply, in geographic mitigation, that this isn't my first time in the Maghreb. 'Morocco,' they'd sigh. Yes, Morocco. 'Ah, Morocco,' they'd repeat with a curl of the lip. 'Disneyland.' And, compared to Algiers, it is.

Nobody's been to Algeria for a decade unless they had a very pressing reason and some very secure connections. The last photographer I knew who tried to do a story here never got out of his hotel room. He went straight back to the airport, thoroughly scared. There were precious few news teams or foreign journalists – eleven years of civil war have been unforgivingly diligent and murderous and terrifying. Threats in Algeria are never empty. They come replete and fatty with promise, dripping with a brutal, dark efficiency.

'Zidane,' I say – Zinedine Zidane is the only contemporary Algerian anyone's heard of. 'Zidane,' they reply, 'everyone was following him, looked to him for pride, for a sign.' Pity about the last match, though, that final headbutt in the 2006 World Cup. 'What do you mean?' a man exploded at me, waving his hands. 'We loved that! That moment! All his life Zidane was acquiescent, silent, a brown Frenchman, and then finally, at the last, he did something properly, authentically Algerian.'

Algiers curls like a sun-bleached spine around a great natural harbour. It is a city of lairs, of shadows. Up front is the icing, the promenade: unmistakably, vauntingly French. Tall white apartment blocks with beautiful Algiers-blue shutters and awnings hanging above shaded arcades of shops and deep, dark bars. There are broad, curving boulevards edged with ficus trees that have been pollarded and topiaried into a suspended, undulating green sunshade. It has that faded and dusty decrepitude that so suits colonial architecture, that lends a nostalgia to the bourgeois snobbery and imposed racism. The French city looks out across the Mediterranean towards Marseilles, its mirror.

The French gave themselves the sea view. Behind them, creeping up the hill in a series of zigzag alleys, is the old Ottoman Kasbah and the bey's keep. It's a crumbling, collapsed, graffitied squalor of tunnels, blind corners and burrows – other, African, sinuous, secret and guarded. It was the home of resistance, of an old anger. Stamped above both cities are the rigour and clumsy thud of communist architecture, the direct beauty of function, the dwarfing blocks of social cleansing. Architectural cod liver oil. Our hotel is a monument to collective socialist hospitality, a holiday barrack containing the cafeteria to unknown heroes. Its decoration is caught in a moment of Algerian optimism, the exuberance of the 1970s, textured concrete, knobbly glass screens, plastic furniture and rubber plants. It's an interior that would have the style editor of *Wallpaper* sucking his thumb with excitement.

There is, though, one small ergonomic hiccup. There is no entrance. They've done away with the welcome. You get in circuitously, nervously, your car checked for guns and bombs by soldiers with Kalashnikovs. Algiers is shell-shocked with a weary fear. There are policemen and soldiers, astonishingly camp motorbike cops in head-to-toe leather on every street, every corner and junction. At night the roadblocks are constant, checks are relentless, a contact stutter, a practised repetition of security for the chronically insecure, the reassurance of a shared terror. All cars drive with their interior lights on so that the occupants can be seen. You slow down. A shadowy, nervous indentured boy from some Berber village peers into the wan yellow light, his knuckles white on the barrel. My driver tells me that he'd been to England for three months as a student. He returned to the city and forgot to switch on the vanity light. Soldiers stopped him at cocked gunpoint, hauled him out of the car. 'We could have shot you,' an officer said. 'Why are you driving in the dark?' The man apologised and said he'd been in London. 'Yes, right,' said the soldier, 'and they don't have checkpoints in London?'

It's hard to credit that there are global security wonks and think-tank nerds who hold up Algeria as a model of a workable, acceptable, doable Arab republic, a possible poster boy for Iraq, now that the horrors of its civil war have dulled the edge of Islamic fundamentalism. There may even be somewhere in this place to interest the Middle East peace process. Seen from twenty storeys up and 10,000 miles away, in the air-conditioned and neon-lit offices, on a pie chart on a screen, Algeria's mixture of socialist, military, secular state with a Muslim population – a Westernish Arab country that wears Nike and drinks beer and wants to sell stuff and buy things – looks like a good bet, a possible way forward. But down here on the street, without the benefit of the graph, the figures, the briefings and overviews, it seems astonishingly mad. The idea that Algeria could be anyone's role model raises only a humourless snigger.

Algeria is a butcher's shop of fury and fundamentalism, violence and vengeance and unresolved injustice. It was the home port of Barbarossa and his Barbary corsairs, who for more than three hundred years robbed ships in the Mediterranean, sacked ports, kidnapped more than a million Christian Europeans as slaves from as far away as Iceland. They made the southern coasts of Spain and Sicily virtually uninhabitable. The pirates were finally defeated by one of the first ever multinational task forces. The American marines' hymn that starts 'From the halls of Montezuma to the shores of Tripoli' refers to this action.

In the great Islamic expansion the original population of Berbers was overlaid by the Arabs, then the Ottomans, and then the area became home to displaced Moors and Jews. Finally, when it had become exhausted and bloatedly corrupt, the French arrived, in 1830, fired barely a shot, and the beys departed.

Despite its unrelentingly vicious history, the French took North Africa to their hearts. Algeria was a colony for more than 130 years. That's longer than any other country in Africa apart from

South Africa and Mozambique. The French didn't just use Algeria for what they could get out of it; they did something far more damaging, far darker. The French fell in love, like an old man besotted by a young girl in a hot climate. The French imagined that with the power of their culture, their charm, their romance and a specially formed army of criminals they named the Foreign Legion, they could woo Algeria to become an exotic member of the family. It wasn't simply a chattel, it was adopted and made part of France. Algerians voted in French elections, had deputies in Paris. More whites moved to Algeria than to any other African country. There were over a million French *pieds noirs*. They farmed a large percentage of the motherland's fresh produce. They took the Bedouins as mistresses and occasionally wives. When the time came for the divorce, it was cruel and desperate. Fanned by great self-righteous self-pity, Algeria broke France's heart and the French behaved like cuckolds. There was no sense of giving the nation back. This was the servants stealing the silver – a national humiliation, an act of betrayal.

Albert Camus, the existentialist who won the Nobel Prize for Literature and played in goal for Algeria in the World Cup, said famously that, forced to choose between his country and his mother, he chose his mother. The war of independence, which lasted from 1954 to 1962, cost a million Algerian lives; the French were finally driven out in an orgy of impotent and spiteful destruction. The war caused the collapse of the Fourth Republic, split the French army, instigated internal terrorism and confronted France with its own perfidy and torture. It also left it with one of the largest immigrant populations in Europe. African countries are marked by the moment and manner of their independence. Algeria's was particularly brutal and divisive. Apart from the casualties, 1.5 million Algerians emigrated; all were forced to leave. Mostly they were professionals, the educated: doctors and teachers and lawyers.

And then there was the terrible score settling with those who would work for or with the French. The traitors were executed in the streets. The French, of course, refused to protect or take in

Algerians who had trusted them, or who'd been forced or bribed to do their bidding. The final reckoning of the war was a cathartic internecine settling up, and it left Algeria with a terrible anger.

Sooner or later, every Algerian I meet tells me with a furious emphasis that they won the war, they beat the French – twice Algerian armies have defeated Europeans, once with Hannibal, once with the FLN (National Liberation Front). 'We beat them, but where is the victory?' a left-wing intellectual says to me (all intellectuals here are left-wing). 'It doesn't feel like victory. We never got our justice.' He sounds like a petulant, thwarted child.

Algeria won its independence in July 1962. It became a 1960s beacon for Africa, a socialist republic that was armed and proud, an inspiration to other resistance movements. For a silly moment, it was the cool country for left-wing European professors of politics, agitprop journalists and people with black polo necks.

Ahmed Ben Bella, the proto-Mandela of the Sahara, enthusiastically played to the international conference stage. At home he became autocratic and reclusive and disengaged. Algeria sank under the weight of its problems, the president's friend General Boumedienne forced a coup, and there followed the seesaw of military and socialist government until finally, in late 1991, the first round of elections was won by the extreme fundamentalist Islamist party, the Islamic Salvation Front (FIS).

With the encouragement of the Americans and the ever-present French, the army once again stepped in to prevent their taking power, forming instead another military government. There followed a civil war quite as brutal as the one fought with the French. Indeed, it drew its lessons from the independence struggle. Muslim jihadists slaughtered villagers. The army did the same. Both sides used roadblocks, torture and the dark to instil competing visions of terror. Journalists didn't come here, foreigners didn't come. Algiers was a fortress of fear.

'You could wake up and find that your immediate neighbourhood, your neighbours, would have had their throats cut in the night,' I am told by a man who closed his business on a whispered threat. Everyone lost someone – a cousin, a brother, a school friend. The countryside was a medieval curse of retribution, and in the middle of all this there was a Berber rebellion and someone had the bright idea of setting up the Saharan wing of al-Qaeda.

Recently, the violence seems to have stalled, sated itself. It's not peace, it's the absence of war – an exhausted and shocked truce. There are still murders, still roads that aren't safe after dark. The army are still everywhere, but it seems better. There have been new elections, but still there is the tight, hard kernel of anger.

I walk in a street with a man who suddenly grows incandescent at the sight of another man in a djellaba, wearing the white cap of a hajji. He's walking with a veiled woman. 'Look at that,' says my companion. 'That's not part of my culture. Algerians have never dressed like that. When I was a child we never saw men with those beards, women didn't have to wear those ridiculous blankets on their heads. It's all imported. Some people, they went to fight in the first Afghan war and came back with this extremism, this religion, and . . .' he searches for the word, 'this intolerance.'

Algeria is the eye of a perfect storm of intolerance, the tsunami of post-colonial trauma coupled with the most nihilistic of 1960s-isms, Third World socialism, as well as authoritarian, reactive military juntas and Wahhabi sharia, all competing in a swamp of mass unemployment. It has a resentfully youthful population – almost a third are under fifteen. They hang out on corners, huddle and plot, race past on secret missions, mooch in gangs in the kasbah looking like greyhounds waiting for the white rabbit of no good to spin past. The boys are malevolently handsome, often strikingly beautiful, and they are the only people on earth who can make shopping-mall sports kit look chic and elegant. The names of the European football clubs on their backs mock the cul-de-sacs of their lives. On every spot of dusty land they kick balls, do press-ups, hang out with pit bulls on chains, tug at their own balls, smoke, have mock fights and wait for something to turn up.

'They're waiting for the Australian boat,' someone tells me. It's a euphemism. In the 1960s there was a rumour that a big ship from

Australia was going to come to the port to take away thousands of men for work and a better life. Every morning men would go to await its arrival. They'd come with their bags and their papers, they'd discuss the rumour of its approach in inexhaustible detail. Officials said it was just over the horizon. The boat became the great, sorry parable for all the groundless hope and unfulfilled promise of Algiers.

The irony of all this, if Algeria really needs irony, is that it is potentially one of the richest countries. There are lakes of oil, mountains of minerals and enough natural gas to inflate a Europe that's desperate for an alternative to the blackmail of Gazprom. But it never seems to happen, or, if it does, to make a difference. Politics, security, intransigence and orthodoxy get in the way. 'Where does the money go?' an intellectual woman in a bookshop asks me. 'Where is the investment for jobs?' You look around and think, it's probably all in security or the military: the old story of a bulky military glutton that eats Third World riches. The nation that used to be France's greengrocer now barely exports olive oil. Mind you, it still has salt mines.

This city feels like a setting waiting for Graham Greene to drop by − beguiling and beautiful, bypassed by the march of international trade and politics. Cathedrals sit beside mosques and synagogues. The Jews, who lived here for three thousand years and were so much a part of Maghreb life, have now all gone. They sided with the French during the civil war. There are small parks where maudlin lovers sit with serious fervour, illicit and fearful, holding covert hands. Each bench holds a tragic operetta of thwarted desire and hapless yearning. You can still sense that this was once a bright and sybaritic city: sophisticated and brilliant, erotic and dangerous, rich and romantic. It was here that the music and mischief of Arabia, Africa and Europe met. But now it takes its entertainment in careful sips behind closed doors.

Yet just along the coast is a little satellite town called La Madrague. There's a marina with yachts, and houses with electric gates, and Mercedes. This is where the small middle class come back to after working abroad. They build with convertible currency. On the beach are busy fish restaurants under awnings, little white tables that could almost be Juan-les-Pins. There are bars with girls and Western pop videos on plasma screens. In one bar a sign commemorates a visit by Brigitte Bardot, and there are clubs with bouncers on the door: tough, sweaty men with lumpy faces and skittling eyes.

Inside, other tough and sweaty men in tight suits entertain girls who look like the prostitutes from Brassaï photographs – so sadly decked out in the gaudy uniform of their calling, eating expensive Western steaks, drinking imported wine. There is something both dangerous and pathetic about all this. It is the imitation of a tacky good time that's being had somewhere else. The Australian ship of nightclubs. I'm taken to a cabaret bar where a general entertains his prostitute. A group of oil workers back from six months' manual labour blow the lot on vodka. A group of shrieking gay men drink themselves into a camp slur. It's dark and atmospheric. Singers take turns to do sets with a radio mic and an electronic organ. They sing traditional, syrupy Arabic love songs. And then the oddest thing: the audience wave money and call them over, and pay to have songs sung about themselves. The chanteuses make up these praise ditties with quavering voices, about oil workers and the general and his dead-eyed companion. The audience become intoxicated with the sound of their own fame. They pay more and more to hear their names and their jobs, and the names and jobs of their friends, sung to the accompaniment of a Hammond organ. My host pays to have me praised. 'Here is our esteemed friend, visiting Algeria from England. We welcome you, Adrian.' So it goes on for hours; hundreds and hundreds of dollars are paid for these nursery rhymes. Everyone claps. The girls with needy thighs sit at the bar and wait and watch the mutual moments of affirmation. It is the most bizarre nightclub I've ever been in. It has a psychotic and depressive sense of cutting to the chase of every night out – you just want to feel good about yourself, be loved and respected by strangers, hear your name in the mouth of a man in a silver blazer and two-tone winkle-pickers.

Along the seafront in the evening, there is a funfair – galloping horses, fire engines and spinning teacups, the chunter of coins and air guns, balloons, candyfloss and great chains of families, the toddlers dressed in bright frocks and bows, eating ice cream, jigging to the tinkly music that always sounds spooky. Fathers shoulder their sons, gaggles of girls look for gangs of boys. The penniless stand at the sea wall, dangling hooks into the surf, and stare out at the oil tankers queuing up in the bay. It's warm, and it smells of sweat and sugar and sewage. This is the carousel at the northern edge of a dark continent. The sky bleeds puce and carmine, and I'm being shadowed by secret policemen. I can pick them out in the crowd. Behind me, a voice whispers: 'Look out to sea, sir, you can take pictures of the sea.' Across this bay, the great municipal pond of civilisations. 'But must not turn round. Please, sir, don't look back.'

Dubai

The only way to make sense of Dubai is to never forget that it isn't real. It's a fable, a fairy tale, like *The Arabian Nights*. More correctly, it's a cautionary tale. Dubai is the story of the three wishes, where, as every kid knows, with the third wish you demand three more wishes. And as every genie knows, more wishes lead to more greed, more misery, more bad credit, and much, much, much more bad taste. Dubai is Las Vegas without the showgirls, the gambling or Elvis. Dubai is a financial Disneyland without the fun. It's a holiday resort with the worst climate in the world. It boils. It's humid. And the constant wind is full of sand. The first thing you see when you arrive is the airport, with its echoing marble halls – it ought to be the welcome for some vast metropolis in a vanishing hinterland. It's big enough to be the hub of a continent. Dubai suffers from gigantism – a national inferiority complex that has to make everything bigger and biggest. This includes their financial crisis.

Outside, in the sodden heat, you pass hundreds and hundreds of regimented palm trees and you wonder who waters them and what with. The skyline, in the dusty haze, looks like the cover of a dystopian science fiction novella. Clusters of skyscrapers lurch out at the grey desert accompanied by their moribund cranes, propped up with scaffolding, swagged in plastic sheeting. Dubai thought it was going to grow up to be the Arab Singapore – a commercial, banking and insurance service port on the Gulf with hospitality and footballers' time shares, an oasis of R&R for the less well endowed. But it hasn't quite worked out. The vertical streets of offices are empty. A derelict skyscraper looks exactly the same as one that's teeming with commerce. They huddle around the current tallest building in the world – a stifled yawn of an accolade, a monument to small-nation penis envy. This pylon erected with the Viagra of credit is now a big, naked exclamation of Dubai's fiscal embarrassment. It was going to be called Burj Dubai, but as Dubai was unable to make their payments, they were forced to go to their Gulf neighbour, head towel in hand, to get a loan. So now it's called Burj Khalifa, after Abu Dhabi's ruler, who coughed up $10 billion to its overextended neighbour.

Dubai has been built very fast. The plan was money. The architect was money. The designer and the builder was money. And if you ever wondered what money would look like if it were left to its own devices, it's Dubai.

My driver gets lost more than once. He's lived here all his life. He says he always gets lost. The roads keep changing. It's a confusion of orange traffic cones and interlocking barriers; access roads peter out into long drops to rubble and dust. Nothing actually goes anywhere. The wide lanes loop around endlessly, and then there's no place to go. No plaza or square, no centre. Nowhere to hang out, nowhere to walk. Why would you walk? In this heat?

You pull over and throw your keys to a valet, and get indoors as quickly as possible, generally, in one of the dozen shopping centres that look like the airports of lesser nations or Egyptian tombs. They echo with the slow footfalls of the security guards. In the boutiques, the glossy assistants stare at mannequins with a mutual mime of cashmere-folding despair. Dubai has been mugged by its own greed. Its consumer economy is being maintained by a hundred families to whom depressions, booms, lottery wins, recessional reason mean little. Riches and wealth are relative terms. But not ones we're related to. The gold market here, where you buy intricate jewellery by weight, is as silent as an Amish bowling alley on Sunday. There is an indoor ski mountain, probably the biggest indoor ski mountain in a desert, where the Arab boys queue for suits and boots and skis. The smarter locals arrive in their own designer après-ski gear, with fur and moon boots. You walk through the doors and it's like *The Lion, the Witch and the Wardrobe* – the land of permanent winter. The fat kids push past carrying their snowboards towards the Tyrolean chocolate shop and Swiss fir trees. The fat boys slide down the hill with a practised arrogance. The girls slither, splay-legged, hijabs fluttering, in the manufactured snow. In the windows, more chubby kids, in American leisurewear, press their noses against the glass to stare as if there were a rip in the space-time continuum.

No one dreamed of this. Twenty years ago, none of this was here. No Narnia. No seven-star hotels. No tallest prick buildings. Just a home of pastoralist tented families herding goats, racing camels, shooting each other. And a handful of greasy, armed empire mechanics in khaki shorts, drilling for oil. In just one lifespan, Dubai has gone from sitting on a rug to swivelling on a fake Eames chair a hundred storeys up. And not a single local has had to lift a finger to make it happen. That's not quite fair – of course they've lifted a finger; to call the waiter, berate the busboy. The money seeped out of the ground and they spent it. Pretty much all of it. You look at this place and you realise not a single thing is indigenous, not one of this culture's goods and chattels originated here. Even the goats have gone. This was a civilisation that was bought wholesale. The Gulf is the proof of Carnegie's warning about wealth: 'There is no class so pitiably wretched as that which possesses money and nothing else.' Emiratis are born retired. They waft through this city in their white dishdashas and headscarves and their obsessively topiaried, humourless faces. They're out of place in their own country. They have imported and built a city, a fortress of extravagance that excludes themselves. They have become duplicitous, schizophrenic. They don't allow their own national dress in the clubs and bars that serve alcohol, the restaurants with the hungry girls sipping champagne. So they slip into Western clothes to go out.

The Gulf Arabs have become the minority in this country they wished out of the desert. They are now less than 20 per cent of the total population. The rest are white mercenary workers who come here for tax-free salaries to do managerial and entrepreneurial jobs, parasites and sycophants for cash. For them money is a driving principle and validation. They came to be young, single, greedy and insincere. None of them are very clever. So they live lives that revolve around drink and porn sex and pool parties and barbecues with a lot of hysterical laughing and theme nights, karaoke, and slobbery, regretful coupling. In fact, like all cases of embarrassing arrested development, these expats on the short-term make don't expect to put down roots here, have children here, or grow old here. Everyone's on a visa dependent on a job.

Then there is a third category of people: the drones. The workers. The Asians: Indians, Pakistanis, Sri Lankans and Filipinos. Those who actually build, make, run and maintain Dubai. Early in the morning, before the white mercenaries have negotiated their hangovers, long before the Emiratis have shouted at the maid, buses full of hard-hatted Asians pull into building sites. They have the tough, downtrodden look of communist posters from the thirties – they are both the slaves of capital and the heroes of labour. Asians man the hotels; they run the civil service and the utilities and commercial businesses; they are the clerks and the secretaries, the lawyers, the doctors, the accountants; there isn't a single facet of this state that would function if they didn't maintain it. No one with an Emirati passport could change a fuse. Yet, the workers, who make up 71 per cent of the population, have precious few rights here. They can't become citizens, though many are the third generation of their family to be born here. They can be deported at any time. They have no redress. Many of the Asian labourers are owed back pay they aren't likely to get. There are reams of anecdotal stories about the abuse of guest workers. I'm told about the Pakistani shop assistant who, picking up an Arab woman's shopping, accidentally passed wind, got arrested and was jailed.

The Arabs live in their own ghettos, large, dull containments of big houses that are half garage behind security walls, weighed down with satellite dishes. We drive by an empty lot, and my driver tells me that this was the site of the house of the son of a rich politician. Daddy had it bulldozed when his boy was caught having a Western-style rich brats' party. There is a growing, unspoken problem with the indigenous youth here. Fat, and spoiled beyond reason, they are titanically rude. They have taken to forming slovenly gangs that have been responsible for random attacks on foreign workers and women simply for the computer-game fun of it. This is a generation of kids who expect never to seriously work – but do expect secure jobs. An Indian manager who runs hotels in Dubai told me that everybody dreads the call from some royal Arab telling them to expect a nephew who will be coming to work. The boy will demand an office, a secretary, a car, wages, deference and an empty schedule. It's a sort of pro-tection shakedown that you pay to do business here.

The Maktoums are secretive and autocratic, as most Arab despots are. The sheikh is always prime minister. Abu Dhabi's ruler is always king. The royal family's public exposure is uni-versally adoring, supine, sycophantic and breathlessly bland. There are rumours, always rumours, about dark secrets. The royal family owes its power to an intricate web of family alliance, patronage and operatic charity. It is sincerely respected.

The Maktoums have taken to horse racing. They practically own the British and Irish bloodstock business. It's a clever and self-serving hobby. Horses are one of the very few upper-class American and European enthusiasms that are shared with Arabs. All racehorses have a little Arab in them. So the Maktoums can mix in the West without that stigma that the Saudis suffer from back home – the public decorum with a private, Western deca-dence. The simple business of betting is, of course, ignored with a disdainfully turned shoulder. Since Dubai's construction-based economy stumbled, the prince has obliviously opened a massive and spectacularly hideous hippodrome, the Meydan Racetrack. The biggest racetrack in the world, it cost $3 billion to build. It's home to the Dubai Cup, the most expensive horse race in the world, naturally. This place couldn't have the second-most expen-sive horse race in the world. The winner pockets $10 million.

The track sits in a wasteland surrounded by the exhausted squirm of motorways. I walk around it and look not at the gal-loping horses and their bright jockeys but back up at the stands. Here in one long panorama is the Dantean vision of modern Dubai – the Arabs huddled in a glass dome, looking like creatures from a *Star Trek* episode in their sepulchral winding-sheet dish-dashas. Next to them are the stands for Westerners, mostly British, loud and drunk, dressed in their tarty party gear. The girls, raucous and provocative, have fat thighs that wobble in tiny frocks. Cantilevered bosoms lurch. The boys, spiky and gelled, glassy-eyed and leery-mouthed. In the last enclosure, the Asians, packed in with families and picnics, excited to be out of the Portakabin dormitories and the boredom and the homesickness of internet cafés. In front of them all are the ranks of wired-up security guards, making sure the layers of this mutually dismissive society don't pollute each other. After the horses have run, Elton John will perform.

Dubai is the parable of what money makes when it has no purpose but its own multiplication and grandeur. When the culture that holds it is too frail to contain it. Dubai is a place that doesn't just know the price of everything and the value of nothing but makes everything worthless. The answer to everything in Dubai is money. In the darkness of the hot night, the motorways roar with Ferraris and Porsches and Lamborghinis; the fat boys are befuddled and stupefied by sports cars they race around on nowhere roads, going nowhere. Taxi drivers of their ambitionless, all-consuming entitlement. Short-changed by being given everything. Cursed with money.

Albania

In the unlikely event of your ever needing to know, Tirana's international airport is called Mother Teresa. It is grimly typical that the Albanians named their runway to the world after a woman who devoted herself to helping people die, and after a Catholic from a country that's 70 per cent Muslim. Mother Teresa is the only internationally famous Albanian; all the rest are infamous.

As you walk across the tarmac, you might notice a couple of planes from Albatross Airways – there is, again, an Albanian inevitability in naming your planes after the only bird that is an international synonym for bad luck, and which doesn't fly anywhere near the Adriatic anyway. Any sentence with Albania in it is likely to get a laugh. Albania is funny. It's a punchline, a Gilbert and Sullivan country, a Ruritania of brigands and vendettas and pantomime royalty.

It's a tragic place. But just at the point in the story where you should be sobbing, you can barely restrain the sniggers. After all, Albania's favourite comedian is Norman Wisdom, and that's the place all over. It's funny because it's not funny. The capital, Tirana, is a rare place, blessed with both fascist and communist architecture. The competing totalitarian buildings strut cheek by cheek down the potholed roads, like an authoritarian tango in marble and concrete.

The Italians, who had the most sympathetic fascist architecture, built the futuristically classical university art school and government buildings, while the communists made the thudding celebrations of workers' triumph and the grim warrens of piss-stained grey boxes for housing the triumphant workers in.

Parts of Tirana look like small southern Italian industrial towns, tree-dappled, lots of cafés, while other bits look like Gaza, ripped up and smashed stretches of urban exhaustion and collapse.

But none of that is what you notice first. The thing that catches your eye and holds it in a sticky grasp, like a child with a humbug, is the colour. The grim apartments and public housing projects have been painted with broad swathes of livid decoration. They look like a giant installation of West Indian scatter cushions.

The multicoloured building was the very, very bright idea of Tirana's mayor, a man who the locals seem to think is suicidal and inspired in equal measure. When Albania's peculiar version of hermetic communism finally collapsed, in 1992, the new man said that, though there was no money to change anything, seeing as they'd been living in monotone grindstone misery for fifty years, they might brighten the place up with a lick of paint. Apparently, they got a job lot of all the colours Homebase couldn't sell in Cheshire and sploshed away. The result is both inspired and ridiculous, and very Albanian. Like a clown's make-up, it draws attention to the crumbling gritty face underneath.

In the span of one long lifetime, Albania has been dealt a full house of political, social and economic experiments. It started the twentieth century as a subservient state of the Ottoman Empire, then it became a playground for every Balkan and Adriatic neighbour. At one time or another, Albania had seven competing armies trying to grab lumps of it. Briefly it was an imposed German monarchy, then an ineffective Austrian protectorate. In 1913 the Treaty of London drew its borders to suit the conflicting demands of Serbia, Greece, Italy, Austria and Russia, which left over half of all Albanians living outside their own country, principally in Kosovo.

At the Treaty of Versailles, the Albanian throne was absurdly offered to C. B. Fry, an English cricketer who was supposed to be such a paragon of masculinity that he was photographed naked and flexing at Oxford, and ended up running a naval prep school of exemplary cruelty with a dykey, sadistic wife. And then they got King Zog.

You really couldn't make up Albania's history. Zog was Europe's last self-made monarch, and a man who made Charlie Chaplin look serious. He favoured light operetta, white hussar's uniforms and waxed moustaches, and cut a mean tango; he encouraged the Italians to come and build things like roads and cafés. The bad news was, the Italians were Mussolini, so Zog had to make a dash for it and ruled in the Palm Court at the Ritz.

Then the Italians lost the war and the partisans took over, which might have been a good thing except they turned out to be run by Enver Hoxha, the weirdest of all Cold War communist dictators, a man of stern cruelty and fathomless paranoia, who decided that the only two allies he could trust should be at the opposite ends of the world. Albania's only mates were China and Cuba, and it became proudly the only Maoist state in Europe.

Finally, long after everyone else had got a credit card and a mobile phone, Hoxha got cancer and died, and his unique chronic communism died with him. So Albania was welcomed out of the cold into the warm embrace of the free market. That should have been the good news, but of course it wasn't.

There's a park in the centre of Tirana that was built by the workers for themselves. They dug a great lake, built an amphitheatre, made a little zoo with a mad bear. You get in by walking through a homeless incontinent's toilet, past the busts of madly furrowed Albanian heroes and the small, neat British war cemetery.

In shady meadows, men cut grass for hay and young men sit on tree stumps staring at nothing. Around the lake, men fish without anticipation; behind them, other men squat and watch. Fishermen-stalking is a feature of former communist countries. As a displacement activity it's about as complete a waste of a day as you can come up with. Old men sit in the sun and play dominoes. Their peanut-butter-tanned bodies are wrinkled and polished like old brogues. They sit on cardboard boxes in those distressingly skimpy second scrotums that the communist world still clings to as attractive swimwear; they grin through bomb-damaged teeth.

These are the flotsam and detritus of the train wreck of a command economy, their jobs and pensions just another cracking

Albanian joke. A man who was once a history professor looks out across the water at the speculative illegal palaces being built in the people's park and tells me how the good news of capitalism came to Albania.

'We didn't know anything about markets or money. Suddenly it was all new, all opportunity, all confusion. And then there comes pyramid scheme. You've heard of this "pyramid"? We put money in. They give you back many times more. You put that money back and much more comes. It was brilliant, this capitalism. Magic. Everyone did it. Maybe 70 to 80 per cent of the country. People gave up their work to live on marvellous pyramid money. This was best two years of Albania's life. Drink and food and laughing, everyone is happy. Everyone has cash and hope.' He stops and looks at the fishermen. 'But it's fraud. Everyone loses everything, not just their savings but their homes and farms, and they borrow and there's no state to help. We have less than nothing. I lose my savings and my job. I don't understand.

'You laugh. We were fools, yes, but what do we know of capitalism? It was a fairy story. And when it's gone, people kill themselves, go mad, fight, scream and cry and want revenge. You understand Albanians have very, very ...' (he searches for the words) ' ... strong emotions.'

Albania was a nation of dupes waiting to be taken and they didn't take it well. Everything you understand or think you know about Albania and Albanians needs to be seen in relation to how they got the way they are. After the pyramid scam, Albania sold the only thing it had left: its people. They handed out passports and waited. There are four million Albanian citizens in the world – fewer than there are Scots. Three million of them live at home, the fourth quarter work abroad, and what they do is mostly illegal. Albania is the hub of the European sex trade, smuggling and pimping girls from Moldova and the Ukraine into the West.

It's said they also run most of the illegal arms trade, the cheapest Kalashnikovs you can buy. They're the Asda of mayhem. After years of being bullied, invaded, ripped off and lied to, the Albanians have grown very good at being frightening. They're not subtle, they don't deal in proportionate responses, controlled aggression or veiled threats. Albanians, I'm told, have taken over the crime in Milan – exporting organised crime to Italy beats selling fridges to Eskimos or sand to Arabs.

In the centre of Tirana there's an area known as the Block. Under Hoxha this was the closed, salubrious preserve of Party members, patrolled by soldiers, forbidden to all ordinary Albanians. Now it's grown into the all-night trendy reserve of the young: cafés, bars and clubs have sprouted back to back along the crowded streets.

In parts it looks like sunny holiday Europe, but then you turn a corner into grim, hunkered, crumbling commie squalor, with kids kicking balls and toothless ancients sitting like lonely loonies on benches, staring at the angry graffiti.

The number and proportion of young people in Tirana is a shock, compared with northern Europe. This is a young person's country; they have large families here who all continue to live at home, so they need to get out.

The cafés on the Block are thick with teenagers, collectively called 'students', though this is a title rather than a vocation – there's precious little work for them to study for. The streets are a slow crawl of large cars: BMWs, Porsche Cayennes, blacked-out Range Rovers, Humvees and the ubiquitous tribe of Benzes – all stolen, of course, from Germany and Italy.

The young lounge and practise their impenetrably tough looks; the boys play-fight. The difference between these kids and their neighbours in Italy and Greece is how they look. With effortless élan, Albanian students are without peer the worst-dressed kids in the Western world. They are obsessed with labels and designers, but all they can afford are the chronically laughable rip-offs and fakes in the markets. Shops here are full of absurdly repellent, tatty clobber with oversized logos stencilled on, and the kids wear this stuff with a flashy insouciance, all looking like characters in search of a comic sketch show.

Albanians are naturally quite modest people. You still see old women in peasant headdresses and men wearing traditional white fezzes, but the youth are desperate to be Europeans, and that means sexy. There are girls with bad peroxide jobs, and minute skirts, and tits-out-for-the-boys tops. They play at being gangster bitches, but it all looks much more like a drama school production of *Guys and Dolls*.

The men have a strange – and, it must be said, deeply unattractive – habit of rolling up their T-shirts so that they look like bikini tops. The Albanians are short and ferret-faced, with the unisex stumpy, slightly bowed legs of Shetland ponies. My favourite fashion moment was a middle-aged man with a Village People moustache and a Hobbit's swagger in a T-shirt that declared in huge letters: BIG BALLS.

Albanian is one of those languages that has no known relative, just an extra half a dozen letters. They say it's impossible to learn after the age of two. They say it with very thick accents. The fact that nobody else can speak it makes it a ready-made code for criminals, but in a typically unintentional way it's also pathetically, phonetically funny. The word for 'for sale', for instance, is *shitel*; carp, the national fish, is *krap*.

I went to a tiny basement bar that specialised in death metal music. This, finally, is a look that even Albanians can get right. I found a seat next to the drummer's mother, a beamingly proud peasant woman watching her son epileptically thrash our eardrums with his group Clockwork Psycho Sodomy Gore.

Groovy Tirana troops into a nightclub with a self-conscious bravado and sips cocktails politely, while the naffest barman in the free world goes through his Tom Cruise bottle-juggling routine, shaking passé drinks and presenting the bill stuffed into the top of his stonewashed hipsters to groups of giggling top-heavy girls.

All this imitation, this desperate wannabe youth culture, is being paid for by cash sent home from abroad. Albania's economy runs courtesy of Western Union and wads of red-light cash stuffed under the seats of hot-wired Audis. Much of it is criminal, but there is also a lot that is the bitter fruit of lonely, uncertain, menial jobs in rich Europe done by invisibly despised immigrants on the black economy. However it's gleaned, this is the hardest earned money in Europe.

I was constantly told to be careful of pickpockets and muggers in rough areas. Over the years, I've developed a bat-eared coward's sixth sense for the merest whisper of trouble, but Tirana felt like a very safe place playing tough. There is very little drunkenness on the street, though they drink copiously. The only drugs seem to be a bit of home-grown grass and, given that this is the vice-export capital of the West, there were no lapdancing clubs or pornography shops. You can't even find a prostitute on the street in Tirana. It's like trying to find lobsters in Scotland: they've all gone for export.

Albania has by far and away the worst traffic record of any Western country, and no Albanian would conceivably wear a seat belt, considering it the first symptom of passive homosexuality. Driving north out of Tirana along the pitted roads, you see an insatiable orgy of construction with barely a nod to need, purpose or planning permission. The outskirts are being covered in country bars and restaurants without customers, and capacious country houses without sewerage, water, electricity or inhabitants. The biggest single industry in Albania is money-laundering, and construction is the easiest and quickest way to turn vice into virtue. There are thousands of buildings without roofs or windows flying an ironic Albanian flag, which, appropriately, is the double-headed eagle looking both ways at once.

The mountains are a landscape of terraces and forests sparsely populated by peasants who still cut hay with scythes, where men turn rotated strips with wooden ploughs behind bony mares as their wives sow seeds from baskets, looking like the posters for a Bertolt Brecht revival.

Tiny villages lurk in high valleys; extended families live on the first floor of stone and mud plaster houses. On the ground floor live the cattle and plough horses. Vines climb the walls; chickens and infants scratch in the dirt; dogs are chained in wicker kennels; hens nest under the sweet hayricks; women bake bread in wood ovens. We're given a lunch of grilled lamb, fizzing sheep's cheese, tomatoes and cherries fresh from the tree. The fields all around are choked with wild flowers; songbirds and turtle doves clamour for attention; tortoises shuffle in the stubble; donkeys moan operatically to each other.

It is as close as any of us will get to seeing what life across Europe was like in the sixteenth century, but living a sixteenth-century life in the twenty-first century is not a smart option. Even sixteenth-century people know that. So the country is emptying, and the peasants trudge to the city to try and lay their hands on a little second-hand vice money.

All across Albania there are decrepit concrete bunkers, thick beehive constructions that smell of mould and foxes. They run in little redoubts up hills, along coverts and through gardens. There are millions of them. Hoxha started building bunkers at the end of the war, and they became a lifelong paranoid obsession that cost a hubristic amount of Albania's wealth. The bunkers follow no coherent battle plan. There would never have been enough soldiers to man them; they are simply the solid pustules of mistrust and fear. Albania has always been surrounded by enemies, but it has also been divided against itself.

There is no trust in this landscape: it is the place of vendetta and vengeance. There are still families here where the fearful men never leave their windowless homes, where male babies are born to die. The rules of being 'in blood' were laid down in the fifteenth century in the Canon of Lekë, an ancient murderer's handbook. That is one of the reasons Albanians are so good at organised crime. The distinctions of religion are nothing compared with the ancient honour of families; everything is secondary to family honour and to making money. Everything is excusable to sustain those.

There is also a divide between north and south Albania. The north is called Gheg, the south Tosk. Gheg is tough, uncouth, aggressive; the south, educated, civilised, Italianate. It's a bit like England.

On the Adriatic coast is Durres, which was once a seaside capital; the beach is a muddy grey, a coarse sand of cigarette ends, bottle tops and those blue plastic bags that are the world's tumbleweed. The smelly, tideless Adriatic limply washes nameless slurry on to the shore, and children build sand villas while their parents roast. Albanians have surprisingly fair skins and they cook to a lovely livid puce. A man calls me over. He's angry. 'American?' No, English. 'Tell them, tell Europe, we don't have tails. You see, we are not apes. We're not another species. Durres is going to be the new Croatia.' There's a thought.

'Norman Wisdom – what do you think of him?' I asked. 'He's very nineties. Now top best comic is definitely Mr Bean.'

Sitting in Tirana's main square, where the moneychangers stand in the shade with their wads, and men sell dodgy mobile phones and repair petrol lighters, I watch the Albanians come and go, and there's something odd. It takes me an hour to work out what it is – hardly anyone wears a watch. Well, why should they? They haven't got anywhere to be.

Stockholm

The ball bearing was patented by an eighteenth-century Welsh wheelwright, but a ball bearing on its own is a mere marble. It took a Swede to see the democratic power of the group and invent the multi-row, self-aligning radial ball bearing. Have no doubt that it's self-aligning radial ball bearings that make the world go round. And Sweden is the largest manufacturer of steel balls on the whole revolving globe. They are a neat and stylish metaphor for modern Swedish society. A collection of contemporary, clean individuals free to move anywhere they wish, who choose to roll all together, making their society smooth and fair and efficient and rather ergonomically beautiful. Volvo was a spare name the ball-bearing manufacturers weren't using. And it was a Swede working for the car company who invented the three-point safety belt, another memorably Swedish invention, managing to be, like its homeland, both unarguably sensible while at the same time irrationally annoying. And one Nils Gustav Dalén, while working on a patented valve that switched the gas off between flashes of fjord warning buoys and lighthouses (halving their expense at a stroke), created what is perhaps the most emblematic of all Swedish appliances: the Aga. Not so much an oven as a declaration of liberal, smug, Scandinavian intent. Nothing said quite so much about the northland as an Aga. In a moment of uncharacteristic self-congratulation, the Swedes awarded Nils the Nobel Prize, ostensibly for his valve, not actually for baking.

Just by chance, as I stand in the steaming, garrulous, striptease lobby of Stockholm's Grand Hôtel, I'm surrounded by Nobel winners. Serendipitously, this is the week of the big dinner-dance and royal diploma handout. If you fell over clutching your chest right here, yelling 'Is there a doctor in the house?', you'd be surrounded instantly by a herd of unmitigated genius, the most overqualified quacks in the world, and I bet not one of them could peel the paper off a plaster without sticking it to his nose. This is a grand place to sit and ponder the greatest of all God's self-aligning jokes. The cleverer people are at the pinnacle of human achievement, the stupider they are at its base. At breakfast I watched the madly brilliant and the brilliantly mad, empty plates in hand, regard the dead fish, flayed pig and various curds of a Baltic breakfast with wild, confused surmise. In the hallways, long-suffering wives tie up scarves and shoelaces and find unhanded gloves for the confused smarty-pants who have more letters after their names than in them.

The lobby has a special Nobel desk, manned by ever-helpful young blondes. I imagine it's there to arrange courtesy cars and woolly hats, but I also like to imagine they help worried laureates with intractable computations and missing theorems. And perhaps offer a dating service ('Brilliant Italian chemist would like to meet inspired biologist with great tits for fun and research; photo and pheromone sample essential').

There is something distinctly bizarre about being here, some-thing surreal, a whiff of *Monty Python* about the Swedes in Sweden. Their very calm, rational common sense invites the lobster of surrealism. And just as I'm pondering the Swiftian lobby, out of the lift steps the great *fruit de mer* himself. Bruce Springsteen, rock music's Mr Bean. He's playing the Globen, Stockholm's megastadium – which, predictably, is the world's largest hemispherical building.

And dancing in the dark is what we're all doing up here. Outside there is barely enough daylight for an owl's nap. And it's cold. Dark, cold, mad, and smells faintly of pickled herring. So why am I here? Why come to Stockholm in the winter if you're not that clever? There is a radiant truth about our world. All hot places are sunny in the same way, but all dark places are singularly crepuscular. Look at the covers of all the supplements and bro-chures and catalogues of foreign promise. They are samely inter-changeable: the view from the resort at the relaxing edges of the world's midriff is sweatily predictable. For as long as we've all had passports and the capitalist's choice of beef or chicken, travelling has meant chasing the sun. But now the sun is chasing us. Hot and greasy is not so much a luxury as a liability. Tourism is as much about fashion as amenity, and the truth of global warming will mean SPF 40 sun cream is going to be next year's nicotine patch.

Why would you want to be in Stockholm in December? For a start, there's the light. The absence of the light leaves not dark but an ethereal opalescence, a glow-light gaslight. The sun lurks just below the horizon. As it briefly shows its face, it casts low, gold rays that bathe and gild the stuccoed house fronts and turn the water lamé. The city is a collection of fourteen islands connected by some sixty bridges, all cast like bread on the Baltic. You're never further than 100 yards from water. The fat, frozen light is bounced and smoothed. This is a place without shadow.

You can walk from one end to the other in a couple of hours. A human-sized city arranged in kitty-sized portions. Each bit has its own specialised style and atmosphere. Palaces and parliaments here, parks and zoos there, restaurants and shopping over here. There are medieval markets and merchants' wards. It's like a collection of well-made, old-fashioned children's toys: intricate building blocks, baroque Lego.

It's difficult to finger what makes a city immediately agreeable. But by the time you've dumped your bags and walked five blocks, you can always tell. You just know that this is a comfortable, interesting place. Nothing is as gratifying and lifts the spirits like meeting a new city and knowing that your first impressions are correct. It's the intimation of small things that promise deeper, broader, lifelong things. Even before I got out of the car from the airport, I knew I would love Stockholm. The driver casually pointed out an unprepossessing triangle of green between road intersections – a sort of municipal off-cut that everywhere else attracts rubbish and dead Christmas trees – that was home to dozens of black bunnies. A few years back, some Swede released a pair that then went at urban survival like rabbits. The motorway warren is fed and protected by local people. It's important that the rabbits are black. They slowly undermine the motorway and elevate the liberality of Stockholmers. Given its political credentials and its artistic heritage, this city should be infested with street mimes. There are plenty of squares and pedestrian precincts for the vermin of static begging. But the harsh winters and the darkness keep them away, although I'm told they have been seen as far north as Hamburg. Keeping street mimes out of the Arctic Circle is one of the best reasons for living a green life.

Stockholm is a parvenu by European standards. It didn't really begin until the thirteenth century. The name means 'place of wood'. It wasn't until the fifteenth century that it grew to become a regional centre. And even by 1600, the population was only just over six thousand. That wouldn't even make an ABBA concert. It still has the sense of a village dressed up in fancy wrapping. What's particularly winning is Stockholm's civility. Civilisation shares a Latin root with the world 'civic'; they grew together and then, as in so many conurbations, grew apart. Most modern cities seem to repel civilisation and incubate barbarism, but Stockholm is a fundamentally civilised, relaxed, safe, inquisitive, sybaritic and ethical place. It has a beauty that is both man-made and natural. The little streets of Gamla Stan, the old merchant quarter, where the bourgeois warehouses face the water and the winding streets are studded with bright little shops and restaurants and neat, cheese-coloured churches. Outside the palace, a splendidly imposing piece of rational baroque, soldiers change the guard, hopelessly uncoordinated in a giggling shambles, their uniforms as dull as a postman's. In less emotionally secure countries, they'd be court-martialled. But what better measure of civilisation than amateur soldiers?

Winter markets are full of sausages and gingerbread. Bright, fatty, folksy jumpers and socks that smell of animal sweat. There are a disturbing number and variety of gonks, trolls and nymphs in the permanent evening. The shop windows glow like pages from hallucinogenic fairy stories. The veneer of simple ascetic good taste and contemporary design, which is so much part of the

Scandinavian essence, barely covers a hand-carved, folksy, once-upon-a-time saga of peasant kitsch.

Twenty minutes from the palace is Skansen, bizarrely amusing set in a wooded park. It's a collation of old shops, houses, churches and farms collected from all over Sweden and made into a sort of outdoor museum and funfair attraction, which is also a market and a zoo. There's peasanty dancing and singing and steaming cobbled-street food. Everyone's dressed in costumes like Strindberg extras. What rescues this from death by whimsy is that it's all disingenuous and free from irony or cultural exploitation. An eighteenth-century peasant in a big woolly hat sells me a flatbread cone filled with mashed potato and fried, smoked elk, doused with warm, fruity, sweet cloudberry sauce. It's a medieval Swedish kebab, and Bergmanishly good, if long-winded.

Food was the great surprise of Stockholm. Not just very good but also very modern, while still being regionally rooted in local ingredients and old-time recipes. Swedes like the conviviality of eating and drinking. They're conservative by nature but experimental by inclination. Drinks are astronomically expensive, but here they work diligently and hard for the right to get legless, and there are plenty of small, intensely warm and foggy dens, like little wooden wombs. People spend so much time indoors that, over the years, they've done about as much to a herring as is possible and decent. Their open buffets of preserved fish, salted fish, warm bread and thin-sliced cheese is as delicious a national cuisine as you could wish for. If you think Swedish women are spectacular, wait till you see the fish. The cold North Sea and the deep fjords produce the best in the world. I found cod the size of fat five-year-olds, the flesh flaking like pages from a glossy encyclopaedia. Stockholm is a midnight feast.

Along with the fourteen islands, sixty-odd bridges, dozens of Nobel laureates and countless varieties of herring, there are also more than seventy museums, which, even by the culturally inclusive nature of modern Sweden, is an impressive smorgasbord of experience. If you only see one, it must be the *Vasa*. It should be inconceivable to go to Sweden without visiting this ship in a box. The *Vasa* is the only seventeenth-century wooden ship in existence. It sank on its maiden voyage in Stockholm's harbour, and it was preserved by the particular quality of the Baltic fjord. Raised in the 1960s, it has been stabilised and displayed in a hangar-like museum. Now if that sounds sort of *Mary Rose* damp-plank dull, trust me – nothing prepares you for the first sight as you walk in and see this towering, astonishing object. The *Vasa* wasn't just an unlucky ship. It would have been the greatest warship afloat, built by the great hero of the Thirty Years War, Gustavus Adolphus. Rarely do objects so successfully and memorably tug you through the portals of history the way the *Vasa* does. They've reconstructed the heads of the skeletons that went down with her. The faces of seventeenth-century Scandinavians stare back at you. It feels like a crimp in time.

The *Vasa* points to a historic fact about Sweden: it was an aggressively bellicose nation, born out of a loose confederation that traded and pillaged up to the Black Sea. The Swedes fought wars with the Poles, Russians, Germans and Danes for two centuries. German nursery rhymes still frighten children with the possibility of Swedes coming in the night. It had a Baltic empire that encompassed Finland and Norway, part of Denmark and Germany – and, weirdly, St Barts, which it swapped with France for bonded warehouses in Gothenburg. (The capital of the West Indian island is still a free port called Gustavia.) Sweden controlled a league that included all the Scandinavian countries, plus Greenland and Iceland. After the plague and the Thirty Years War, it was left as the most powerful country in northern Europe, and the most intolerant.

Having been the last continental nation to accept Christianity, holding on to the Norse gods well past their rape and pillage date, the Swedes got Calvinism and became intolerant fundamentalists, crusading in Finland and Germany. It was illegal to have any other religion. Swedes who converted or fell out with God were exiled. It was a country ruled by aristocrats who spoke French but worked by a few million of the poorest, most backward peasants in Europe.

At the turn of the twentieth century, some 15 per cent of

Swedes, the fit and the young, migrated to America. Mostly to Minnesota, where they took their hardiness and their resourcefulness, their bleak religion and tough seeds, and farmed land that no one else had been able to put a blade through, in a climate so hostile it reminded them of home. They made the prairie a sea of wheat and fed the modern age.

The point of all this history is that Sweden was once the diametric opposite of everything we associate it with today: warmongering, intolerant, reactionary, superstitious, hierarchical, and dirt-poor. And then, by some cataclysm, by some late-night depressive flash of enlightenment, a sauna and schnapps-induced reality check, they decided, all together, synchronistically, to change, not just the cushions and curtains, but everything. To be different. To be pluralistic, liberal, modern, sexually relaxed, culturally open, democratically inclusive, peacefully non-aligned, committed to comprehensive social welfare and the common wealth, health, happiness and Bergman movies. I can't think of another country that has so dramatically proved that national characteristics aren't bred in blood and bone but come from years of bad practice, prejudice, fear, snobbery and abuse. The Swedes dug up their roots and became the international standard for caring, the paragon people. And that's remarkable. Stockholm looks and feels like a composite, comfortable European city. It has all the redeeming things that we like to associate with the best of us and very few of the concomitant blights.

I have a prejudice that all really great cities are built on water: rivers, bays, ports, lakes. Water is the wallpaper, carpet and drapes of Stockholm, a city that continually presents twinkling, reflected vistas, glimpsed through arches, across squares. Everywhere, the water calls to you.

On an inflatable dinghy in the Baltic, it's bloody cold. I'm dressed in a thermal Arctic survivor suit. My gloves have their own mittens. It's fabulously beautiful: an archipelago of little islands sits in the polished smoke-grey water under a soft, mauve-grey sky. Everything except me is still. The trunks of the silver birches stripe the shore, their naked branches cross-hatching the frozen air. On the islands, people build simple, calm houses, painted the colours of Scandinavia, in particular a rusty, clotted red that comes from an iron-rich earth. Their roofs are pitched against the weather, and on jetties are little windy house-saunas with fairy lights in their windows. Everything is comfortable and practical and welcoming. Everything talks in a whisper. Nothing boasts. There is a Swedish word for this: *jantelagen*. It's the unwritten law of equality. It means not getting above yourself. Not taking on airs. It's anti-bling, anti-greed, and it's the social oil for the ball-bearing people. This is where the unobtrusive and invisible rich have their holidays. And in the summers, with the endless mornings, they sail and swim and fish and eat long, pickled buffets, probably in the nude. But now it's cold and elegant, under the serene, silent, gull-grey light.

Sicily

Palermo's airport is named Falcone e Borsellino. It sounds like a seventies American cop show, and you'd be forgiven for not knowing who either of the names belong to. They were a pair of mortally brave magistrates who tried to finally break the ancient grip of organised crime in Sicily. Both were assassinated.

They don't like to talk about the Mafia to strangers here; it's an embarrassing family concern, none of our business, a private tragedy. Sicily is a secretive place. You can sense it in the blackened, baroque streets of Palermo, the capital, where the bomb damage from the 1943 Allied landings still hasn't quite been cleaned up and where the tenement palaces are inhabited by North African refugees. It's a watchful and masculine place, beautiful and thwarted.

Sicily's history is as mordant and miserable a romance as any in Europe – well into the 1950s these were among the poorest peasants in the Western world. For centuries they eked out a meagre life, suffering constant vendettas and feuds, injustice, exploitation, honour killings and murderous codes, all surrounded by the smell of mandarin blossom and incense. In Sicily, blood called to blood for blood down the ages.

The Capuchin monastery in Palermo is a discreetly blank building. It sits in a quiet square beside a graveyard, across town from where, in 1992, the Mafia settled its account with Magistrate Borsellino. Outside the door, tucked into a corner, are a couple of hawkers peddling postcards and guidebooks; inside, a friar sits behind a table selling tickets and more postcards and votive trinkets. It's a slow day; he reads the paper.

Down a flight of stairs, past a wooden statue of Our Lady of Sorrows, is the door to the catacomb, the waiting room of the dead. Surprisingly large, with high, vaulted ceilings and long corridors stretching away at right angles, it's cool and dank and smells of sour, spiced dust and rotting cloth. The windows are high and diffuse the sunlight into a pale glow. Fluorescent bulbs vibrate, adding a medically forensic, anaemic brightness. Hanging from the walls, propped on benches, resting in their decrepit boxes, are nearly two thousand dead. They're dressed in their living best, the uniforms of their earthly calling. There's no one else down here.

In Europe the desiccation and preservation of corpses is a particularly Sicilian affair. There are other examples in Italy, but the great majority are in Sicily, where the relationship between the living and the dead is especially strong. Nobody knows how many there really are, or how many have since been removed from catacombs and buried in cemeteries by priests uneasy with the theology of keeping votive corpses. The phenomenon provokes an instant question: why would anyone do this? Why would you exhibit decaying bodies?

I walk down their ranks with that awkward confusion of trying to make sense of what it is I'm actually feeling. In the West we don't often see dead bodies – the absence of life is shrouded and hidden. These dead have a mystique; they come with an attitude and previous convictions. Examining the corpses with a morbid interest – so this is what death looks like – I realise that the big difference between the living and the dead is that you can stare at the dead with an intense, close-up curiosity that the living would never tolerate. And then I think they really ought to be playing Michael Jackson's 'Thriller' as background music, given how like prosthetic, schlock-horror-effect zombies these bodies look, how comically and pathetically the great denouement of nature mimics not just art but cheap art. Their jaws hang open in silent yowls, rotting teeth grin with menace, eye sockets stare bleakly, shreds of hard skin cling to shrunken cheeks and arthritic knuckles. These people are mostly small, their arms crossed as they sag against the wire and nails that hold them upright, their heads lolling on shoulders, bodies slowly collapsing with the effort of imitating a past life.

The corridors are segregated into religious folk and professional, meaning doctors and lawyers and a couple of vaudeville grand soldiers in their *carabinieri* uniforms. There's a women's corridor where the guide points out that we can admire the fashion of the past. The skeletons stand in shredded rags, grimed and bleached a murky grey. There is little to admire. A side chapel is devoted to those who died virgins, especially poignant and by contemporary mores a pathetically cruel appellation to carry into eternity. When they were interred here, they must have appeared as symbols of purity among the decay.

And then there is a small chapel for infants. The children are dressed in their party frocks, propped up like living-dead dolls. One sits on a nursery chair with a little skeleton on her lap, perhaps a younger sibling, unbearably pitiful and simultaneously laughably grotesque.

This isn't like the catacombs of Rome, an archaeological excavation of tombs. Here the bodies were always meant to be seen, and they charge you a small fee for the pleasure. There are signs to remind you to be respectful and not take photographs, but they sell them. It's not clear if this is a religious experience or a cultural one, but it is a tourist attraction.

The first and oldest mummy is a friar: Silvestro da Gubbio, standing in his niche since 1599. (The word 'mummy' is from an Arabic word for bitumen, which resembled the blackened resin the ancient Egyptians used as a preservative.) Most of the bodies are from the nineteenth century. To begin with, they were exclusively friars and priests attached to the monastery. As time went on, the religious men were joined by benefactors and dignitaries and notables.

No one knows exactly what started the mummification; probably by chance it was discovered that a body left in a crypt with a particular atmosphere of coolness and porous limestone would actually dry out rather than rot. Then a system was devised. The newly dead were laid in chambers, called strainers, on terracotta slats over drains, where their body fluids could seep away and the corpses slowly desiccate, like prosciutto. After eight months to a year, they'd be washed with vinegar, put back in their best clothes, and either placed in coffins or hung on the walls.

Preserving ancestral bodies is done in any number of places, but they're rarely displayed like this. Sicily has so many cultures, so many people came here with their practices and beliefs and were assimilated, that little bits now and again rise to the surface, their origins long forgotten. It has been suggested that perhaps the practice is the residual echo of a much older, pre-Christian rite – belief in the shamanistic power of corpses. Not every corpse would have dried out; some must have rotted, and so the preservation of others might have been an intimation of God's will, a divine hand keeping certain individuals as they were as a mark of a particular worldly goodness. As saints' relics are used to aid prayer and belief, maybe these bodies were thought to have been preserved by God to reinforce faith. Or perhaps the catacombs were made as a great vanitas, a memento mori, an illustration of the passing of all worldly ambition and the inevitability of death and the vanity and foolishness of storing up wealth on earth.

In later years some of the bodies were more elaborately preserved by means of chemical injections, taking the responsibility out of the hands of God and leaving it to undertakers and science. In one of the chapels a little girl, Rosalia Lombardo, lies in her coffin. She appears to be sleeping under a filthy brown sheet. Unlike many of the other strained and dried mummies, she has her own hair, which hangs in doll-like curls over her yellow forehead, tied up with a big yellow silk bow. Her eyes are closed, the eyelashes perfectly preserved. If she weren't surrounded by the grinning skulls and rot of this place, she could be just a child dozing on the way home from a party. The naturalism and the beauty are arresting; the implication that life is a mere breath away, disturbing and spooky. Rosalia was two when she got pneumonia and died. Crazy with grief, her father asked Alfredo Salafia, a noted embalmer, to preserve her. The effect is dreadfully, tragically vital, and the grief still seems to hang over this little blonde head. (Salafia sold his mummification fluid – keeping the formula secret – to funeral homes in the United States, as the fashion for embalming spread after the slaughter of the civil war.) In Palermo, Rosalia is mentioned as a sort of semi-deity, a magical little angel. The taxi drivers say, 'Did you see Rosalia? *Bella.*'

Savoca is a silent village that crawls up the side of a hill until it reaches a view across the eastern end of the island to the sea. A tightly wound place that corkscrews back on itself. This is where Francis Ford Coppola filmed *The Godfather*. The bar where Michael and his tragic wife had their wedding reception sits on the tiny square looking exactly as it did thirty-seven years ago on-screen. There's no obvious sign mentioning the movie. They don't like the association; most Sicilians I ask profess never to have seen it.

At the top of the hill is a convent, a place that looks more like a youth hostel than a gothic medieval institution. There are only two nuns here, both Indians from Jharkhand. They wear woollies and jackets over their saris. In a side room, laid out in temporary plywood packing cases, are a couple of dozen cadavers that are being studied by a trio of scientists.

They're an unlikely team: Arthur Aufderheide, an octogenarian American from Minnesota who started as a pathologist and moved on to become one of the world's top mummy experts; Albert Zink, a big German who is the director of the Institute for Mummies and the Iceman in northern Italy; and a young Sicilian, Dario Piombino-Mascali – excitable and nervous, constantly worried, enthused and driven and possibly brilliant – who has a bolt through his eyebrow and a jacket that has 'Boxfresh' written on the back, apparently without irony.

I find him leaning over a very unfresh box and delicately lifting the surplice of a nineteenth-century priest. He is looking for an unobtrusive piece of organic material for Professor Zink to do tests on. 'Ooh, is this what I think it is?' We all poke our heads up the vicar's frock and concur that it probably is. A thin pouch of powdery dry skin comes away in his hand. A half-centimetre sample is labelled and packaged. He's not going to miss his scrotum now.

An enormous amount can be gleaned from dead bodies about the day-to-day lives of the past – diet, illnesses and life expectancy. Knowing more about diseases like syphilis, malaria, cholera and tuberculosis centuries ago can help us get the better of them today. The scientists move methodically, checking the corpses' heights and ages, examining skulls and teeth, looking for the ridges inter-rupting enamel that signify years of malnutrition. Two mummies are gouty. Five show signs of degenerative arthritis. Almost all these people suffered horribly from dental conditions – tartar build-up, receding gums, caries and abscesses.

Abdomens are checked for missing organs. One of the bodies has had its soft tissue removed, and others have been stuffed with rags and leaves, including bay leaves, perhaps to mitigate the smell, or because they were supposed to have some preservative value. Filling out the shrunken forms would have made them more lifelike. The skin has the waxy quality of parchment, the clothes feel sticky and damp, the faces bloat and yawn, mouths give up wizened larynxes and shrivelled tongues for examination.

The scientists are respectful of the bodies, never losing touch with the fact that they were human – they were like us – but still they refer to each one as 'it', to keep a distance, a dispassion, when they're pulling a molar out.

A few years back these bodies were vandalised in their crypt. People broke in and poured green paint over them. Lurid and humiliating, it spatters and dribbles across their faces and coats and shoes, making them look even more like characters from a funfair ghost train. The nuns who are keepers of this strange congregation look on with pity and distaste. They tell me the bodies should be decently buried, allowed to return to dust. One says there's nothing spiritual or uplifting to be learned from all this.

The paint-spattered, rag-filled bodies will soon be returned to their empty niches. At the moment the arched alcoves along the wall hold nothing but hundreds of dried, dead centipedes. A number of bodies are still kept in their elaborate coffins. Gingerly I lift a heavy lid that may not have been moved for over a century and peer inside. The air seems to escape with a thick sigh, and the smell grabs the back of my throat – not a rotten smell but the odour of beef tea and the clogging aroma of dry mould and fine, powdery layers of human dust. It's a smell that is dramatically unforgettable, the tincture of silence and sadness, the scent of repeated prayer heard in the distance, or of remorse and regret, a smell that's both repellent and intimately familiar. Something sensed for the first time, but also with a strange and compelling sense of *déjà vu*.

We will never know for sure what these corpses meant to the congregations who laid them out and dressed them. They remain one of Sicily's many mysteries. We are left with our own concerns, thoughts and doubts when confronted by these comic and tragic visions of death. It is difficult to untangle the feelings aroused by the bodies, frozen on the journey between nothing and nothing – the mysteries, fears and hopes, the contradictions of life and loss, that are eternal and universal.

The beautiful town of Novara di Sicilia has a large and piously decorated church. In front of the altar is a secret door to the crypt, and at the press of a hidden button the floor opens electronically, just as in a James Bond film. Down a flight of steps is a room with carved stone niches containing the variously and now familiarly sagging bodies of six more prelates. On a high shelf stacked with skulls is a box containing two cats, naturally mummified, like a faint shadow of ancient Egypt. They got trapped in the crypt, a reminder that, even with nine lives, there's only one end.

Danube

I. The River

Take the path into the woods, over the mossy stones, the roots and brambles, down into the shadows under the bank of a meadow. In a bowl of smooth rocks springs a spigot, no more than a twist of water fetched from the thick earth. It splashes in puddles, pauses for a moment, then sprints helter-skelter away into the forest. It slides past boulders and over gravel, runs without thought or apparent purpose into the decline of least resistance. People come here and dip tin mugs, and sip a toast to a new start, to great journeys, to small things growing into mighty things. It's a communion with an ancient animism: the power of water and wood and the earth that bears them. This is the Black Forest, and this stream is the start of the Danube. This is the farthest you can get from its final debouche, 2,860 kilometres away to the east. The Danube, the Donau, the Dunaj, Duna, Dunav, Dunarea, the greatest river of Europe, the longest outside Russia, a river that belongs to no one country but waters ten. Here in the dark, sighing wood it isn't yet old enough to be called the Danube. It's the Breg, an infant that will become a torrent.

Above the stream there is a commodious café where you can get thick slices of real Black Forest gateau, served by real Black Forest girls in dirndls who bulge and wobble with a coarse, whipped-cream-and-cherry hilarity. The forest is strident with Germans. Committed to a cardiovascular efficiency, they march in shorts with backpacks and sticks covered in those little enamel shields that are mementos of places they've sung tumpty-tum songs over: Ulm, Regensburg, Passau, Vienna, Stalingrad.

Just up the road in the local town of Furtwangen, there's a clock museum. The cuckoo clock, despite what Orson Welles tells us, didn't come from Switzerland, but from here in the Black Forest, a place of desperate medieval poverty where men would take to the roads as travelling cuckoo-clock salesmen. It seems an unlikely enterprise for starving peasants, but, as ever, we underestimate at our peril the hard work and ingenuity and the macabre inventiveness of the desperate German. The bird was pressed into a homely stardom, not because of any innate timekeeping ability but because its call is the easiest to imitate. There were experiments with ducks and owls, and possibly two-headed eagles.

The Breg leaves the forest and continues east where it meets another ingénue sprite, the Brigach. They come together at Donaueschingen, where the Danube officially begins, in a big garden beside a big house belonging to the von Fürstenbergs, the local nobs. It springs from an ornamental pond – a water feature with a baroque statue of a chilly woman scolding a pair of naked children. She is the female spirit of the region, telling the little rivulets to grow up and play nicely. The water runs underground for a moment and exits from a classical gazebo. It's all a bit humourlessly, Teutonically kitsch, a vanity to pretend you can own a river. This was a favourite spot for Kaiser Wilhelm, who started the Great War, to come and shoot ducks with his English guns, modified for his withered arm. I walk a little way down the river. A pair of mallards start noisily. A solitary man walks a dog. The wind flickers the leaves of the poplars. The local hotel is bright and jolly in a gloomy sort of way.

The Danube is the great fault line of Europe. It was the natural boundary of the Roman Empire. To the west and the south is classical Europe, the empire of reason and intrigue, poetry and order. North and east was barbarian Europe: bearded and clannish, homespun, superstitious, the Europe of the forest and the troll. The river is also the boundary between Catholic and Orthodox Europe. It marks the furthest advance of the ten centuries of Islamic expansion. It winds through the shifting barneys of the Balkans, and it passed unstoppably from the liberated lands through the Iron Curtain to the Warsaw Pact. It is the river of Jason and the Argonauts, of the earliest human European settlements. But more than all that, the Danube is the great artery that fed Mitteleuropa, that amorphous place of ideas and commerce that existed as much in books and concert halls as in geography; a place of chocolate and cafés, psychology, philosophy, romance and rebellion, riches and music – as much music as a conductor could shake a stick at. It was the great portal for new thinking, for science and invention; a way of thinking and being, a culture that is still the leaven in our collective character.

But we rarely come to look at the centre of our continent; far less often, and with less fondness than we go to the reverie of the south. We prefer olive-oil Europe to goose-fat Europe – it seems showier and sexier down there. Yet it was along this wide stream of consciousness that the deep and real idea of Europe came, and it begins quite quietly: a stroll through a lilting country of time-bred villages and well-fed, beery indolence. In the past I've had trouble loving Germany, but here it is pretty and light, and amused and sybaritic. Northern, Protestant Germany is hard-working, organised and serious. The south is Catholic, bucolic, nostalgic – Germany with the German taken out. Northerners despise south-erners as obese, greedy, stupid peasants. The southerners call northerners *Saupreuss* – 'pig Prussians'. I like it down here. It's a bit Krauty-Irish.

The first big stop on the river is Ulm. Ulm is beautiful and stalled. The city made a late medieval fortune from trade, and then it all dried up, and it subsided into a pretty penury. As with most beautiful German towns, what you see only reminds you of what is lost. The RAF visited just the once, in December 1944: much of the old town was destroyed in a firestorm. They filled in the gaps with striking modern buildings, from the Ulm school that replaced the Bauhaus. But mostly this is famous for having the tallest church tower in the world. It's Lutheran, built on the border of Swabia so that Catholic Bavaria can see the towering marvel of the Reformation. It was the tallest building in the world until the Eiffel Tower. They started in 1377 and didn't finish until 1890. It's an unnerving climb to the top: you circle inside a pinnacle like a corkscrew until you're finally drawn out with a pop, into a blasted panorama that I'm sure is spectacular, but it is a bizarre scientific fact that all elevated views are forgotten by the time you've climbed down.

Inside the church the carvings of the choir are remarkable, a series of portraits and figures of philosophers, scholars, clerics, cuckolds and drunks. They're touchingly earthy and whimsically ethereal, and escaped the wave of Protestant iconoclasm – perhaps because carving is a modest peasant's decoration. The art came slyly through the craft and, after all, Christ himself was a carpenter. The city's heraldic symbol is a sparrow. They have a holiday for it, make chocolates of it and call their football team the Sparrow. The story is that a wagonload of timber for the cathedral arrived at the city gate, but the logs were too long to get through the doors. The Swabians scratched their heads, and probably their stomachs, and were about to demolish the gates when someone noticed a sparrow carrying a twig to its nest. It turned its head sideways to get through a crack in the wall. Eureka! This confirms everything the northern Germans think about the south. Not just that they're more stupid than small birds, but that they're so stupid they continue to tell the story. Then there was the tailor of Ulm, who in the eighteenth century made a flying suit, leapt across the Danube and fell straight in. Everyone laughed at him, so he drank himself to death. He has a statue. Surrounded by all this rollicking idiocy, what is remarkable is that Ulm is also the birthplace of Einstein.

The river leaves the gentle green towpath and continues east to Regensburg. But first a detour to Dachau and the guilty contradiction of going to visit a concentration camp. Of course we should bear witness, but not as part of a holiday. It is wordlessly sad. Now neat and silent, with an exhibition explaining German culpability. They knew. Everyone knew. School kids are bussed in; they're naughty and bored and interested only in each other, which is a sort of redemption.

Regensburg town centre is a UNESCO World Heritage Site. There is a very old, immense bridge, but my guide – an American who has become a born-again Bavarian – is most interested in the local beer. I manage to locate the last great hat shop in Germany –

probably in Europe, and therefore arguably the best hat shop in the world. They embossed my initials in gold on a green felt trilby: AAJ. Albrecht Altdorfer and the astronomer Johannes Kepler came from here; it has been home to the current Pope and to Oskar Schindler.

The river picks up speed and makes for the border. Passau sits on the confluence of three rivers – the Danube, the Ilz and the Inn from Innsbruck. The city made a not inconsiderable living charging tolls from passing barges, and was politically powerful, poised on trade routes and borders. It doesn't feel German. The proximity of Austria has put a fey waltz into its step. Italian craftsmen came here to build the gleaming baroque cathedral. Every so often the river leaps up and douses the place, like shoving the head of a teacher's pet down the bogs.

We get on a boat, the *Avalon*, one of the many cruise ships that start here, full of immensely old and fit Americans and Australians. They are hardened cruise veterans. As we leave and look back at the view of Passau, sitting bright and baroquely Latin with just a hint of a rococo flourish, we can see that the river flows in two colours – the green of the Inn, and the dark, muddy grey of the Danube. We cross into Austria. The old towpath is now used by cycles: you can pedal all the way to Vienna.

Occasionally on the banks we see couples entwined beside abandoned cycles, overcome by the loveliness of it all, and each other. I love our boat; it's as luxurious as a provincial motel, and I am introduced to the joy of travelling with the adventurous old, those who live against the clock. They are up for everything – trips to abbeys and distilleries, operas, folk dancing, chilli-pepper factories, afternoon quizzes, evening singalongs ... They talk optimistic and dress pessimistic: a good lesson for travelling.

Now the river really takes over. All rivers have their own narrative; they flow like old songs, and we let ourselves be hummed into its rhythm. In the morning I'm absurdly happy to see its dappled light bounce around my cabin. Linz is a European cultural capital and it wears the responsibility with all the ease of a *Bürgermeister*'s chain of office. The city has splurged on concert halls, museums, installations, sculpture parks and an eye-bulging collection of contemporary art. Linz has always been rich, home to merchants and industrialists and moneyed power-broking. It has the gaudy good taste of public philanthropy and social aspiration. The city takes me out to dinner and plies me with press packs and pens and CDs, and a *Linzertorte* – a cake of jam and almonds with a hundred secret recipes, all of which are the oldest ever recorded. The city's new, arty motto is 'Linz: A City Livens Up', which as a tourist slogan needs some work.

Linz straddled the Russian- and American-occupied zones after the war. The Danube was the border, the Nibelungen bridge a checkpoint. On the north bank they starved in the dark and the cold, and despised an ignored enemy – Cold War pawns. Over the water, the other Linz lived in the economic resurgence of the 1950s. The rest of Europe forgets how very close Austria came to being dragged behind the Iron Curtain. Linz has grown fat on its industrial wealth, which was assured by the largesse of its most famous son: Hitler moved the factories here, the steelworks and the chemicals. Hitler is not the only famous old boy; Fritz Austerlitz also came from Linz, and he was the father of Fred Astaire.

The river runs on, through a romantic landscape of vineyards and orchards, of apricots and plums, pastoral villages, neat farmhouses, a rich land with big, expectant barns; an unfurling green banner of heartiness, husbandry and heavy harvests, and deeply conservative prosperity. Here, on an eminence, is the immense abbey of Melk, a staging baroque lump of iced Catholicism. It has an impressive library, an exceptional series of brutal and vigorously devotional Germanic paintings by Jörg Breu, and a church that has so much gold in it, it's like being inside a giant rapper's mouth. All I could think of was how many punnets of plums and apricots, how many bottles of sweet wine, veal calves and apple strudels it must have cost the local peasants to build and maintain this house of devotional bling. On the altar is a Latin tag that says 'Without a just battle there is no victory' – the worldly evocation of the strong-armed Church as corporate Pope-enforcer. While your jaw hangs open at the sheer extravagance, Melk reaches in and pulls prayers out of your throat like exclamatory adenoids.

Further down the river is Dürnstein, the castle where the troubadour Blondel sang his songs to discover Richard the Lionheart, who was held for ransom after the away match of the third crusade. It looks like an idealised romantic folly, put here to delight amateur watercolourists and passing Australian octogenarians. Somewhere along here they discovered the Willendorf Venus, who at 30,000 years old predates the Greek goddess by more than 20,000 years. She's carved from ivory, a fecund and bootilicious woman with a seedpod or a basket for a head. She is the very earliest representation of us, the mother of creation, an image of self-awareness, of symbolism. Finding her in southern Austria seems unlikely, but it is proof that people have lived here for as long as there have been people.

As the boat draws up to Vienna, I look out and wonder where the city's gone. The Viennese don't have much to do with the river – perhaps because it involves sailors, swearing and all the rough and rude business of trade and sex. The city was founded as a garrison for Roman cavalry. Austria means 'eastern border' – they were here to keep people out. Their spirit lives on. This is an odd place, charming and repellent in equal measure, often simultaneously. The city looks like it was built for a species of semi-divine giants who are now extinct, and is inhabited by an order of starch-obsessed curators. Everything about it is huge and mythological and naked and violent, or made out of marzipan. The national museum of art is a delirious vision of counter-Reformation sado-masochism; vast canvases depicting erotic mutilation and ecstatic agony. Vienna marks the farthest expansion of Islam. In 1683, the insatiable Turks were finally halted at the gates of Vienna. The Viennese made it by the slimmest of margins, mainly thanks to the intervention of the Polish King, Jan Sobieski, who forfeited his own country to the care of the Virgin Mary for the sake of Christendom. He commanded the largest cavalry charge in history. The Turks left coffee behind them; the Viennese invented cappuccinos and croissants modelled on the Ottoman crescent. The Turks also dropped their musical instruments, giving the West the dubious cultural bonus of military brass bands. Vienna marks the descent of the Iron Curtain. Beyond here, until 1989, ships straying downstream would be met by gunboats.

From here the land changes, becomes harder, poorer, battered and abandoned. We drive the short distance to the next capital. The responsibility of leadership apparently took Bratislava by surprise, as if someone with a clipboard had knocked on the door and said: 'Congratulations, you have been chosen to be the capital of the new sovereign nation state of Slovakia. Good luck!' The divorce from the Czech Republic was heart-warmingly, liberally amicable. I mentioned this to a couple of locals, who rolled their eyes. 'Don't be so gullible. They split the country because they couldn't agree who was going to get all the post-communist money, the businesses, the international loans, the investment. Two countries, twice as many corrupt politicians with their faces in the swill.'

The first thing you notice about Bratislava is the inhalingly hideous socialist slab of a bridge, with a triffid UFO growing out of it. It has a restaurant and a discotheque. Ex-communist countries are immensely keen on discotheques; they are modern and trendy, with forbidden, imported music and licentiousness. But they also have comforting queues, and good socialist crush and discomfort. They say the view from the top is spectacular. It was closed. They also said there was an interesting Jewish museum. That turned out not to be open. And in the tiny baroque centre of town, there is the room where Napoleon signed a treaty after the Battle of Austerlitz. That was being renovated. There was a heavy-metal festival in the town centre with at least half a dozen people there enjoying themselves; I saw a bald man in camouflage with a live chinchilla on his head. Nobody famous has ever come from Slovakia but, per head, they've put together more cars than any other nation on earth.

I grab a seat on a waterbus, crowded and companionable, hot with sweat and garlic sausage, onions and plum brandy. We grunt and grumble down the river to the Hungarian capital, the 'Queen of the Danube'. Budapest is something else, somewhere else. For so much of its existence it's been the patronised junior partner of Vienna, but through national pride and a natural flamboyance, the people have built a gloriously exuberant and dramatic place. The parliament building was based on Westminster, but with added architectural Botox and the addition of a vast dome. It was put up when they weren't even an independent country. Budapest is a kaleidoscope of other places – sometimes it's London, then Paris, Berlin or Milan. The baroque is shuffled with fantastic secessionist buildings. It has castles, cathedrals, the river's best bridges and a Valhalla of music. In the afternoon I heard Alfred Brendel's farewell performance in Liszt's concert hall.

Walking through the city, I suddenly realise what's been missing, what's been rationed up till now – it is laughter, a sense of humour. This is a funny place. It eats well, it drinks a lot, it talks and argues and boasts and waves its hands about. It is a city of nous and galleries, a centre for photography and journalism. All its enthusiasm has grown out of a lot of misery. Hungary had a bad war and a worse peace, a badly failed uprising and some very bad retribution. They've made a museum out of their terror. It's one of the best modern museums to ideas that I've seen anywhere. But we had to drag ourselves away from the paprika and the gypsy violins and continue downstream. For an afternoon I stopped in the south of Hungary and cycled along the river, through fields of poppies, rye grass and wheat. There were scarecrows and vines and beans, and on the horizon you could just see the towers of a distant cathedral. The river kept me company, and it was perfect.

Vukovar is a shock. A medium-sized town in Croatia, surrounded on three sides by Serbia, it was besieged in the Balkan war. The burnt-out houses and shops now burst with lilac and dog roses. The still-broken city sits shell-shocked, caught in its moment. It is twenty years – a generation – since the Serb militia emptied the hospital, took the wounded and the sick to a local farm and massacred them. The hospital's basement is now a desperate, raw memorial, and there is a water tower they keep, blasted but erect, so you can still see it from Serbia. The countryside is silent and sullen. There are graves in the woods. The river washes nothing away.

One hundred kilometres downstream is Belgrade, the capital of Serbia, set on the confluence of the Danube and the Sava rivers. I stand on the battlements of its castle, looking out at yet another panorama, and my guide – an intense professor of self-serving history – tells me proudly that Belgrade is the only city in Western Europe to have been properly bombarded. Five times in the twentieth century: twice in the First World War (which, incidentally, they started) by the Austrians, the second time with the Germans; twice in the Second World War, first by the Germans, then the Allies; and finally by NATO. Despite the amount of ordnance it has absorbed, Belgrade is a very grand city, with vast cathedrals, the obligatory opera houses, parks and boulevards, but you realise its defining characteristic is a terrible sense of self-pity and injustice. Serbia has always wanted to be one of the great states of Europe, always saw its destiny thwarted by the jealousy and unkindness of others – the Ottomans, the Austrians, the Germans, the Russians; the perfidy of their allies the French, and the Italians, and then NATO. Add to that the ingratitude of the rest of the Balkans, and there's barely a country on the Continent that hasn't offered Serbia some buffet to its vanity. Not wanting to get into an argument, I turn and mention how beautiful Serbian women are. And they really are – unsmiling, ice-blonde, skin-tight pneumatic and terrifying. The food is surprisingly good and the citizens are cosmopolitan, friendly, fun and flirtatious, just as long as you don't mention Kosovo. I particularly enjoyed Marshal Tito's tomb, with his collection of ornamental relay batons and hunting rifles. And, of course, the zoo, which has only white animals.

The river gathers pace and enters its most spectacular phase: the Iron Gates, towering cliffs where the water chicanes and boils, and the castle of Golubac. We pass into Bulgaria, though on the left bank it's Romania. Romania: the old Dacia and Scythia, conquered by Trajan and embossed on his column. Romania is still a classical country. Its alphabet is Latinate; the language sounds like a Geordie with a cold talking Italian. Somewhere along the bank the Goths, being pushed by the Huns, crossed as refugees to the eastern Roman Empire, and thereby began the long, precipitous collapse of Rome. In the villages, horses outnumber cars, there are haystacks and a muddy confusion of agriculture. Small, hunched women in black headscarves and bright shawls sit on rustic benches like characters waiting for a fairy story.

Bulgaria is Cyrillic and Slav, smells of roses and boiled plums. Pretty villages with low, painted chalets and hidden, ancient, bedizened churches. Every brick cottage has a front garden neat with beds of potato and cabbage. The river sniffs the sea and runs on past the abandoned factories of communism, the sunken barges and rotting jetties. This great wet way once carried the exotic of Africa, the wealth of the East and Constantinople, the furs of Rostov up to northern Europe, and brought down salt and timber and craftsmen's skills. Now there is barely any trade. The river is barren. We pass occasional barges, but mostly the river runs alone until it disperses into a broad delta of islands and causeways, choked streams full of eagles and storks, cuckoos and pelicans, water snakes, frogs and mosquitoes.

In the sodden islands and floating bogs, secretive people build temporary homes and boil huge, slimy catfish. The delta is a strange place, lawless and lost at the very edge of Europe. The river splits. Some channels run past Moldova and Ukraine, but to the west it catches a canal that ends on the Black Sea coast with the last town of the Danube, Constanta. A Roman city where Ovid was exiled, it languishes in a pointless decrepitude. A great white baroque casino sits on the promenade, a gamble that failed. The sea slaps the land with a salacious familiarity. It smells of ozone and pizza. The muezzin calls the faithful to prayer, his voice drifting out to Asia. I walk back past an old synagogue that is collapsing. Through the broken window I see the golden Hebrew letters – the writing on the wall. The Jews are the absent heart of this story. This was their river as much as anyone's. There was a thriving and brilliant Jewish community in every city along its reach. This was the heartland of the Jews in Europe, and they've gone. The shade of the millions that once were, the millions that might have been, is still here – in the architecture, the shops, the cafés and the banking, the dumplings and the spices and the schmaltz, the gold, the poetry, the psychiatry and the politics, and the violins that yearn with a blissful ache the length of the Danube.

The Stoics said no man crosses the same river twice: both the man and the river will be changed. Yet it is also true that men and rivers change little. Rivers roll away time. They're part of the brotherhood of sweet water. All are stories, great narratives, as deep as sorrow and as shallow as laughter. To trace the length of a river is to be part of a parable, to float on a metaphor. We each of us see not just time and history, commerce and power reflected in the water, but the inexorable passing of our lives.

II. Vienna

Ronald Reagan was a man who knew the diplomatic form. He also had a showman's ear for a tune. So when, at an official dinner, the marine band slipped into 'Edelweiss', he stopped mid-anecdote, rose to his feet, placed a reverential hand over his heart and stared into the blank mid-distance out of respect for the Austrian national anthem.

This possibly calumnious story pulls out a truth not so much about American presidents but about Austria. It is a greatly misunderstood and trivialised country. Being justly and stiffly proud and protective of their extraordinary musical heritage (Berg, Bruckner, Haydn, Mahler, Mozart, Schoenberg, Schubert, two Strausses and Webern are just the ones you can hum from memory). Austrians fail to see the humour in the fact that around the world their theme tune is a musical written by two New York Jews, and that those of us who wouldn't know whether to blow, swallow or applaud *Die Zauberflöte* all know that doorbells and sleigh bells and schnitzel with noodles are a few of Austria's favourite things. And Vienna – where Mozart lived and Mahler directed the opera – has a signature tune from a British film played on a Russian stringed washboard (*The Third Man*). Vienna is a city that's made a virtue out of rising above the slings and arrows and mockery of cruel fortune with a pose of glacial disdain and the sigh of the socially martyred. It all clings to a scuffed dignity. Despite all their illustrious ancestors, still the most famous Austrian is Christopher Plummer.

There's a funny thing about Vienna. You don't notice immediately; it creeps up on you and hits you between the eyes. The doors all open the wrong way. The Viennese just decided contrarily to have doors push into the street rather than pull into the hall. Perhaps it's a small act of rebellion against being mistaken for Germans. So you spend a lot of time *drücken* when you should be *ziehen*. For some time I've had this feeling about Vienna – a *Fledermaus* squeak of synchronicity. Its name came up once too often; I had a sense that it's a coming destination. It's a city with so much behind and so much front that it's about to happen.

It was suggested that I took my newish twins. So mother, babies, nanny and Tom the photographer and I all went to Vienna for a winter weekend. Weekend breaks have become a feature of the northern European life that cuts leisure time like cucumber sandwiches into little triangles. We need the crust off our holidays, and since the opening of the land beyond the Danube and the euro, the cities of far-flung Europe from Barcelona to Riga have been overrun by berserk, Hunnish hordes of gel-haired drunks in matching T-shirts and squadrons of feral bridesmaids with matching Brazilians. The Continent is where we go to act out and up. But not Vienna. This is no place to let your hair down or get your buttocks out. This is grown-up Europe, a city for adults. You don't act your age here, you act a couple of decades older.

The waiter looked at the double buggy the way a French polisher might regard a lawnmower on a dining table, and suggested ever so politely that he could put it somewhere else. 'It's not in the way,' I said, 'not blocking a corridor or fire exit.' 'No, but it could go out of the way.' I realised his objection in this gingerbread and crystal coffee and cake emporium was aesthetic rather than practical. 'But,' I added, 'it's got a pair of children in it.' 'Yes,' he said uncertainly, realising that this probably brought the conversation to a close, but not quite understanding why.

Vienna isn't child-friendly. But it's not just children. It isn't anybody-friendly. Frail, loveable humanity isn't Vienna's bag. Watching the Viennese go about their daily business, you see they're not people people, not particularly warm to each other. What they are instead is polite, with immensely good, lightly starched manners, and this is such a joy after coming from a social climate of enforced, instant mateyness and small talk. The thoughtful formality of etiquette is a blessed relief. You forget what a strain friendliness is until you don't have to do it.

Viennese restaurants don't have dress codes – they don't need to, because Vienna has one. Often rather eccentric, there is a lot of rural, musical hunting gear worn by both sexes. Furry pig's arse on green felt hats, double rows of horn buttons, military-fetish goat skin and things made out of carved antlers. I found an old jewellery shop that specialises in setting teeth in silver, which is both compulsively fascinating and perineum-clenchingly shuddery – and which is true of so much of Vienna. Nothing can quite prepare you for the incoherent cacophony made up of marble expletives and hysterical, psychotic plaster-laughter. The buildings silently bellow and leer at you. For a start, it's their sheer scale. Utterly unhuman, they all start with the assumption that everything needs to be XXL, the size of a seventeen-platform railway station built in the municipal classical style, with a Babel of pedestals, columns, pilasters and assorted architraves, then decorated with a giant confectioner's piping bag with figures and images whose associations would defy the imagination of a priapic, visionary hermit. Naked angels riot with double-headed eagles and fight the fish-people, naked bodybuilders club goatmen, lions are strangled by alligators, ethereal brass bands and Valkyrie cheerleaders helter-skelter across the roofs. A rampant cornucopia of bodacious, perky, muscle-bound, up-for-it nudity.

On the street, the Viennese are the most conservatively buttoned-up, primly polished people in Europe. Just above their heads there are godly roastings and snuff orgies like baroque cartoon thought bubbles. It's no coincidence that Freud came up with the id, the ego and the subconscious in Vienna – it's no coincidence because Freud said there are no coincidences, but it does make you wonder what psychiatry would have been like if he'd lived in Belfast or Belgium. Vienna looks like a city that is always trying to prove something to itself. It lives on civic steroids. Other places had bigger empires, more money, more successful armies, but nowhere ever proclaimed itself to itself with such grandiose ardour. But the most striking and impressive object in Vienna is the simplest and the most modern, and the one I expect the Viennese resent and dislike the most: it's Rachel Whiteread's mordant stone library, which is the memorial to Austria's lost Jews.

Vienna has always been on Europe's turbulent edge, the front line against Ottomans, Huns and columnists. It was a fulcrum, and for all its whiskery probity and pursed-lipped snobbery, it has produced more staggeringly impressive first-flush culture than any other European city – not just music but science, philosophy and art. The secessionists Klimt and Schiele, the writers Joseph Roth, Rilke, Schnitzler (who was imprisoned for the uncompromising sexual play *La Ronde*), and that most Viennese of socialists and utopian essayists, Leopold von Sacher-Masoch, who wrote *Venus in Furs* and painfully gave his name to the world as masochism. Sacher-Masoch: half spanking, half cake – so very Viennese.

Although the buildings are monumental, the city is very human sized. You can walk everywhere. The streets in winter are effulgent with the thick smells of gingerbread and *Glühwein*. The shop windows grin and shimmer with pastries and cakes and chocolates and carmine G-strings. There is a laughable number of lingerie shops with mannequins quite as explicit as the baroque decoration. All Vienna's interiors are terribly overheated, so you see lots of women wearing vast fur coats in the street with plainly very little on underneath.

Despite all its über-civilisation, Vienna's principal gift to humanity is the café. Thanks to the coffee left behind by the Ottomans and the chocolate donated by the Spanish branch of the Hapsburgs. Vienna invented the most perfectly civilised venue in all human culture. Cafés have spread to every corner of the world: from the high Himalayas to the oases of the Sahara you can sit in a café. They are Vienna's gift to all of us. Properly egalitarian, they belong to everyone – you can read a paper, talk bollocks, write a book about alienation or discover an Oedipus complex. Cafés aren't just the transcendent examples of civilisation, they are the crucibles of culture: more great thoughts have been had in cafés than in all the world's universities, and Vienna has the finest and the best.

Demel is perhaps the most famous cake-maker who fought a ridiculous, Roald Dahlist legal battle against the Sacher hotel about who had the original secret recipe for *Sachertorte* – did the apricot jam go under the icing or in the middle? The café has waitresses in old-fashioned black and white uniforms, and glass cases of cakes and pastries that look like jewels. There are jugs of the finest hot chocolate and alpine ranges of whipped cream. It all exudes that slightly spooky feeling of a cautionary fairy tale. You can watch the patissieres wearing floppy chef's hats that no other cook has worn for eighty years, hand-make iced cakes in the shape of naked women – of course – and animals. I watched a girl spend ten minutes getting a white-spotted sugar pig just so. Vienna is one of the last places in Europe where the making of things that are important – like spotted iced pigs – is done to a nostalgic tradition, not a commercial equation.

At the end of the war, the Germans looked at their shattered country and their flattened industry and made the decision to take the American cash and build a whole new economic miracle. It seems that, confronted with the same catastrophe, the Austrians chose instead to rebuild the past, to wrap themselves in the comfort and the glory, the whipped cream and good manners, and the understanding that the best Austria could ever hope for was already behind them and the closer they kept to their history, the better.

Vienna is a city without a future, and that's the way they like it. It's also the way I like it; a marvellous, echoing place of ghosts and white horses and music. And if you come away with anything, it should be the fact that Christopher Plummer isn't now the most famous Austrian. Arnold Schwarzenegger is.

Iceland

(December 2008: after the banks' collapse,
before the Eyjafjallajökull eruption)

In the summer of 1783, there was a volcanic eruption in the south-east of Iceland that vomited lava into the Skafta River, which boiled and ran with fire like a mythological Nordic curse. The volcanic gases were toxic and poisoned animals in their byres. Seething clouds of opaque ash plumed into the sky, blotting the sun. Everything that photosynthesised withered and died. There was a famine that killed a fifth of the population – a fifth of the people who had survived the smallpox epidemic that had previously seen off a quarter of all Icelanders.

So the penury of the Icelandic banking system, the collapse of its currency, the parlous implosion of its economy that relegated it from being, per capita, the second or third richest nation in the world to being the shivering *Big Issue* seller of Europe, bobbing in the queue somewhere behind Albania and Moldova, is not actually the worst thing that ever happened to this island. That would have to be the two occasions when the plague wiped out more than half of everybody. Iceland didn't have any rats, but they got Europe's worst case of bubonic deaths without them. That's unheard of. That's virtually impossible – but that's how Iceland's luck is. It's said you make your own luck; it's never said that your luck also makes you.

Iceland and Icelanders have been forged on the anvil of hard knocks. The unfair thing about this latest paper calamity is that it happened just when they thought things were going so well. There were restaurants that sold food to people who weren't hungry, there were international bars for international folk, there were boutique hotels with ambient music, and candles for smell, not illumination. Iceland was chic and cool, not just in a cold way. 'This summer,' a pretty girl with a red nose and a pink scarf told me, 'everybody was here on a small patch of green in front of the parliament' (which itself is smaller than Elton John's guesthouse). 'We came to cheer and drink, because Iceland had won a silver medal at the Olympics for handball,' she said. 'It was huge. We'd never won a medal before.' Who came first? 'Who cares? We came second. Everything was going so well.'

Reykjavik is littered with the detritus and shells of things that were once going so well and now aren't going at all. Like the big four-wheel-drives, bought on a promise and the never-never. The biggest is a Babel-ish building site, palisaded by protective cranes, which was hoping to be a music hall, the Sydney Opera House of the far, far north. There is still a visitors' centre, with a girl on the phone looking for a new job. There's a toy model of what it is now unlikely to look like. You can peer through a telescope at nobody working. I watched one ancient traffic warden give a ticket to a solitary pick-up, abandoned on a patch of rutted wasteland that was going to be a smart amenity area. This was all financed by Landsbanki, one of the raiding banks that spent like mullered fishermen and borrowed like agoraphobic Vikings, who leveraged the economy into the stratosphere without a Keynesian parachute, along with every other bank in the monetarist world.

The difference here was that, in every other city centre, they can run home to Daddy Government and have their gambling debts paid off. The Icelandic government is a dozen shepherds and a couple of grocers in Specsavers and M&S suits. One of the reasons they say the financial risk was so precipitous was that the entrepreneurial pool is so small. The bankers and the regulators, the ministers and the judges are all the same people – they've known each other all their lives, their wives and their children are friends, and nobody wanted to be the one who said no. And why should they? It was all going so well.

Down by the container port, where the derricks droop idly, is a car pound the size of half a dozen football fields, circled by defunct iron boxes. It's full of hundreds, perhaps thousands, of cars. Behind them, across the grey fjord, black pumice crags are scarred with snow. The cars are going nowhere, dumped here at the end of the world: a great, windswept, conceptual monument to the hubris of Mammon, laughed at by black-backed gulls. These testaments to excess are now the most tasteless things to be seen in. They call the puttering Range Rovers 'Game-Overs'.

Further down the shore is a speculation of modern flats, expensive, insubstantial urban penthouses that may well remain empty for ever. A young man passing by, dressed in the winter uniform of Icelandic youth – skinny jeans, T-shirt with ironic postmodern slogan, Converses and a bit of a useless scarf, hunched shoulders and a general air of thermometer-denial and hungover insouciance – stops and laughs: 'Who did we ever think was going to live here? Now we look back and it seems mad. Anyone could have told them. I could have told them.'

Outside Reykjavik there are suburban developments for new commuter suburbs. They put in roads and street lights but the houses have yet to be built, or stand blankly unfinished. Outside, a little girl plays in the gloaming with her sheepdog. It's a strangely surreal image: the silent cul-de-sac, like a model of the middle American burbs, with just this child, a character snatched from an Edward Hopper painting.

Further along a road called End of the World we find a self-employed electrician. His company is called 'Why Not Me?'. When he has finished here, he is going abroad to find work – 'Poland, probably' – and he smiles a crooked Icelandic smile. It's a joke. There used to be lots of Poles here doing the dirty bits of the economic soft times. Now they have all gone home because the Icelandic krona has become shrapnel in the explosion of free markets.

Kaupthing, Landsbanki and Glitnir sound like characters from *The Lord of the Rings*, and there is an element of fairy-tale come-uppance to these three backwater banks. Only when you're shown their headquarters do you realise how bizarre and unworldly their success was. They look like small city shops, branches of Bradford & Bingley. One of them was run from the floor above a fast-food restaurant. As with every great disaster the world over, the moment after it happened, the scales fell from every eye and all could see that it was inevitable. Where were the white-collar jobs for the commute back from the brave new garden suburbs to come from? Where was the black-tie audience for the opera? How could Iceland have the sharpest cashiers in the world? How could this nation sustain just two main industries: cod-fishing and international high finance? And, most importantly, most damningly, how did they ever think they could buck the Icelandic luck? Now everyone looks back at the road they've just travelled and wonders why none of them mentioned it was made of marzipan and Rolexes.

The act that tipped the last Icelandic bank off the edge of the cliff was delivered by Gordon Brown, who froze Icelandic assets in the UK using our new, gleaming anti-terrorist legislation. The Icelanders mind that – they're hurt by that. You see, they always imagined they were one of us, not one of them. But Gordon needed to do something cheap to look competent, so he beat up a smaller kid. Not just a bit of a slap, but a vicious kicking. Showing off to impress the girls. He would never have started it if the banks had been German or French, or even from Liechtenstein.

The Icelanders mind about the terrorist thing. They don't even have an army. They barely have a jail: it's more of a drop-in centre. The police drive you home if you're too drunk. This is the most liberal, reasonable, hard-working, decent, moral, amusing and well-educated people on the continent; a nation who are temperamentally the furthest away from terrorism. Remember that about Brown – the man who said he wanted to prevent the export of terrorism. Remember it when he puts on his Save the World, Mr International Harmony hat. He put an ally into intensive care for the sake of a headline and three points in a weekend poll. Perhaps he didn't notice. Perhaps he was looking through his glass eye.

Let's just be clear about what Iceland really is. Most people think it's the size of the Isle of Wight with the population of, say, Holland. It's bigger than Hungary, bigger than South Korea, which has a population of fifty million. There are just over 300,000 people in Iceland. So that's a country the size of Portugal with the population of Bradford. Those are Mr Brown's terrorists.

Iceland imagined that Europe and America would help it out. After all, it has always helped us out. Keflavik was a vital NATO base between the east coast of America and the west coast of Europe in the Cold War. We were all in this together. Except, as they were to learn, we were only in it together if we were fat enough to buy ourselves the solution. The Russians bailed Iceland out: Reykjavik could be a very useful place to launder money and cock a snook. And the Faroe Islands, bless them, population 48,000, lent £34 million. Everyone in Iceland signed a thank-you card. And finally the IMF came up with a rescue package.

Oh, but Gordon Brown – or you and me, as he is known abroad – leant on that so that fat, stupid English councils could get their greedy noses in the trough before Icelandic children got a banana. That's not hyperbole – because they have so little foreign currency, imports are graded into three categories: essential, necessary and luxury. Exotic fruit is a luxury, but then in Iceland a tree is an oddity. If you want fruit, eat fish liver or a puffin.

Sitting in the happy, healthy organic cafés of downtown Reykjavik where the hippie kids blog (there are more bloggers here than anywhere else) and girls with blond babies laugh at each other, you wouldn't know this was an economically dead country walking. In the 101, a New York-brittle boutique hotel built and patronised by the bankers and speculators, you couldn't tell that nobody here has a pension or savings. The groups of svelte and confident girls flick their hair, neck cocktails and make blatant passes at the men with face hair like mangy seals who are downing beer and shots. Icelanders react to bad news the way they always have. It's the same way they react to good news; they get hammered. Properly Valhallaed. The bars and clubs are full, the booze is expensive, and they toast each other with a grim irony. There are still redundancy payments around – they're cash-happy. The crunch will come in the New Year when the brass handshakes run out.

People may be hurt by Brown and the British, and embarrassed by the gluttony and ineptitude of their own businessmen, and they are angry with their government. They want an election and someone to be Icelandic enough to grasp the blame and responsibility. But about themselves and the future they are remarkably, Nordically sanguine. A very direct woman in a bar said: 'All that money, all the things and the stuff, it's very un-Icelandic. The wanting, the conspicuous consumption, the avarice and ambition, the pathetic jealousy, that isn't us. A great weight has been lifted now the money and the desires are gone. We can get back to being who we are.'

Who the Icelandics are is one of the great enigmas of northern Europe. They speak an ancient, pure Scandinavian. They are horrifically hard-drinking, maudlin and prone to flights of dark nihilism and lengthy bitterness. They are taciturn fishermen and farmers; stoical, practical and moral. They have published more books and produced more chess grandmasters per head than anywhere else. They read more and write more, they sing and play instruments. Everyone here can change a tyre, strip an engine, ride a horse, sail a boat, dress a sheep and cure a salmon. They have grown through a hard Calvinism to a moral atheism while maintaining an open mind about elves.

Roads are moved to avoid the homes of the hidden people: elves have to be asked permission before new buildings are built, and country folk see them regularly, not always when drunk. The fairy folk who share this empty island with the humans are Adam's other children: the unwanted, cloaked by God in invisibility.

There is also a deep hand-made seam of nostalgia that links all Icelanders. Families are going back to the old ways – to buying the autumn-culled sheep. Traditionally you get an odd number, and the whole family comes to make *slatur*, a sort of fatty haggis sausage that is boiled and tastes like warm, meaty fat. The warming cabinets of convenience stores offer vacuum-packed, ready cooked, laterally sliced halves of sheep's heads, which I'm told are selling like boil-in-the-bag halves of sheep's heads. The women are going back to knitting rough, tarry wool into the mentally geometric jerseys that feel like wearing St Francis's wife-beater. A big second-hand shop has become a smart and fashionable place to shop, though not for anything that is fashionable or smart. The contents are commendably and pathetically meagre and practical. The boxes of second-hand records hum the contradictions of Iceland's long winter. There are lots of romantic choral works, home-grown folk songs from men in third-degree knitting, and heavy metal and prog rock. On the second-hand magazine rack are piles of practical outdoor activity manuals and a copy of *Hello!* commemorating the death of Princess Diana.

The designer interior decorating emporiums that sprung up in the last five years now stand empty and sulky, like party-dressed girls with panda eyes waiting at morning-after bus stops. There's a large new mall on the outskirts of Reykjavik, neon-bright and desolate. The girl who takes me there says, 'A mall – nothing could be less Icelandic than a mall. All this will go', and waves a mittened fist at the prefab warehouses, the new homes and the loneliness of the long-distance car park with its flapping flagpoles, 'and we can stop pretending to be little Americans, or Danes, or British'.

There is something invigorating about Iceland at this moment – like being with people waking from a dream. It's exciting and instructive. It's a patronising cliché to say that people have wealth beyond mere riches. Nobody is better off for being poor. But this tight-knit, undemonstrative community at the edge of the world has been woven together from sterner stuff than I think we could muster. 'We'll be all right – we're not going to starve,' a shopkeeper told me. 'We have fish and rye and mutton and barley. We can grow the odd tomato in a polytunnel. We have skills – useful skills, practical skills. And, you know, they're underheating the pavement outside my shop so it won't freeze in the winter. All our energy is thermal and free. So maybe I can't have a new mobile phone, but when I get drunk and fall over, the pavement will keep me warm.'

From the twelfth century a miraculous thing happened here: one of those eruptions of creating that defy the laws of culture and make civilisations briefly pyrotechnic. A series of books was written to illuminate the dark: sagas, secular stories of life, of mystery and mythology, of lords and farmers, politics and revenge, love affairs and voyages. Stories that were the first to be written as narratives with parabolas of plot and evolving characters. Nobody anywhere else had ever done that before. It is the birth of literature. They are as inexplicably, breathlessly awe-inspiring as the conception of the Renaissance a hundred years later. It was the Icelandic sagas that inspired Tolkien to write *The Lord of the Rings*, because he wanted Britain to retrospectively have a creation myth. Nobody knows what inspired Iceland or what precipitated this volcano of clear, collected genius. It was just Iceland: out there, sparse and treeless.

In the howling gale where the water boils and the volcanoes rumble, and the earthquakes make the ground liquid, and black shores crash and smoke, it is a landscape that fills you with either dread or stories. And it's shared with the hidden people and the heroic solitude, a brooding presence to measure your height against.

Iceland has grasped this weakness, this greed, this business with money, and turned its back to take an unsentimental look at itself. They will be all right. This is the nation that made the first democratic parliament – the Althing – that fought the Royal Navy to make the first sustainable fishery in the northern hemisphere, produced three Miss Worlds and one Nobel literature laureate – then came second at handball. You are measured by how squarely you stand against bad luck. Not how you squander good luck.

Copenhagen

(December 2009: climate-change conference)

Let's be frank. There is far more irritation than inspiration in the whole hot-air, finger-wagging, tooth-sucking, guilty-gifting, mud-slinging, misery-mongering, muesli-munching, fun-puckering green movement. But it's the pleasurable sort of irritation. The kind you want to grumble over and wallow in and pass on to strangers.

'Did you see all the private jets at the airport?' asked the Copenhagen taxi driver, taking me to the biggest, grandest climate-warming conference in the whole world ever (ask the Met Office). 'You must have seen them. They say there are twenty, maybe thirty.' No, I can't say I did. Perhaps they were hidden behind the helicopters, and the Zeppelin, and the space shuttle? And Father Christmas.

Then there's the story of the hundreds of extra-stretched Humvees imported from Germany to ferry the bloated delegates to the divans in the grand auditorium. I never saw anything but clapped-out old Peugeots. The Danes don't go in for ostentation. Most people travel by bus or metro. But don't let that dampen your ire-works.

Collecting and pinning out hypocrisy is a particularly Scandinavian pleasure, especially when environmentalists are involved. Mention the convention and everyone has to start with the joke about the amount of hot air given off. All the CO_2, expended in getting everyone here. 'All those bean-eaters: more farts than a McDonald's beef herd,' chuckled a newspaper vendor. The jokes are as thin as the ice around Greenland.

Granted, a global conference to cut greenhouse gases is a big round oxymoron. But it's also something else. It's a triumph. In the imperial Roman sense. Copenhagen is a victory parade, although it doesn't look like one on the first day, when the world and his delegates turn up at twelve sharp to register their presence.

The Danes, while anally efficient about many things – such as breeding policemen who are a foot taller than the European average and look like blond Chippendales who are pleased to see you but have real guns in their pockets – are immensely lax about some other things. Like signposts, and building an entrance. For the largest ever conference in the world ever, there is no sign, just a couple of cones on a motorway, beside a bit of temporary fencing, under the metro flyover.

The Bella Centre is the only incontestably hideous built thing in Copenhagen. An underconceived, underdeveloped industrial estate. Like the O_2, but without the O. Outside it, there is three hours' worth of queue, vibrating in the Baltic cold. It looks like a dystopian illustration from a children's book that invites us to meet the people of the world. For some reason, the closer to the equator they live, the more the delegates feel the need to wear their national costume. The Indian contingent have all arrived dressed as Nehru and perch their little white food-hygiene hats over knotted scarves and balaclavas. South Sea islanders shiver in borrowed Lap blankets; Africans, stoical as ever, suffer miserably in army greatcoats. One of the small miracles of African life is that they somehow can always find an army greatcoat.

The queue is like an open audition for a global disaster movie, which is not far from the truth. It is entertained – make that annoyed – by a street theatre band banging boxes, chanting 'Greenpeace in da house'. Small street-theatre demos are one of the best arguments for turning up the patio heater and waiting for the sky to turn puce. I'm accosted by one very brave man, the only dissident here: the Solzhenitsyn of dissent. He palms me a pamphlet claiming the global warming is all a conspiracy insti-gated by Prince Philip.

The crowd are surprisingly good-natured, given the great dis-tances and hardships they've had to endure to get to a flyover in Denmark. They slowly edge into a big room where we are sep-arated into further queues, like the branches of a great Amazonian tree, or the triage in a detention centre. A line for NGOs, one for media, for delegates, for the unattributed and one for the United Nations and VIPs. Very ungreen to have VIPs. For many, the queue itself is their first taste of a new age, an eco-cooperative novelty. I watch as a covey of girls from some South American country has the concept of queuing explained, slowly, three or four times, by a polite security guard. They giggle and sigh. I think they believe they are being taught a Viking version of the samba. They face the wrong way until gently turned round.

Standing here for half an hour to get my accreditation, which is all done by Danish schoolgirls with impeccable mockney accents, I realise that I am standing on one of those ley lines of history, a joint in the space-time continuum. I am stepping across an invisible border, balancing, Nureyev-like, on a pivot of a remarkable moment, a moment of moment. This chilly melee is the tipping point. Not the climatic one – more important than that. Copenhagen is where the principle and the process of environmental change and global warming have gone from being the exclamation of a pressure group, and a charity whine, to being the orthodoxy, the accepted wisdom, the mainstream. The environment was outside the big tent. Now it's inside and it makes absolutely no difference what opinion polls or referendums say. It matters naught that the Green party has singularly failed in every democracy. It doesn't matter that they're all as boring and righteous as goodness. It doesn't matter that scientists fake messages and bury statistics, that they do everything in secret. None of this matters now. It doesn't even matter if it's actually going to happen. All that matters is that the people who matter think it matters.

When the heads of nearly every government turn up here to make promises, sign agreements that they will undoubtedly break and fudge and chuckle over and lie about, that's not what's important. They may bounce the cheque, but they won't bounce the reason for writing it. They're on board for global warming.

Global warming is where the momentum is. Global warming is the future. The deniers, the sceptics, are now the crusties, the Swampies, the loonies with the sandwich boards, the swivel-eyed Cassandras. They will, of course, go on complaining and gainsaying, they will pick nits and write books and turn up on late-night cable TV shows. But they're out of the big room. This is the new deal.

Inside the Bella Centre you notice a number of things. First, that the Danish don't make pastries and, second, that there aren't any signs. They don't like to tell you what to do.

I spend three days dazed and lost, aimlessly skidding round thousands of folk in bits of tribal costume sitting in makeshift huddles round the communal computer. Talking endlessly and tapping ancient rhythms into their keyboards. There is a distinct absence of hippies, although there are three Asians dressed as trees. There aren't any ponytails; there are hardly any beards or home-knits or hand-woven things. The people here aren't the ones you see in the demos. They're not wearing Peruvian hats. They haven't shaved up the sides of their heads while drunk and they're not the kids outside doing street theatre.

This is the third generation of eco-warrior. It started with the wild prophets in the 1970s, who wrote books in woad and became hermits in distant wildernesses, listening to Gaia and talking oblivion. And then it was their students, the alternative geeks, the white rastas, the furless models, skinny boys in bands, fashion designers, folk who made cider and grew hemp. But they're all gone. Now there's traction. And it's being made by professionals. The technocrats.

The room is full of thousands of the overqualified, who are softly spoken in four languages. They're the people you find running NGOs and huge charities and UN agencies. The alternative bureaucracy of the world and they're almost all under forty-five. The ecology thing has become too big, too momentous, to be left to romantics with nits. Let them write blogs, build cycle paths. In here, it's about arranging the world economy for the next century.

So big business is here. Car manufacturers, airlines, oil companies. Energy providers. They know which way the wind farm's blowing. They all want to be inside the tent. They understand that environmentalism has edged closer to the axis of power and cynicism. There are untold fortunes to be made in fighting global warming, in technology, innovation, carbon trading, grants and guilt. Guilt is big money. And the people you want as customers are all here: young, clever, savvy, global civil servants. In the southern, developing world, apart from tourists the only people you see on aeroplanes are locals flying to environmental and medical conferences. This is where all the smart cash is, not with the ancient sceptics or deniers. They aren't going anywhere. They're not buying anything. Their only aspirations are to keep everything as it is and win a Test match.

None of this could have happened without the laptop. Everyone here has one; everyone is constantly lit from beneath, like a character from a gothic movie. They call it the green movement because that's what it makes you look like. None of them will ever complain or campaign about the carbon expended on the web, or by search engines, or the resources used in manufacturing laptops, or the wages of the workers who have to make them. These tools are their swords of burning gold, their chariots of fire. The ecology movement was made possible by the web, the blogs and the e-mails and computer modelling. Fifteen years ago, nobody would have been here. That, of course, doesn't mean there's no more paper: there're unfeasible reams of it. Every stall, every nation, every special pleading NGO prints acres and acres of booklets and pamphlets and study documents, all scribbled in a densely illiterate techno-speak. The entire convention is of course plastic-bag free, so they hand out printed and dyed cotton bags instead, which are far more wasteful and damaging and expensive.

In the two main halls (all the rooms are named after famous Danes: the biggest one is Isak Dinesen, who you'll remember had a farm in Africa) the bureaucratic official business creeps along with all the wit, excitement and warmth of a receding glacier. There are the points of order, the bland language of government, the weight of an international organisation being built like a great pyramid, with none of the excitable shouting or enthusiasms of a student demo. The delegates fit in their nationally adopted seats, dying of jet lag, boredom and incomprehension. This for a moment is the world turned upside down, the first are last and the last are first. The developed, industrial, post-colonial world is at the bottom of the pile; the pariahs who must do the most to catch up. On top are the specks of land, the minute and unvisited corners. So let's hear it for the Solomon Islands, the Marshall Islands, Tuvalu and Togo.

Few things infuriate quite as much as the constant reference to indigenous people. Everyone has to say indigenous people at least once in every statement. I fight the urge to put up my hand and shout: Please, sir, can you point out those that are not indigenous persons? Which of us is a dis-indigenous human? Which the Caliban-bastard, unconnected to even a square foot of this earth? The patronising of indigenous people is hideous. Indigenous, of course, means pre-historic, ancient, pettable. The indigenous are spoken of like endangered hominids elevated to the iconic status of pandas and polar bears. Their pictures, in colourful Victorian anthropological outfits of fur, feather and face paint, grace every stall and poster. Because we're up north, Eskimos abound in kayaks, hunting with spears, something they haven't done in a generation. Eskimos hunt with rifles in plastic boats with outboard motors, wearing North Face parkas. The reason polar bears are scarce in Greenland is not because the ice is melting so much as they are being shot to shreds by unemployed Inuit with nothing better to do.

One of the things that is most depressing and disturbing about this whole green thing is that they seem to have no sense of taste at all. They don't care what they eat, they don't care what they wear and they don't care what's on the walls. They have no concept of their own culture, only of other people's, which they revere without criticism, grabbing bits and pieces of primitive pattern, handprint and rock carving. All the delegates are dressed appallingly in Lego shoes and flappy fibrous urban survival gear, sporting that old school tie of liberal sensibility, the ethnic scarf. Even communism and fascism managed to translate their philosophies into an aesthetic. The green movement is just too crap and shabby and unimaginative. It doesn't have time. It doesn't think it's worth it. It's too glued to its models and its blogs to even make up some decent protest music. No art: nothing but some sadly punning slogans and the most uninspired, turgid and solipsistically verbose writing.

But, despite that, what makes the green movement triumphantly successful is that it has the most important and precious of things: it has a story. It is telling us our own saga, the adventure of saving the world. This has all the elements of a great myth, the impossible trials, the dragons and giants to be defeated, the magic seeds to be found, the wells and fountains of health and youth, the band of brothers, the implacable enemy. The princesses to be rescued. The kingdoms to be won.

If you look at the global warming debate as simply the first draft of the first new creating myth to be invented in thousands of years, then you see why it's irresistible. Who wouldn't want to be part of their own fairy tale?

Maldives

You don't expect palm trees in Copenhagen, but the place was lousy with them – palm trees and rainforest. Palm trees, rainforest and Samburu herdsmen. Actually, the Samburu didn't look too happy, shivering in the blustery northern twilight along with the Keralan fruit farmers. Last year's climate change conference brought all the delicate and sensitive bits of the planet – the people who dress in blankets and feathers – together in a sort of dystopian theme park, with sneezing and cardigans and complaining. It was odd to walk through the halls of hot air and be confronted by a Korean dressed as a whale, or a Solomon Islander done up like a Florida real-estate agent.

The undoubted Mickey Mouse of this Disneyland of extinction was Mohamed Nasheed. The name may not be instantly recognisable, but if you're a change-spotter, then you'll know him as the first eco rock star. He is the president of the Maldives, and among the alpha males of the political world who dropped into Denmark this slight, telegenic man stole the spotlight. He led the '1.5 group' – a collection of island nations that will drown if the temperature rises by more than two degrees. He has a natural PR's ability to grab a photo and sew a headline. He held a cabinet meeting underwater, had his desk moved out into the surf.

The Maldives is a long atoll of more than a thousand bits of exploded volcano, which lie like pale whales with only their backs above water. They are as vulnerable and endangered as a white tiger in a Chinese chemist. We are pushing them under by the way we live.

That, of course, is the hot dichotomy of the Maldives; the irony, the contradiction, the fly in the ointment. Its position on the edge of the world becomes clear. What is sinking the nation is carbon emissions. What's keeping it afloat is the carbon emissions of tourists. Dropped by vast, pregnant, intercontinental jumbos, these are folk with the sootiest footprints on the planet. The queue for customs is about as ecologically aware as the cosmetics department at Harrods. But you must be aware. You should understand. This is not hypocrisy. This isn't cake and eat it; it isn't doing one thing and saying another. This is the rock and the hard place brought together. A nation in the middle of nothing, next to nowhere.

Before the international hotels came, the Maldives' main industries were dried tuna, exported to Sri Lanka, and the RAF base on the island of Gan. Sushi and bombs isn't exactly the green option, and there is nothing else for the Maldives to do except make coconut matting, so it has to be tourism.

I'd been before, twenty-five years ago, when they'd just opened for tourism. Then you had to stop over in Sri Lanka, and it was all rather dull and youth hostelly, with awful international food: stroganoff flown in from Singapore. Now you fly direct to Malé, the capital, then go on, by boat, to your choice of island. This time I and the Blonde and our pair of two-year-olds are staying on Reethi Rah. It's a resort that goads PRs into the most ecstatic, hallucinogenic brochure clichés: 'Barefoot luxury', an awful oxymoron that manages both to insult the barefoot and to devalue luxury, trips lightly from many tongues. There are clouds of euphonious ways of saying 'Relax, unwind, let go, de-stress, chill out'. There is a holiday island tropical assumption that people who do lots and lots of nervy, shouty business in the First World need to go to the Third World and listen to birdsong and panpipes to stop. The assumption continues that the more tightly wound your life is, the further you need to travel to untangle it. Oddly, my experience of the very rich is that, back home, they do very, very little. One of the universal talents shared by all successful plutocrats is an ability to delegate stress with a beatific nonchalance. They don't even carry their own bags or children.

Reethi Rah is an astonishing place. I've sat on a lot of desert islands, and, after ten minutes, the expectation and assumption evaporate into the experience of sandflies, trade winds and rotting seaweed – all of which is overcome by a desperate, wrist-sawing boredom. Reethi Rah, though, is somewhere else. Reethi Rah is what God would have made if he hadn't already found a home for heaven. It has a spookily ethereal quality, as if it's hiding something. Perhaps, underneath it, a James Bond villain is building a space rocket. Maybe it's the set of a huge, elaborate reality porno movie. This is somewhere else because it never used to be here. It wasn't a place at all until someone decided to build a hotel.

The Maldives is a tiny atoll in very deep water. Nothing much lives here, except for the questing ghost crabs. They've imported an ideal of a holiday – shipped in thousands and thousands of tons of sand like sugar icing, planted a nirvana of palm trees and tropical flowers to make the jungle from a children's book, dappled and neat and friendly.

Our room is a house. It comes with all the largesse and effortful detail that people who travel without carrying anything demand: three sorts of incense, a butler (I asked the butler: what's the first thing most people ask a butler for on a desert island?' Internet access, he said, of course) – and one hundred channels of TV, movies on demand and two fridges, with three sorts of water from three continents.

Water is a concern here – the island has its own desalination plant, its own generator, its own waste disposal and seven hundred staff, hidden like Japanese soldiers in the Rousseau-like jungle. We have his and her bikes and a golf buggy, and through the big French windows, beyond my personal dining area, over my own black swimming pool, across the personal beach with its hammock and outdoor thatched post-perambulatory double bed, is my very own bit of ocean. There are three restaurants – they've improved the food. An alfresco Lebanese, quite as good as the Edgware Road; a Japanese restaurant on stilts where Roy Scheider-sized nurse sharks glide through the floodlit water at your feet. In the main dining room they bake bread from around the world and think juicing is an art. There is a sweet, sweaty, pallid Irish chef who serves the sort of food the unwinding entitled expect; the exotic and the rare made accessible and polite, with the crusts cut off. There is a health spa that could service a Premier League football team and a Brazilian brothel. Half the guests are Russian, paunchy and determined men with defensive eyes, aggressive hair and holiday clothes that have been bought by assistants who don't like them. Most of them have lady friends whose second names they haven't yet grasped. These girls undulate in slicing and engorged bikinis and survey through predator glasses their new partners and everyone else in the way that undertakers look at old people.

The rest of us are the usual dumb smattering of slack-jawed, bruised and carpet-burned honeymooners, made incoherent by sex and the dawning realisation that this is the only sex they're ever going to have, a few happy pensioners who've cashed in the insurance and international CEOs with their pterodactyl second wives.

I've realised I'm not making this sound very alluring. It is actually blissful, but surreal. A sort of avatar bliss, conjured from a thousand concierges' suggestions, designed to be the evocation of hot Valium, a set of a play that nobody can be bothered to write. There is nothing to see, nothing to be anywhere for. I imagined I was going to write a book, make busy. But the laptop sleeps in its neoprene case, and I lie in the hammock and swing and sleep.

One day, I stepped off the sandy path into the woods – a thing you're never supposed to do in a children's book, and there found long greenhouses growing miles and miles of orchids, to be beheaded and nonchalantly strewn in scented baths and on courtesans' pillows. It was strangely distressing.

If you lie here on a hammock, you can watch a man slowly walk the beach, pulling a rake. He's doing outdoor housework, stroking the sand into a herringbone pattern, and you can wonder at the yin and yang of tourism, consuming the thing it protects.

I cast my mind back to Copenhagen. All those chilly activists in their Peruvian hats demanding change, a new frugality, the end of capitalism and progress, rationing and hobbling, demanding with a shrill sadness that we do it now to save the pristine, azure scatter of the Maldives. This island is really not what they had in mind.

Arctic

Cold. We spend our lives getting out of it, away from it; our whole human history has been spent avoiding it, wrapping up against it, fighting and escaping it. Cold shoulders, cold stares; vengeance is cold, corpses are cold. Who wants to be cold? Hot is good, hot bodies, hot dinners, hot sex and holidays. Hot or cold is no sort of choice, except for some, the contrary, chilly few for whom the very, very cold has a clear and harsh allure. The cold places of the world have a troll's call; they give us goose pimples, those frozen lands, the keening of the north wind. And they're going. By popular demand, the heat is winning. The cold retreats, melts before our eyes. We need to feel it while stocks last.

So when someone asked, did I want to go to the Arctic, I said yes, absolutely yes, before they could add – 'camping'.

It's all about the kit. The finding it, the losing it, the lists, the sizing, the ordering, the web hunts, the unpacking, the trying on, the taking off, the mirror work, the turning and flexing, the thumb and forefinger testing, the folding and packing, the little piles and secret stashes, the stuff in the corner of my office that grows and grows like a glacier of wool and feathers, Gore-Tex and Velcro.

People who travel to destinations without room service or flushing toilets get fixated by kit. What they talk about is not vistas or customs or ruins or trails, but socks and torches. Unwrap any explorer and you'll discover a closeted closet obsessive. And while the rainforests and oceans, the deserts and savannas all make their demands on packing, nothing and nowhere compares to the top and tail of the world. Nowhere demands the propitiation of kit like the cold. And few places are as cold as Svalbard.

I happened to bump into Sir David Attenborough. I don't know David well, but, like the rest of you, I think I do. 'I'm going to Svalbard,' I said, and instead of glowing enthusiastically, a shadow of alarm crossed his familiar face.

'Really?' he whispered. 'It's very cold now. Very, very cold. Why are you going there?'

'To look for polar bears,' I answered, like a perky Cub Scout.

His eyebrow twitched: 'Polar bears are dangerous, you know, really quite dangerous. And the thing about extreme cold is everything is fine until it's not. You walk along and it's okay, but lose a glove and you'll lose your hand.'

'Thanks for the tip. Where are you off to next?'

'I'm going home – Richmond.' And he went.

Along with the clothes list – longer than the one I had for boarding school – I was told I'd need fitness level four. I had no idea there were Michelin stars for aerobic muscles, so I asked what sort of activity a four would normally expect to undertake. Someone e-mailed back, tersely: 'Five would expect to climb Everest.' So I packed my gear in my new waterproof North Face bag and, with Tom the photographer, staggered to Heathrow feeling about a two and a half.

It takes some time to get to Svalbard. You fly to Oslo and from Oslo to Tromsø, which is a very long way north, then again from Tromsø for an hour and a bit, until you find Longyearbyen, on the island of Spitsbergen. Longyearbyen is named after an American, Mr Longyear, who bought a coal mine here. Spitsbergen is the Dutch name given to it by the explorer Barons who discovered the place and died up here. Svalbard is the Norwegian name for this collection of islands. It means 'cold coast'.

When Norwegians call something cold, it's not just parky. This is the furthest north anyone lives permanently. This airport is the most northerly runway. This is 78 degrees north – the Pole is 90 degrees. Above us there are only a few seals, walruses, a huddle of scientists, a couple of hunters, and one or two eager public schoolboys lugging sledges on behalf of cats' homes. Svalbard was too hardcore even for Eskimos.

There are no indigenous people here. This is where we met the rest of our team: a pair of identical twins – extreme adventure journalists from Idaho, Kit and Kody (one took pictures, the other wrote, and I never worked out which did which); Craig, a Californian banker in his mid-fifties whose solitary hobby is taking pictures of big predators; Anastasia, a nineteen-year-old Siberian fashion student; David, a Taiwanese-American businessman; Chai Chai, an enthusiastic and excitable Thai electronics executive; and Florie, a petite PR who is a perky Pollyanna. Then there's Max, our grizzled Swedish polar bear expert, and two Norwegian guides. 'Oh, my God,' hisses Tom, 'this is the cast from a seventies disaster movie.' We do make an incongruous and possibly doomed group, standing in the foothills of our new kit. We have all come to be guinea pigs, or perhaps lemmings, to camp in the wilderness where nobody has been fool enough to holiday before.

Longyearbyen is built on stilts, out of attractively functional Scandinavian kit houses that hover above the permafrost, ready to run away if things get really bad. The town huddles in a valley between precipitous hills at the head of a fjord. There's a small church, a university, a couple of hotels, a supermarket, some shops selling serious, gritty kit and chewing tobacco and, bizarrely, a bewildering variety of liquorice.

The town is dominated by an impressively menacing chimney that blows elegant smoke into the clear air. Longyearbyen's reason for being was the coal that's now too expensive to export, and just heats and lights the town. Across the hillside, the black derricks that once carried the coal cradles to the port straddle the hills. There is a cemetery containing the permanently frozen bodies of sailors who died in the great flu pandemic of 1918–19, and there is a war memorial inscribed with the obligatory British names. This place was flattened by German battleships and was home to lonely radio operators listening to the static voices drifting up from a distant war.

Svalbard had a disengaged relationship with the rest of the world. Before the 1920s, when Norway gained control, it had been no-man's-land, visited only by whalers and explorers. It's not covered by the Schengen Treaty, and anyone can come to live here. After Norwegians, the second most popular nationality in Longyearbyen is Thai – a couple of families who work in hospitality. Nobody is actually from here: babies are born on the mainland. Everyone's here by choice, happenstance or despair – people who love extremes, people who want to ski into the nothingness. Flags are all at half-mast here. I wondered if it was for the skier killed in an avalanche the day before. No, said our guide, it was for the teenage girl who killed herself. There are a lot of suicides: the absence of light, the relentless weather. Svalbard is the end of the line, the suburb at the edge of the habitable world. But for me, on a visit, it's more exciting than a month of white Christmases. I lie in my little hotel room, oddly and sparsely decorated with pictures of past mayors, and stare out at the blinking northern sky, sleepless with anticipation.

The next day, we're taught how to get dressed. I thought I'd had this down as second nature for five decades. Apparently not. This was like the stewardess's safety instructions, except we were all concentrating. So this is what I had to get into to go out: two pairs of longjohns, one thin, one thick, both merino wool; one thin merino vest; one waffled wicking Patagonia T-shirt; one zip-up thick merino jersey; two pairs of merino socks – one thin, one thick; one pair of ski tights; man-made trousers; one pair of down-filled waterproof overtrousers with braces; a down waistcoat, a down Arctic parka with a tunnel hood and coyote-fur trim; a pair of Baffin boots the size of two garden sheds, with removable silver thermal inner slippers; a thin sex offender's balaclava; a thick Captain Scott balaclava; silk inner gloves – important, these, because anything metal that you touch outside with your bare hands will take the tops of your fingers off – and huge mittens on a string, like in infant school. Wear gloves with fingers and you'll lose yours down to the knuckle. Finally, a hat, made by my mate Eggert in Iceland out of sea otter, with fox-fur flaps. I have UV-protected glasses so dark it's illegal to drive in them, and getting dressed is like preparing for some murderous sport crossed with a workout at the gym. But I only have to do it the once. For the next week most of this stays on. In the Arctic, nobody can smell you. Except the polar bears.

The laws of thermodynamics insist that all the heat we're going to get we have to make ourselves. These layers, overlapped, buttoned, zipped, laced and double-stitched, are to make sure we leak as little as possible. We are heat misers. But overheating is as dangerous as freezing. If you sweat and the sweat freezes, you die, or bits of you turn black and die on their own. It's a constant fiddle of ventilating and battening down, a bit like being half man, half Aga.

We get our snowmobiles, which are motorbikes on skis. A snowmobile is easier to drive than a shopping trolley, and as difficult to steer, and far easier to flip over. I hate motorbikes, but swap tarmac for snow and they're spectacular fun. Svalbard has more snowmobiles per capita than anywhere else on earth. Locals drive with a hell-for-sealskin nonchalance, Nordic easy riders with rifles slung in holsters at their sides. You're not allowed to leave town without a gun. If you don't have one, you can rent it at a local shop.

The day is blue and white, the shadows purple and pink. The air sparkles with the diamond dust of fine ice crystals. As we speed through the long valley out of town into the wilderness, we quickly learn the limits of kit: even the faintest sliver of exposed skin is frostbitten in minutes. And while your breath freezes on your balaclavas, man-made material wicks moisture up under your goggles, where it instantly freezes, blinding you. I discover with joy that the mittens I've tracked down to an Alaskan website called Midnight Mushing, which look like black crab claws and have special nose-wipe patches, are far and away the best. My hands are constantly warm. Everyone else has to count their fingers.

We stop on a frozen seashore, boulders of wind-scarred ice caught in a freeze-framed ocean. Opposite, spotlit in a shaft of sun, is a great cathedral, an icy temple. This is a place of solemn grandeur, a landscape of high nineteenth-century romance. We get off our machines and the world is suddenly still and silent, but we are not quite alone. At our feet are tracks – crisp and sharp and not yet smudged by the wind. Polar bear. They are huge. I place my black cartoon hand in one. It looks like a child's. This foot is the size of a hubcap. The Norwegians pull out their rifles. The steps trace across this bluff above the frozen sea. You can sense the silent padding, feel the deliberate gait, imagine the swaying head with the most sensitive nose of any mammal. A polar bear can smell a human across fifteen miles of wilderness.

The next day, we start early, pulling sledges steepled with tents and sleeping bags, cooking utensils, dried food and a toilet seat. We leave the town in a single file past moss-digging reindeer, and point towards the east. Five hours through valleys, traversing moraine fields, round mountains and down passes so steep they feel like fairground rides, where to lose your nerve and tug the brake is to risk being thumped on the back of the head by a hundredweight of kit. Across a glacier, we arrive at a short, blind valley on the coast in the early evening and set up camp. As we begin to unpack, the weather starts to close down, the wind gusts, the sky seems to free-fall, the white closes in. We put up the tents in a hurry. There's nothing fancy about them – standard two-person Glastonbury jobs that only keep out wind and snow. Tom and I dig out a basement: somewhere to store the bags and stand in to change clothes. Fixing camp is a race against the wind and the tumbling barometer. You need your fingers to work, but they instantly freeze, and the silk gloves are shredded on Velcro, unquestionably the invention of a cold devil. There is already a mess tent here, a portable Russian poly-hut made of two layers of plastic sheet. Inside are two tables, a couple of benches, a minute cooking area, a paraffin stove and parallel washing lines strung at head height. It's 12ftx10ft and held down by hawsers. The last thing we put up before the light goes is the tripwire fence attached to explosives.

The best defence against bears are dogs: dogs bark, bears stay away. But we're here to see bears, so we haven't brought dogs. A rifle hangs outside the mess hut.

We grab a hot supper and go to our tents to sleep inside a down sleeping bag inside another down bag. I wear a New Zealand possum-down hat and, before exhaustion hits, read with a head torch a couple of pages of Icelandic sagas: 'I ask you, unblemished monks' tester, to be the ward of my travels. May the Lord of the peaks' pane shade my path with his hawk's perch.'

We have to zip our heads into the bag: anything exposed gets flayed in the night. The temperature inside the tent is much the same as the temperature outside. Cold turns toothpaste into minty cement, snaps the glue-binding of books, drains batteries; it's as cold as rejection, as cold as infidelity, as cold as loneliness. It's colder than any of us have ever been before. It freezes the back of your throat, scours your eyes and welds hard bogies up your nose. It burns skin with the pain of a branding poker.

In the morning, the inside of the tent has a thin layer of snow created from our breath. The wind is sparring with these new blots on its pristine landscape, clearing its throat with a bad temper, muttering runic threats and warnings, but it never manages to drown out Tom's snoring. The barometer unravels, and the temperature leaves the mercury standing in a pool at the bottom of the thermometer. The wind gets into its stride and the world goes white. You can't see 5ft in front of your nose. The snow is a heaving, undulating, living thing. It feels as if the surface of the earth is sloughing its skin. It eddies and spews like a hard river in spate. It carves out a new landscape; where there was hard ice yesterday, now there is a 6-ft drift. We constantly sink up to our hips. Anastasia the Siberian asks how anywhere can have weather this bad.

So we sit in the little mess tent, thirteen souls listening to the weather, imagining that it's getting a little brighter for one day, then two days, playing chess, reading, making up quizzes: the capital of Moldova, three famous Norwegians, three famous Finns, how I lost my virginity, how I met my wife. We are like foxes in a den, or blocks in a Rubik's Cube – if one moves, we all have to move. And we talk about our bowels.

Going to the lavatory is a serious expedition. About 20ft from the mess tent is a flapping plastic box, the sort of thing navvies put over holes in the road. Inside is the collapsible lavatory seat.

You wait till the last possible moment – to the point of colonic no return – then grab a biodegradable plastic bag, inform the room that you're just going outside and may be some time, which never ceases to raise a smile, and stumble through the white wind to the little bivouac, and dig in the snow for the paper, which isn't wet, because only defrosting snow is wet, and begin to pull off the woolly layers with stinging fingers. 'How did you go to the loo?' everyone asks. The answer is: very, very quickly indeed. There was a peeing stick for the men to piss against, instantly buried. The little holes in the snow grow from a healthy straw colour to deep, renal ochre as we take on less and less liquid.

The snow pours down the valley, burying the snowmobiles, sidling up the tents. It pushes through the flaps, fills our basement, hides the baggage, blankets, sleeping bags. In the mess hut we sit and make up new dishes. Mine is best: cocoa with Tabasco. The weirdest is porridge with brown boiled cheese and red jam, which turns out to be what Norwegian children eat for breakfast. The room is padded with piles of coats, dripping sealskin mittens and reindeer skin. The washing lines sag with gloves and balaclavas, scarves and hats; the room is a slow Mexican wave looking for lost kit, lit by head torches, candles and the paraffin stove. Shadows flicker, faces glow, we tell more stories, the floor beneath us melts into pools, our socks steam.

Aerden the Norwegian mentions that he skied across Greenland. Even by Arctic endurance standards, that's impressive: Greenland has four time zones. 'What was it like?' We settle down for a saga. 'It's flat, it's white. On the seventeenth day, a small bird came to my tent. I fed it. It flew away, and I went on.' That's it? That, apparently, was it.

On the third night, the temperature drops again. The wind grows Wagnerian. We sing songs, play nursery games with folded paper. Anastasia draws constantly. Tom takes pictures. We tell travellers' tales. The light dances, the time passes. Outside, the weather is an animal, prowling and roaring, intractable, vicious, relentless. We sit in our dripping burrow. There is nobody to come and get us, no helicopter or snowplough. There is no plan B, nothing to do, nothing to be done – the wind and cold have wrested all control. There is a calm in the detention; the imperative of getting on, of making a decision, is all blown away. We can only sit it out. The world has been possessed and shredded down to a few feet. This is all we have. In this wilderness, this is all we are.

That night, the snow buckles the tent struts. It presses in on us like concrete. I lie and watch it creep up the walls. The wind now sounds like an express train wrapped in cellophane. It comes from afar, bellowing and crackling, and gusts past at 30 or 40 knots. The tent shakes and flaps with an animate, mortal agony. We sleep fitfully.

Around 3 a.m. I hear someone digging outside. Aerden's head appears. 'Get out,' he says, 'Get out now. Bring what you can carry.' We're about to be entombed. The Norwegians' tent has also gone. We all fit into the mess tent and sleep for a couple of hours. As the dawn comes up, the snow relaxes into its hard-edged serpentine architecture. The blizzard has blown its full, and we've lost thirteen snowmobiles, eleven sledges, two tents.

Between us we have three collapsible spades. Because of the days spent crouched and supine, everyone grabs the physical work with a joyful eagerness, and we manage to dig them all out from under 6ft of snow. Watching the excavation of my tent is strange. Seeing my belongings pulled out of an ancient grave – a pillow, a book, my possum hat – I expect to see myself lifted out, rigid in the bag.

Now we have a choice: we can abandon the camp and make the trip back to Longyearbyen that will take twelve, possibly fourteen hours, or spend another rough night here and go for the coast – have one cast for the white bear. It's unanimous.

The next morning, we set off in single file. The land and sky are the same pale polar hue. There is no horizon. For an hour it looks as if we're rising through clouds, ascending to heaven like Valkyries. The coast is spectacular. The air clears, the curtains are pulled back, the landscape is revealed in all its vast, sublime harshness. Great crags of blue, shimmering ice, granite boulders cast aside by glaciers, distant, serrated shores over a sea held in parentheses by ice. Fulmars fly with us, the albatrosses of the northern waste and harbingers of spring, skimming the still billows to glean some meagre thermal. And there's a cliff-full of black guillemots, flinging themselves about our heads with furious precision.

This is an epic landscape, a land of saga, of awe, of romantic vision. Late in the afternoon, the Swedish expert points across the wide, hard dunes of ice, the humpback granite, the frozen rubble of the sea. We follow his finger, squinting into the distance, and there is a dot, a lone exclamation, moving slowly across the ice. It's him. The *isbjörn*, the ice bear, old-tooth yellow against the land, three hundred yards away.

The binoculars quarter the distance. A large male out hunting. He surfs the frozen waves on enormous feet, head carried low – listening for seals under the ice, listening to the wind, listening to the rhythmic crunch of snow under his claws, listening to his breath, tasting the air. Polar bears are the most solitary animals on earth. These males are shunned by all living things, including their own kind. They seek no solace in company, no warmth in togetherness. Mary Shelley sent Frankenstein's misbegotten monster to this distant vastness. This bear is the parable at the end of the world. Lord of the bleak, haunting, sighing silence, listening to the loneliness.

Polar bears aren't rare: they're not like black rhinos or giant pandas, tigers or beluga sturgeon. There are more polar bears than there are Starbucks. They won't become extinct – not like the quagga, the thylacine, the passenger pigeon or the great auk. They'll be bred and kept in gated communities. The polar bear is rare in Greenland, where the Inuit hunt them to oblivion, but there are overpopulation problems in parts of the American Northwest. In Churchill, Alaska, they'll come right up to a tour bus. And the best view you'll ever get will be on telly. What is rare, what is memorable, is to see them in this landscape.

The ice bear has become the symbolic mascot of the shrinking cold, its life irrevocably entwined with the receding ice and glacier, this pale land that is melting away. The bears now have to look longer and further afield for the seals, their marginal lives even more marginal. Two bears turned up in Iceland last year – that's a big swim from Greenland. 'What happened?' I asked the Icelander who told me. 'We shot them, of course.'

Polar bears aren't particularly interesting biologically. Their fur is hollow; they have an unusually short gestation for such big animals, giving birth under the snow to semi-formed, bald, blind cubs that must find a nipple to cling to instantly or be recycled. They are the only wholly carnivorous bear, but they'll probably adapt. Bears have been successful because they're adaptable. They can – and as temperatures rise, more frequently do – meet and mate with grizzly bears. And the offspring in turn can breed, which questions whether polar bears are in fact a true species. But that's not the point. It's a traveller's truism that how you make the journey is more important than where you end up, and that all destinations are just stops on one long journey. What is really important is who you travel with and who you meet on the way. And to go through the top of the world without the polar bear would be a great and emblematic loss.

We spent an hour walking with this big old bear, travelling part of the way with him. Even now, I have the sense of him up there beyond my horizon, on that blasted shore, sniffing the chill, padding through the ice, hearing the cry of the fulmar. We are still on our journeys, separated by 12 degrees of distance, and 58 degrees of temperature, parallel but apart.

Haiti

(April 2010: after the earthquake)

Children's wards in emergency hospitals don't get any easier. Knowing what to expect just makes it worse. But I've learnt not to talk. You just can't trust your voice. And don't let them see you choke. The one thing they really don't need is any more expensively imported Western tears. The tented wards of this make-do hospital are pitched in the courtyard of an old concrete and brick one that was untouched by the earthquake, perhaps protected by the little icon of the Virgin Mary. The sick and injured won't go back inside. They're terrified of another shock, of being trapped in their beds under this sorry, suspended, crushing weight. So it hangs empty.

Outside is the Cité Soleil, on the edge of Port-au-Prince, which was, even before the earthquake, the worst place on earth to be a child. This corrugated slum, built of slime and shit, with its open veins of infectious effluent, is also, by a fathomless irony, shaken but unshriven by the hand of God. It still sprawls triumphant, in all its malignant, blighted horror.

The maternity tent is a mixed, sweet and salt place. Babies are all blessings, tokens of hope, and most mothers lie on their little camp beds, safe for the moment in the bubble of relief and joy that birth brings. But this is no time or place to be an infant or a new mother. Most of these women have lost family, their own mothers, and have no homes to return to. A woman sits, bent and shrouded in misery, on her lap a tiny sprite of a thing, baggy in its own skin. His eyes flutter, head lolls, too heavy for the spindly neck. I've seen this before, this mite, havering in the doorway of life. A doctor whispers that he has hydrocephalus. An hour or so away, in Florida, they'd fit a pipe in his head and drain the liquid. 'But we can't do it here, and, anyway, he'd need regular medical help over years. That isn't available.' His prognosis? The doctor shrugs. The little heart pounds in its chest, the stubborn breath stretches the ribs. Only when it's hopeless, when death waits impatient in the corner for the final count, do you truly comprehend how tenaciously fierce, how brave the imperative mechanics and the vital spark of life are. In the cot next to the dying child is a bright little boy wedged between cushions. He has huge eyes and beams up at me, holding out his arms. 'He likes to be hugged,' says a Belgian logistician. 'He trusts everybody. He was left in a rubbish bin.' A Haitian rubbish bin, a post-apocalyptic cess-skip. He was missing a finger. 'Probably eaten by rats', which is not as nightmarishly rare as you might think. Rats come in the night and eat toes, fingers, sometimes noses. He is about nine months old.

This isn't a newly unwanted child – not a guilty secret or a family sin. Someone looked after this little lad for as long as they possibly could, and then in the midst of horror, of death and the earth-moving despair, they made him rubbish. He chuckles and stretches his hands out to me, and I know that if I pick him up it will be impossible to ever put him down again. What have you called him, I ask. 'Herod.' Say that again? 'Herod.' You named this child after the man who ordered the murder of the innocents? There is no tragedy so utter that a Belgian, with the best will in the world, can't make worse.

This earthquake was a women's tragedy. It was, of course, a nation's tragedy, but it leant particularly heavy on women. There are no figures, but it seems that more women died than men. It was the time of day, the late afternoon, women were at home cooking, making the children's tea, when the sky fell. In the amputees' wards my rough count finds twice as many women as men, and the hospitals are beginning to see an increase in the number of rape victims. There is a lot of muttered gossip about the vulnerability of girls, their families smashed, orphaned, foisted on neighbours and distant relatives in overcrowded camps, themselves mostly built and maintained by women, who still do all the washing, cleaning and cooking and protect the young. On the benches, women wait to see the doctor. Quiet and serene, they hold each other's hands and mantle wan children with their arms, hard, capable fingers resting in laps, their faces ironed by grief, set with a brutal resolve. There's something else I've seen before that's difficult to explain; there is a terrible, calm beauty in calamity.

I was last in Haiti for its despairing bicentennial in 2004. It was the most frightening place I'd ever been to. I was gassed, shot at, threatened with voodoo zombies; there were bodies in the streets. I watched the army beat up students, and a lad was shot and killed in a gang fight in front of me. The streets were run by trucks of thugs and murderers known as the *chimères*. It's said they answered to President Aristide, a one-time Catholic priest who was rumoured to use voodoo practices to hold on to power. The place seethed with fury and lashings of violence. It wasn't anarchy. Anarchy implies a philosophy, a rough purpose. It was a howling chaos. The one belief that united most Haitians was the conviction that the country was, and always had been, cursed. As I left, I thanked God I'd never have to come back to this bleak and benighted place. Be careful what you're grateful for – you may get seconds.

The new airport is a surly chaos of duffel bags and boxes. Most of the people milling helplessly appear to be groups of American fundamentalist Christians. There are a lot of kids on God-sanctioned adventures dressed in African safari gear and T-shirts proclaiming their goodness. They are excited and crass. The other half are Haitians returning home to find family, to pick through rubble, bringing money and blankets and CD players. We were held up on the runway in Miami for three hours; a group of excited Baptists passed huge bags of beef jerky over the heads of the people they were coming to offer holy succour to.

The fenced-off airfield is a vast dump of stuff: military tents, warehouses, helicopters and equipment. There are hundreds of charities here, NGOs, international bodies, thousands of workers, volunteers, professionals, some more useful than others. They all need beds, food, water, Western sanitation. The first concern of all these organisations is the health and safety of their members –

an enormous amount of the logistics is used to support the pur-
veyors of logistics and the mongers of prayer.

The American army and the UN police and peacekeepers sit
behind their barbed wire, maintaining themselves with a bored,
grumpy, fat indolence, occasionally motoring up the road in
armoured personnel carriers and mirrored Ray-Bans. They don't
go to the plastic and tarpaulin cities if they can help it. And they
can help it most of the time.

At first sight, Port-au-Prince looks remarkably as I remember
it – even before the disaster it was the crumbliest, most backward
and pitiful capital in the western hemisphere. As we get into
town, I start to notice the collapsed buildings. Tectonic plates are
capricious in their choices. Random houses fall in on themselves;
their neighbours remain upright. Buildings pushed on to their
sides split open to reveal the eerily empty dollhouse rooms of
domestic probity. Rubble spews into the street in great emetic
mounds. Electric cables swag the traffic, supermarkets, offices,
hotels, the presidential palace, cathedrals, all rent and laid low by
Haiti's geology. On hillsides, the poorest breeze block and concrete
homes have collapsed into forlorn heaps, throwing up pathetically
mutilated furniture, ragged, bright clothes, crockery, shoes, shattered ornaments, kitchen utensils, shredded books and fluttering
photographs of the dead, all like a bitter harvest of chattels. It
looks so insignificant. So undramatic. So bereft of gravitas and
dignity – just annoying rubble. The air is hot and heavy with
moisture, stiff with the stench of rot and dung, and sometimes
you stumble into the sickly-sweet stink that is unforgettably a
corpse. The smell of departed souls, the gagging odour of sanctity.
Bodies still lie entombed under slabs. Nobody knows how
many.

Just to get this straight, lest we forget, this is the greatest, most
cataclysmic disaster of the modern era. The worst natural organic
event since the demise of Christ. The official death toll is somewhere around 230,000. Local people think it's much higher. If
you're into top-ten lists of misery, you might argue that the Asian
tsunami was worse, but that was spread over two continents. This

happened in the space between London and Brighton in a nation of barely ten million.

The survivors do their living in the streets. On every piece of flat land, there are lean-tos and shacks. The bivouacs of the displaced choke petrol station forecourts and lay-bys. The parks are like human beehives. Laundry is strung from trees, charcoal fires smoke, pigs and chickens pick through the syrupy rubbish. Ranks of throat-scarring portable loos cling to the outskirts in a vain attempt to stop the shit infecting everything.

As there is no regular or clean water, it has to be brought to the city every day by tanker. Urchins sell small plastic bags of water that tastes of chlorine. This doesn't feel like it's a short flight from Florida, or one half of an island that is a golf-strewn, five-star holiday getaway. Haiti has always seemed more African than Caribbean. It's like Accra or Freetown. Haiti has held on to its slave roots, the dark pride of being the very first black republic. The first black army to defeat a white one since Hannibal. The only non-European army to lay Napoleon low. The French extracted a terrible price for this humiliation. They took Haiti's entire hardwood forest as reparation, which led to the worst soil erosion of any country in the world. Now the main industry is aid, drug- and gun-running, and stitching cheap T-shirts.

The first wave of disaster relief has departed, and with it the news crews. I can find only a desk man for AFP diligently trying to rustle up a story a day, and a camera crew from Al Jazeera. Contrarily, and without apparent irony, the preferred story in a natural catastrophe is a good-news one: miraculous rescues and escapes, acts of heroism and bravery, selfless rescue workers from Rotherham, sniffer dogs from Barking, saintly surgeons from Surbiton. As the hope of more wide-eyed victims being plucked from the grave diminishes, as the disaster medics wrap up their kit and go, so too do the twenty-four-hour rolling-news teams. This is very expensive stuff, and nobody has the budget or the audience for the grim, dull depression of resurrection.

The emergency hospitals are no longer dealing with trauma. They have to see to the grind of exacerbated poverty, the infantile diarrhoea, the constant respiratory problems, the infections and sores. In the makeshift hospital run by the Swiss, the most common complaint they're treating is MUPS – Medically unexplained physical symptoms. Aka grief. Or the need for a bed. Or the yearning for some attention, or the hope of a pill that might make it all right.

A young doctor, eyes bright with messianic ire, tells me about the initial response to the crisis: 'We are finding people in the shanty slums with the metal armatures, the rods, the broken legs still in place. People holding their medical notes who were treated and dumped. There is a woman we found living in a plastic-bag tent. She had fourth-stage breast cancer. In the West it would be considered too far gone to operate, but someone flew her to the Dominican Republic, gave her a mastectomy, stitched her with metal staples and somehow brought her back and left her in Port-au-Prince. She has a CD with her medical records. A CD. Her wound is infected – we don't have the equipment to remove the staples. She is still dying. Who could do that? And the people the Americans took away – the ones with crush injuries, the respiratory trauma, who needed breathing tubes. They went to the aircraft carrier. Where is it? Gone. Where are the patients?'

There was so much haphazard, arbitrary emergency medicine, so many children flown around the globe towing film crews. Surgeons and doctors from rich, First World hospitals took pride in giving First World treatment, began long courses of drugs and procedures that nobody can afford, from pharmacies that don't exist. There was an assumption that someone else would arrive in their wake and turn this into a real, functioning country.

There are hundreds and hundreds of amputees. The most common injury among survivors is the guillotining of an arm or a leg, severed by a wall or a ceiling. There are many children without feet or hands. The amputations were done quickly; victims had often been lying for hours or days, crushed. Now that they have to be given prosthetics, the long process of rehabilitation, of exercising atrophied muscles, must start. A lot of stumps were left raw and weak. The victims have to have their legs re-amputated. A woman wails beside a bed, waving her hands, imploring God. Her husband and sons are dead. She is with her daughter, who lost a leg and now must have it cut again. Is there no end to the pain, to the disappointment? She cries hopelessly.

But medicine is no longer the most pressing concern. There is a boiling, unreported problem with logistics. It's getting practical aid to the millions who live under plastic. This is the second wave of the disaster. If they drive a truck full of tents, or buckets, or beans – just about anything – into a refugee camp, there is a riot. The charity workers are bullied and beaten, the goods are fought over, destroyed, stolen, to reappear again on the black market. There is no infrastructure, no order, no way to distribute aid. The government has no power. The NGOs are young volunteers who can't police themselves; the UN and the Americans have no mandate or desire to get physical; and the victims, struggling every day without practical help, grow angrier. They know that huge amounts of money have been given for their relief, they know that third-rate pop stars and reality show contestants are covering saccharine power ballads for their benefit, that stand-up comedians and over-the-hill soap-opera actors are running marathons on their behalf, but they're not seeing it. What they see are streets jammed with 4x4s in the branded logos of charity, driven by white kids. This is a country that has only ever existed as a kleptocracy – a masterclass in corruption. Everyone knows that the money, the goods must have been stolen by businessmen, by charities, by American Christians, and they're being sold. So people are beginning to take desperate measures – they have started kidnapping white aid workers as a lever to get back what should be theirs. This is also kept unreported.

Médecins Sans Frontières, whom I travelled with, have just had two nurses kidnapped. They were freed after a few days, unharmed. MSF say no ransom was paid – they never pay. The police say someone paid. There are rumours about other NGOs; nobody wants to make this public, but executed bodies have appeared, and it changes the whole shape of the problem – makes everything much, much more fraught, much harder, more cautious, and slower.

The two or three expensive hotels left in the old colonial part of the city are packed. Not with charity workers but born-again baby-nappers and businessmen, here to make an opportunity out of a disaster. There is a good deal of potential here – a lot of money to be spent. Sharp-eyed buccaneers sell phone masts and digging equipment. Experts hawk their expertise. T-shirt moguls are in the market for T-shirts.

A half-trashed, ferrety little expat Englishman buttonholes me at a bar. He's selling protection: 'I cover all of Latin America.' He's doing a brisk trade in bodyguards, drivers, kidnap insurance, all the belt and braces kit of paranoia. It's expensive, but, he says, charities pay to protect their staff, or, rather, the people who pay charities pay. It all comes out of the aid budget. He nods at a large and threatening Haitian standing in a corner. 'There's my security. Of course he carries a gun – probably won't need it, but I wouldn't go out after dark without him.' I give the bloke a long look. I wouldn't go out after dark *with* him. 'You should think about it,' he says. 'You're high-profile, work for a rich international company.' Thanks, but I think I'll stick with my tried and tested strategy. 'Oh yeah, what's that?' Hysterical begging and soiling myself.

We drive to the outskirts of the Cité Soleil to deliver tents to a small community. On the way, we pass ghost camps; smart local entrepreneurs put up fake rag towns, like Venus flytraps, to catch unwary charities. There are signs on the road saying simply 'Help'. The distribution has taken days to arrange. The community appointed a leader, a dignified and stalwart woman. There is a list of which families will get tents. The team of MSF workers hold a masterclass in putting them up. The community has spent a couple of days clearing the land; they've organised their own security. It's friendly and jolly, but it's an awful lot of work for a very small distribution. Getting here, we drove up the wrong road and came across a gang from the slum, their faces obscured with scarves and balaclavas. They cut the attitude of hard men the

Third World over, and turned us back. They're guarding the city's landfill, a broad plain of smoking detritus, the stuff that has been thrown away a dozen times before it gets here. This is their fiefdom, the last scavengers at the end of a long train of disposable, replaceable Western civilisation, the violent vigilantes of filth. And underneath the smoking, stinking field that is their harvest, are bulldozed 100,000 mangled corpses.

Another winning top-ten fact: this is a disaster that uniquely cost more than the country is worth. Haiti is technically an insurance write-off. In New York there is a donor conference where they're asking governments, philanthropies and charities to stump up $17 billion. That is 120 per cent of Haiti's value. Bill Clinton said that if the international community put Haiti back to the way it was the day before the earthquake, it would have failed. This is a once-only opportunity to build a whole new country from scratch, perhaps to offer something of the good wishes the new nation should have been given two hundred years ago. The big, blue-sky idea is to build a brand-new city. This port is silted up and unusable. For this sort of money they could just abandon Port-au-Prince to the dead, leave its cursed slums to the zombies. But right now, the aid distribution of the tents, the food, the plastic legs, is a race against time and the patience of the survivors. The rains are coming. There is the serious threat of mudslides. Nobody knows how the newly fractured geology of the city will behave.

We go to another shanty town built up a precipitous hillside. They call it, with a marvellous irony, Tapis Rouge – the red carpet. In the ruins at the top of the slum, two boys hold a wailing, ecstatic service of mourning in a collapsed house. From up here you can see right across the city to the sea. The main street slaloms away with rills of red, foaming water, like pale blood. The first thunderstorm of the year has just passed. Everything gleams, the streets are full of people, vivid, and energetic. Children shout and jump ropes, kick balls and fly tiny tissue kites. Neighbours sit on boxes, chat and listen to radios. 'Hey, *Blanc*,' the girls shout, '*bonjour, Blanc*.' The girls flirt, with hot, teasing energy. They look directly and quizzically deep into your eyes, with a hooded mischief. They flash their teeth and poke the tips of their pink tongues out. The girls, hands on their hips, sashay and shimmy. They do it not for money, nor from desperation, nor really in the expectation of any consummation, but for the quick, intense pleasure of being able to, for the exercise of their power. To feel attractive, not to waste the terrific force of their youth, and for that fleeting thrill that is lifted out of this grief like a little tissue kite. Flirting is sowing a seed of human contact, blowing a kiss to another world, a moment's light optimism, and it's heart-breakingly touching, and funny, and unnerving.

We slip down the hill in a cappella clucking of sucked teeth, clicked fingers, skipping songs and laughter. At the side of the muddy track, wet children sell mud cakes, smooth, round biscuits made of water and soil and a little fat, baked in the sun. They are eaten by the starving: fill your mouth with earth, your stomach with the grave. I have never seen these anywhere else in the world. Mud cakes are a Haitian speciality.

We're here to see the slum's head man, to organise the giving of survival packs – a basic starter box of life: a tarpaulin, a bucket, soap, water-purifying pills, sanitary towels, nappies and some food. We find him in a lean-to, sitting behind a desk, flanked by silent muscle and lots of children. There are mobile phones, a telly, a DVD player, a satellite decoder. He is instantly recognisable – it's the black Tony Soprano surrounded by the trappings of his power. He's amused and friendly, with an edge of smiling psycho-menace. With an air of a man who's rarely been told 'no', he tries to make these negotiations for aid sound as if they were organised by him on behalf of his people. The MSF negotiators are firm and poker-faced. He does what bullies do: he pats children and makes light of the things he can't get. His lieutenants look stony. The children weave between their legs like cats. They're all aware that disasters like this only happen once in a millennium. This is an oppor-tunity – they're strung and tense, waiting to catch the wave.

We leave and I ask why they're doing business with the gangs, these malevolent bloodsuckers who've blighted Haiti since the Tonton Macoutes, who make the poor poorer and a lot of them dead. 'At the moment, these are the only people who can guarantee the security of a distribution.' But they'll give it to their cronies, sell it, use it as leverage. 'We hope not. We will do what we can, but it's more important to get this stuff into the community until we can deliver so much it loses its value.' These are the hard truths of charity.

The late afternoon light is soft and warm. The distant sea shimmers like lamé. The slum could almost be homely, lounging in the silky red earth. On the crowded street a teenage girl bathes from a bucket; naked to the waist, she's skinny as a whip, glossy with bubbles, and gasps with a flashing white smile, her hands held in a simple, supplicant blessing as her mother pours water over her back. It is a small baptism – washing away the cruel earth, the dust of death and grief, the loss, washing away the past, leaving a laughing girl bathed in the shining, golden light.

Index